Mental
and
Emotional Injuries
in
Employment Litigation

2000 Cumulative Supplement

Mental and Emotional Injuries in Employment Litigation

2000 Cumulative Supplement

James J. McDonald, Jr.
Fisher & Phillips LLP
Newport Beach, California

The Bureau of National Affairs, Inc., Washington, D.C.

Library of Congress Cataloging-in-Publication Data

Mental and emotional injuries in employment litigation / James J.
McDonald, Jr., Francine B. Kulick, editors.
p. cm.
Includes index.
ISBN 0-87179-832-8
1. Personal injuries—United States. 2. Damages—United States.
3. Discrimination in employment—Law and legislation—United States.
4. Psychic trauma. 5. Affective disorders. I. McDonald, James J.
II. Kulick, Francine B.
KF1264.M46 1994
346.7303′23—dc20
[347.306323] 94-15827
CIP

Published by BNA Books
1231 25th St., NW, Washington, DC 20037
International Standard Book Number: 1-57018-216-7
Printed in the United States of America

ACKNOWLEDGMENTS

The author is grateful to Francine B. Kulick, Ph.D., Paul R. Lees-Haley, Ph.D., Mark S. Lipian, M.D., Ph.D., David R. Price, Ph.D., Robert I. Simon, M.D., and the late Sara P. Feldman-Schorrig, M.D., for their insightful work on the forefront of forensic psychiatry and psychology.

The author additionally gratefully acknowledges the support of the law firm of Fisher & Phillips LLP and the assistance and encouragement of Timothy J. Darby and the staff of BNA Books.

ABOUT THE AUTHOR

James J. McDonald, Jr. is a partner in the Irvine, California office of the national labor and employment law firm of Fisher & Phillips LLP. Mr. McDonald received his law degree cum laude from Georgetown University in 1984, and he is a member of the California and Georgia Bars. He was senior editor of the first edition of *Mental and Emotional Injuries in Employment Litigation,* and he is the author of numerous legal publications on mental health and employment law. Mr. McDonald teaches labor and employment law at the University of California at Irvine, and he is a member of the Labor and Employment Law Section of the American Bar Association, Division 41 (Psychology and the Law) of the American Psychological Association, the American College of Forensic Psychiatry, the Society for Human Resources Management, and the Defense Research Institute.

SUMMARY CUMULATIVE TABLE OF CONTENTS

*In this supplement, the title of this chapter has been amended to reflect the fact that the *Diagnostic and Statistical Manual of Mental Disorders* (4th ed. 1994) changed the name of the relevant disorder by eliminating the hyphen in "post-traumatic."

DETAILED CUMULATIVE TABLE OF CONTENTS

*In this supplement, the title of this chapter has been amended to reflect the fact that the *Diagnostic and Statistical Manual of Mental Disorders* (4th ed. 1994) changed the name of the relevant disorder by eliminating the hyphen in "post-traumatic."

CUMULATIVE LIST OF EXHIBITS

PREFACE

As recently as a decade ago, mental health issues were of little interest to most employment attorneys, and the workplace was not a focus of great attention for most psychiatrists and clinical psychologists. Then, the enactment of the Americans With Disabilities Act in 1990 (with its protection for employees with mental disabilities) and the Civil Rights Act of 1991 (providing for emotional distress damages in federal employment discrimination lawsuits) began to bring about what we referred to in the Preface of the Main Volume as the "psychologization" of the workplace. Mental health issues became salient in a number of respects in the workplace, not the least of which being the mental and emotional impact of adverse employment events such as wrongful termination, discrimination, and harassment. As mental and emotional injuries became compensable, mental health issues began to grow important in employment litigation. The co-editors and authors attempted, with the publication of the Main Volume of *Mental and Emotional Injuries in Employment Litigation* in 1994, to begin to collect and analyze the legal and clinical principles that would likely guide the development of this new area of the law.

Much has happened since the publication of the Main Volume in 1994. Emotional distress damage claims have become a significant factor in virtually every employment lawsuit, and "dueling mental health experts" have become a common feature in the trial of many employment cases. This also is an area often characterized by strident ideology on both sides. Particularly in sexual harassment cases, where psychological issues often play a prominent role, shrill cries of "Blaming the victim!" frequently emanate from the plaintiff's side, while accusations of "Hiding the truth!" often come from the defense.

In the six years since the publication of the Main Volume, three important trends have highlighted the development of the law and clinical practice concerning emotional injuries in the workplace.

The first trend involves the ongoing and intensifying conflict between a plaintiff's right to privacy and a defendant's right to a fair trial. The most basic issue with respect to virtually every emotional distress damage claim is whether the plaintiff suffered an injury and, if so, *what was its cause?* Just because a plaintiff (1) was fired and (2) is depressed does not necessarily mean that the firing produced the depression. Perhaps the plaintiff was chronically depressed prior to ever having come to work for the defendant. Perhaps the plaintiff suffered a significant loss outside of the workplace around the time of the termination. If the plaintiff seeks an award of money damages from the defendant for depression, due process requires that the defendant be given an opportunity to explore whether it is truly responsible for the plaintiff's depression before being made to pay damages. This is where expensive and time-consuming—and often bitterly fought—discovery battles typically begin.

As a result, a considerable amount of law has developed over the past few years on issues such as whether (and under what conditions) the plaintiff should be compelled to submit to a Rule 35[1] mental examination, whether the defendant should have access to the plaintiff's medical and psychotherapy records, and whether the defendant may conduct discovery into various aspects of the plaintiff's sexual history. Thus far, the law has not developed uniformly. Congress, for its part, and over the objection of the Supreme Court, amended Rule 412[2] of the Federal Rules of Evidence in 1994 to limit the discovery of the sexual history of a sexual harassment plaintiff. The line drawn by Congress is a fuzzy one, however, and it fails to distinguish adequately between prior *consensual sexual activity* with persons other than the alleged perpetrator(s) (which ordinarily is of little relevance to the issues in the case) and prior *sexual trauma* (which ordinarily is of extreme relevance).

The difficulty with the new Rule 412 and similar judicial efforts to safeguard the privacy of plaintiffs is that although they may protect some plaintiffs from abusive discovery tactics designed to achieve little more than embarrassment and intimidation, in many cases they constitute significant impediments to finding the truth.[3] There is a troubling trend in the law toward creating ever more privileges and restrictions on discovery. Justice Scalia lamented this trend in his dissenting opinion in *Jaffee v. Redmond,*[4] which recognized a psychotherapist–patient privilege under federal common law. Scalia wrote:

> The Court has discussed at some length the benefit that will be purchased by creation of the evidentiary privilege in this case: the encouragement of psychoanalytic counseling. It has not mentioned the purchase price: occasional injustice. That is the cost of every rule which excludes reliable and probative evidence—or at least every one categorical enough to achieve its announced policy objective. In the case of some of these rules, such as the one excluding confessions that have not been properly "Mirandized," . . . the victim of the injustice is always the impersonal State or the faceless "public at large." For the rule proposed here, the victim is more likely to be some individual who is prevented from proving a valid claim—or (worse still) prevented from establishing a valid defense. The latter is particularly unpalatable for those who love justice, because it causes the

---

[1]FED. R. CIV. P. 35.

[2]The full text of Rule 412, as amended, is set out in Appendix A of this Supplement.

[3]*See* J. Gibeaut, *Shield a Prosecution Sword,* A.B.A. J. 36 (Dec. 1997) (describing how "rape shield" laws may deprive defendants of their right to due process).

[4]518 U.S. 1 (1996).

> courts of law not merely to let stand a wrong, but to become themselves the instruments of wrong.[5]

Likewise, one must wonder whether the stated purpose of the 1994 amendments to Rule 412 of encouraging victims of sexual misconduct to institute legal proceedings against alleged offenders[6] can ever be sufficiently weighty to justify the amended rule's use as a tool for preventing the discovery of relevant evidence that is critical to a defendant's ability to mount a valid defense.

The second trend is the increasing willingness of the courts to examine the role of a plaintiff's own prior psychological problems in the genesis of the workplace dispute at issue in litigation. Most often these prior problems take the form of a personality disorder,[7] which is a chronic and pathological means of perceiving and interpreting one's environment and relating to others. An employee with a borderline personality disorder, for example, may initiate sexual-related conversations with co-workers and then suddenly accuse the same co-workers of sexual harassment when they respond. A manager with a narcissistic personality disorder may be insensitive to the needs of his subordinates and unable to comprehend why his abusive manner produces a high rate of turnover.

The most recent and comprehensive recognition to date by a court of the role of personality disorders in the context of harassment and discrimination claims occurred in *Pascouau v. Martin Marietta Corp.*[8] In that harassment lawsuit, the court concluded that "the conduct that could be described as harassment was not based on gender, but rather on Plaintiff's demonstrated lack of interpersonal skills."[9] In its discussion of the facts of the case, the court described at some length the plaintiff's pre-existing psychological problems, many of which arose from the plaintiff's dysfunctional childhood. The *Pascouou* court explained the relevance of the plaintiff's personality disorder:

> The personality disorder is a condition, largely the product of being raised in a dysfunctional home with dysfunctional parents, in which Plaintiff did not learn how to solve problems effectively or to communicate effectively with other people. The disorder leads to the formulation of implausible perceptions and thus different kinds of conclusions about what other people's actions and behavior mean as distinguished from what a reasonable person not subject to such a disorder would perceive them to mean.

---

[5]*Id.* at 1932–33 (citation omitted).

[6]FED. R. EVID. 412 advisory committee's note on December 1, 1994, amendments. The full text of the note appears in Appendix A of this Supplement.

[7]For a full discussion of the role of personality disorders in employment disputes, see Chapter 4, "Personality Disorders and Traits," of the Main Volume and this Supplement.

[8]994 F. Supp. 1276, 76 FEP Cases 651 (D. Colo. 1998), *aff'd in relevant part,* 185 F.3d 874 (10th Cir. 1999) (table).

[9]*Id.* at 1282, 76 FEP Cases at 657.

> Consistent with this disorder, Plaintiff makes judgments that are highly personalized and overly emotional. She sees things in black and white terms rather than shades of gray that permit allowances and generally feels whatever goes wrong is someone else's fault and she had no role in the misadventure. Persons with this disorder take no responsibility for what goes wrong in their lives.[10]

The *Pascouau* court then remarked, concerning the testimony of the defense psychiatrist:

> When asked if Plaintiff's allegations had any role in the causes of Plaintiff's disorders, Dr. Plezak replied that the situation is reversed in that the disorders are causes of the allegations. The incidents Plaintiff related were characterized by misinterpretations of events and interactions with fellow employees that were far more intense than would be interpreted by a reasonable person.[11]

This is a dramatic acknowledgment of the important role that many plaintiffs' own prior psychopathology plays in the genesis of harassment and discrimination cases. This case is particularly significant because it indicates that testimony of psychiatric or psychological experts may be directed to issues of liability as well as damages. As an increasing number of experts focus on possible personality pathology ("Axis II disorders" in psychiatric parlance)[12] on the part of the plaintiff in addition to emotional distress damages, the need for adequate discovery into the plaintiff's psychological history is even more acute, increasing the likelihood of skirmishes over the scope of permissible discovery. Often times, however, the diagnosis of a personality disorder on the part of the plaintiff can supply the key to an understanding of the events that led up to the lawsuit—particularly in difficult "he said/she said" cases where there are no third-party witnesses to break the impasse.

The third trend involves the increasing scrutiny by the courts of expert testimony, designed to ferret out "junk science" that may seem impressive to a jury but that is scientifically dubious.[13] This trend began with the Supreme Court's decision in *Daubert v. Merrill Dow Pharmaceuticals Inc.,*[14] which established the trial court as a "gatekeeper" to ensure that only scientifically sound evidence reaches the jury, and it continued with the Court's most recent decision in *Kumho Tire Co. v. Carmichael,*[15] which extended the *Daubert* rule to expert testimony that does not involve pure science.

Such scrutiny is particularly warranted where the testimony of mental health experts is involved. In numerous cases, such "experts" lack the requisite

---

[10]*Id.* at 1279, 76 FEP Cases at 653–54.

[11]*Id.,* 76 FEP Cases at 654.

[12]*See generally* the discussion of Axis II disorders in Chapter 4, "Personality Disorders and Traits," of the Main Volume and this Supplement.

[13]For a discussion of "junk science," see Chapter 11, "Avoiding 'Junk Science' in Employment Litigation," in this Supplement.

[14]509 U.S. 579 (1993).

[15]526 U.S. 137 (1999).

training and qualifications, or they fail to employ commonly accepted diagnostic protocols, or they administer psychological "tests" that are really little more than subjective symptom inventories, or they cite to "research" that purports to prove a link between adverse workplace events and a variety of mental disorders but that in fact proves no such thing. Although psychiatry and psychology differ from "hard" sciences such as chemistry or physics, they are sciences nonetheless, the basic principles of which are derived through the scientific method. As such, particularly after *Kumho Tire*, they should be no less susceptible to a *Daubert* analysis.

Even though much has happened in the six years since the publication of the Main Volume, the law in this area is still just beginning to develop. Employment attorneys on both sides of lawsuits, mental health professionals, and the courts continue to struggle with psychological issues in the workplace, and this struggle has sometimes produced peculiar results. For example, one judge derisively characterized the Minnesota Multiphasic Personality Inventory (MMPI)—the most widely used and extensively validated personality inventory in existence—as a "mind control device."[16] Another court affirmed a jury award for emotional distress damages, noting that the plaintiff's psychological expert had diagnosed posttraumatic stress disorder (PTSD) as a result of her being terminated and having to listen to foul language in the workplace[17]—a plainly invalid basis for a PTSD diagnosis.

Yet another court conducted an exhaustive, seven-week hearing on psychological damages for a class of successful sexual harassment plaintiffs, at the conclusion of which it issued a 416-page decision thoroughly analyzing each plaintiff's claim.[18] Although the court awarded damages to each of the plaintiffs, it awarded relatively nominal amounts to those plaintiffs whose backgrounds revealed significant alternative stressors. For example, it noted that one plaintiff had been sexually molested as a child by her grandfather, which caused her to have nightmares of a man chasing her and which led her own doctor to diagnose delayed onset PTSD. This plaintiff also was the victim of date rape, a violent relationship with her mother, and a violent relationship with her ex-husband (which included forced sex at gunpoint). The court noted that the plaintiff's reported nightmares about being chased by a co-worker named "Bob" bore a "striking similarity" to the content of her nightmares about her grandfather. The court rejected the plaintiff's expert's conclusion that sexual harassment was the sole cause of the plaintiff's emotional problems due to the expert's failure to employ standard diagnostic procedures and failure to consider the plaintiff's medical and social history, but the court awarded the plaintiff $6,000 for mental anguish resulting from sexual harassment at work. After the National Organization for Women filed an *amicus* brief accusing the trial court of gender

---

[16]Usher v. Lakewood Usher Eng'g & Mfg. Co., 158 F.R.D. 411, 66 FEP Cases 558 (N.D. Ill. 1994).

[17]Baty v. Willamette Indus., Inc., 985 F. Supp. 987 (D. Kan. 1997), *aff'd,* 172 F.3d 1232, 79 FEP Cases 1451 (10th Cir. 1999).

[18]Jenson v. Eveleth Taconite Co., 1996 U.S. Dist. LEXIS 17617 (D. Minn. 1996).

bias, the Eighth Circuit issued a scathing reversal, finding that the lower court had allowed too much discovery, applied the wrong legal standards, and awarded too little in damages.[19]

Cases such as *Jenson* add to the confusion in this already uncertain area of the law, as one court's painstaking application of standard clinical principles to claims for emotional damages (and where other potential stressors also were in abundance) is attacked as sexist by a leading rights organization and summarily reversed by a higher court. Justice and due process will not be achieved by avoiding the difficult issues addressed by the lower court in *Jenson,* however. Unless the courts—aided by informed plaintiff and defense counsel and qualified mental health professionals—are willing to step away from the ideology and emotion inherent in these matters and rationally and objectively examine these issues according to established scientific principles, the quality of justice will be greatly compromised.

James J. McDonald, Jr.
(April 2000)

---

[19]Jenson v. Eveleth Taconite Co., 130 F.3d 1287, 75 FEP Cases 852 (8th Cir. 1997), *cert. denied,* 118 S. Ct. 2370 (1998).

CHAPTER 1

THE LEGAL CONTEXT

Actions in Which Emotional Distress Damages Are Available

Common Law Bases for Recovery of Emotional Distress Damages

Intentional Infliction of Emotional Distress

As indicated in the Main Volume, plaintiffs in harassment and discrimination cases also often plead state law claims for intentional infliction of emotional distress, in an attempt to collect damages exceeding the $300,000 limit on federal compensatory and punitive damages imposed by the Civil Rights Act of 1991. Case law developed to date, however, indicates that a federal Title VII violation does not necessarily equate with a state law cause of action for intentional infliction of emotional distress.

In *Hadley v. VAMPTS,*[1] the court held that the standards of proof are different for recovery of emotional distress damages under Title VII and for the common law cause of action for intentional infliction of emotional distress. The plaintiff in *Hadley* was awarded emotional distress damages on his Title VII claim, but not on his claim for intentional infliction of emotional distress. He argued that there was no difference between the two claims, but the court disagreed. It explained:

> While it is true that compensatory damages under Title VII can overlap with actual damages suffered as a result of intentional infliction of emotional distress, the severity of injury necessary for each is markedly different. In order to be compensable, emotional distress under the state law of intentional infliction of emotional distress must be severe. There is no such requirement for compensable emotional harm under Title VII.[2]

This difference in standards of proof has become relevant to claims for intentional infliction of emotional distress based upon an organization's failure

---

[1]44 F.3d 372, 67 FEP Cases 186 (5th Cir. 1995).

[2]*Id.* at 372, 67 FEP Cases at 187.

to promptly remedy sexual harassment. In *Codrington v. Virgin Islands Port Authority,*[3] the court held that the employer's failure to take prompt remedial action following a claim of sexual harassment constituted a violation of Title VII but was not conduct "so outrageous and so beyond all bounds of decency to be considered atrocious and utterly intolerable in a civilized society so as to support a cause of action for intentional infliction of emotional distress."[4] In *Prunty v. Arkansas Freightways Inc.,*[5] by contrast, the corporate employer was held liable for intentional infliction of emotional distress based upon a vice president's knowledge of a manager's sexual harassment of a subordinate and the vice president's failure to take corrective action. The court reasoned that the vice president, on behalf of the corporation, had ratified the manager's harassment. The court noted, however, that liability for intentional infliction of emotional distress will not arise out of an "ordinary employment dispute." Only in "extreme and outrageous" situations will liability attach.[6]

Loss of Consortium

In *Brown v. Youth Services International of Baltimore,*[7] the court noted that "federal courts almost unanimously have dismissed loss of consortium claims based upon federal civil rights violations."[8] The *Brown* court went on to point out that although Congress amended Title VII of the Civil Rights Act of 1991 to provide for compensatory damages for various forms of loss, it did not specifically provide for loss of consortium. The *Brown* court concluded that it was inappropriate for a court to add a remedy that Congress had failed to provide.

Proof and Calculation of Emotional Distress Damages

Proof of Damages

As explained in the Main Volume, plaintiffs who are victims of unlawful discrimination are not automatically entitled to recover emotional distress damages. They must prove in addition that the unlawful discrimination caused them to suffer mental or emotional injury.

This point, recognized by the Equal Employment Opportunity Commission (EEOC) in its *Policy Guide on Compensatory and Punitive Damages Under*

---

[3]911 F. Supp. 907, 70 FEP Cases 213 (D.V.I. 1995).

[4]*Id.* at 915, 70 FEP Cases at 219.

[5]16 F.3d 649, 9 IER Cases 911 (5th Cir. 1994).

[6]*Id.* at 654, 9 IER Cases at 915.

[7]904 F. Supp. 469, 69 FEP Cases 991 (D. Md. 1995).

[8]*Id.* at 470, 69 FEP Cases at 992 (*citing* Godby v. Electrolux Corp., 65 FEP Cases 211 (N.D. Ga. 1994); Quitmeyer v. Southeastern Pa. Transp. Auth., 740 F. Supp. 363 (E.D. Pa. 1990); Tauriac v. Polaroid Corp., 716 F. Supp. 672, 48 FEP Cases 1256 (D. Mass. 1989)).

1991 Civil Rights Act,[9] grows out of the decision of the U.S. Supreme Court in *Carey v. Piphus.*[10] In that case, arising under 42 U.S.C. §1983, the Court held that compensable emotional distress damages must be proven; they will not be presumed to have been suffered even if liability is established.

In *Jenson v. Eveleth Taconite Co.,*[11] the Eighth Circuit noted that plaintiffs were required to show that sex discrimination and sexual harassment were "substantial factors" in causing their emotional harm.[12] Although the Eighth Circuit differed in a number of respects with the lower court's handling of the plaintiffs' damage claims, it found no error of law or abuse of discretion in the lower court's rejection of the plaintiffs' attempt to divide their mental anguish claims into separate impairments (for example, anger, shame, wounded pride) and seek a separate monetary award for each type of impairment.[13]

Other courts have varied in the standards that they have required plaintiffs to meet to qualify for emotional distress damages in employment cases; no single, clear standard has crystallized to date. Most courts have held that a plaintiff's own testimony is enough to sustain an award for emotional distress damages, although many courts subject awards based solely upon the plaintiff's own testimony to greater scrutiny than where other objective evidence of such injury also exists.[14]

In *Patterson v. P.H.P. Healthcare Corp.,*[15] the Fifth Circuit, relying on *Carey*[16] and the EEOC's policy guide,[17] expressed some doubt that mere "hurt feelings" on the part of a plaintiff can justify an award of emotional distress damages. Rather, maintained the *Patterson* court, the proof necessary for an award of emotional distress damages

> requires a degree of specificity which may include corroborating testimony or medical or psychological evidence in support of the damage award. Hurt feelings,

---

[9](July 7, 1992), *reprinted in* 8 FEP MANUAL 405: 7091–7102 ("Emotional harm will not be presumed merely because the complaining party is a victim of discrimination. The existence, nature and severity of emotional harm must be proved.").

[10]435 U.S. 247 (1978).

[11]130 F.3d 1287, 75 FEP Cases 852 (8th Cir. 1997).

[12]*Id.* at 1294, 75 FEP Cases at 857.

[13]*Id.* at 1290 n.5, 75 FEP Cases at 854 n.5. *See also* Reynolds v. Octel Communications Corp., 924 F. Supp. 743, 69 FEP Cases 1178 (N.D. Tex. 1995) (although plaintiff was discriminated against based upon both her sex and her age, she suffered but one injury and cannot recover the same damages twice).

[14]*See* Price v. City of Charlotte, 93 F.3d 1241, 1251, 71 FEP Cases 1289 (4th Cir. 1996) ("A survey of the case law reveals that a plaintiff's own testimony, standing alone, may support a claim of emotional distress precipitated by a constitutional violation. . . . Equally, however, the case law reveals that courts scrupulously analyze an award of compensatory damages for a claim of emotional distress predicated exclusively on the plaintiff's testimony." *Id.* at 1251, 71 FEP Cases at 1296 (citations omitted), *cert. denied,* 520 U.S. 1116 (1997).

[15]90 F.3d 927, 72 FEP Cases 613 (5th Cir. 1996).

[16]435 U.S. 247 (1978).

[17]POLICY GUIDE ON COMPENSATORY AND PUNITIVE DAMAGES UNDER 1991 CIVIL RIGHTS ACT (July 7, 1992), *reprinted in* 8 FEP MANUAL 405: 7091–7102.

> anger and frustration are part of life. Unless the cause of action manifests some specific discernable injury to the claimant's emotional state, we cannot say that the specificity requirement has been satisfied.[18]

The *Patterson* court noted that "a number of our sister circuits have recognized that a claimant's testimony alone may not be sufficient to support anything more than a nominal damage award."[19] It went on to vacate the lower court's emotional distress damage award of $40,000 and to hold that no more than nominal damages may be recovered where the plaintiff presents no corroborating testimony in support of his damage claim and offers no medical or psychological evidence. It vacated an award of $150,000 in favor of a co-plaintiff on similar grounds. The court noted that although a retaliatory discharge "caused a substantial disruption" in the plaintiff's daily routine, no proof of actual injury existed, and an award of more than nominal damages was unwarranted.

In *Forshee v. Waterloo Industries Inc.,*[20] the Eighth Circuit overturned an award of emotional damages in the amount of $9,631 in a sexual harassment case, holding that the district court erred in submitting the issue of emotional distress damages to the jury. The plaintiff had alleged that her supervisor had made a sexual advance which she rejected, and that she was subsequently terminated as a result. The court noted that the plaintiff's evidence of emotional distress was based entirely upon her own testimony. The plaintiff had testified that after being terminated she went home and cried about it for the rest of the day and that she was thereafter forced to work at two lower-paying jobs. The court observed that "[w]hile a compensatory damage award may be based solely on plaintiff's own testimony," the plaintiff "did not identify and describe the kind of severe emotional distress" that warrants a damage award. The court further pointed out that the plaintiff suffered no physical injury, was not medically treated for any psychological or emotional injury, and no other witnesses corroborated any outward manifestation of emotional distress. It noted that the plaintiff found a new job almost immediately and although it was lower paying, her award for lost wages would make up for the difference. Finally, while the court recognized that the supervisor's sexual advance was "disgusting," it did not humiliate the plaintiff in front of her co-workers and that the plaintiff admitted that his remark was not the cause of her emotional distress.[21] The *Forshee* court curiously refused to disturb the jury's finding that the plaintiff's rejection of the supervisor's sexual advance resulted in her termination, yet held that no emotional distress damages were recoverable because the plaintiff attributed her emotional distress to the loss of her job as

---

[18]90 F.3d at 940, 72 FEP Cases at 623–24.

[19]*Id.* at 938, 72 FEP Cases at 622 (*citing* Fitzgerald v. Mountain States Tel. & Tel. Co., 68 F.3d 1257, 69 FEP Cases 163 (10th Cir. 1995); Gunby v. Pennsylvania Elec. Co., 840 F.2d 1108, 45 FEP Cases 1818 (3d Cir. 1995); Erebia v. Chrysler Plastic Prods. Corp., 772 F.2d 1250, 37 FEP Cases 1820 (6th Cir. 1985); Vance v. Southern Bell Tel. & Tel. Co., 863 F.2d 1503, 50 FEP Cases 742 (11th Cir. 1989)).

[20]178 F.3d 527 (8th Cir. 1999).

[21]*Id.* at 531.

opposed to the sexual advance. *Forshee* may be of questionable precedential value, therefore.

In contrast to purely emotional injuries (which in the view of most courts may be established without expert testimony), where workplace events (or the stress produced thereby) are alleged to have caused or exacerbated a *physical* disorder, expert medical testimony is necessary. For example, in *Hrabak v. Marquip Inc.,*[22] the court granted the defendant's motion in limine to exclude evidence of the plaintiff's miscarriage. The court held that, without presenting the testimony of a physician, the plaintiff could not attempt to show that emotional distress resulting from sexual harassment caused her to miscarry. In *Shea v. Icelandair,*[23] by contrast, the plaintiff put on the testimony of medical witnesses to the effect that his unlawful demotion caused his Parkinson's disease to worsen, caused him to suffer cardiac problems, and caused him to suffer emotional distress. Although the courts reduced the plaintiff's compensatory damages award by $75,000, it held that the plaintiff could still recover $175,000.

In *Karcher v. Emerson Electric Co.,*[24] the court cited the testimony of the plaintiff's treating psychiatrist and treating psychologist in rejecting the defendant's argument that a jury award of $150,000 for emotional distress in a sex discrimination case was invalid. The court noted that the two doctors had linked the plaintiff's depression and emotional stress to her job-related problems.

Hedonic Damages

Courts thus far have largely rejected attempts by plaintiffs to collect damages for the loss of enjoyment of life, known as "hedonic" damages, in employment cases.

The Civil Rights Act of 1991 allows for recovery of damages for "loss of value of life" as a type of compensatory damages recoverable in federal employment discrimination cases.[25] Nonetheless, at least since the Supreme Court's decision in *Daubert v. Merrill Dow Pharmaceuticals Inc.,*[26] courts generally have rejected testimony on hedonic damages as lacking sufficient scientific reliability. Thus, in *McGuire v. City of Santa Fe,*[27] the court barred the plaintiff from putting on testimony by a psychologist and an economist to the effect that the alleged harassment and termination of the plaintiff caused him to suffer "lost pleasure of life" damages amounting to between $1,430,000 and $2,300,000.[28]

---

[22]58 FEP Cases 908 (W.D. Wis. 1992).

[23]925 F. Supp. 1014, 70 FEP Cases 1544 (S.D.N.Y. 1996).

[24]94 F.3d 502, 71 FEP Cases 1651 (8th Cir. 1996).

[25]42 U.S.C. §1981a(b)(3).

[26]509 U.S. 579 (1993).

[27]954 F. Supp. 230 (D.N.M. 1996).

[28]*See also* Kurncz v. Honda N. Am. Inc., 166 F.R.D. 386 (W.D. Mich. 1996); Ayers v. Robinson, 887 F. Supp. 1049 (N.D. Ill. 1995); Hein v. Merck & Co., 868 F. Supp. 230 (M.D. Tenn. 1994); Sullivan v. U.S. Gypsum Co., 862 F. Supp. 317 (D. Kan. 1994).

Even prior to *Daubert,* one court rejected a discrimination plaintiff's claim for hedonic damages, noting that the plaintiff already had been awarded back pay and "[t]o allow hedonic damages on top of the back pay would be equivalent to a double recovery."[29]

Availability of Damages for Stress of Litigation [New Topic]

With increasing frequency, plaintiffs in employment cases attribute some portion of their emotional distress to the stress of litigation, such as testifying at depositions and in court, undergoing a mental examination conducted by a defense examiner, and encountering an ex-boss, harasser, or co-workers at depositions or court proceedings. The law almost uniformly holds, however, that damages for litigation-induced stress may not be recovered.

In *Blakey v. Continental Airlines Inc.,*[30] the court noted that some of the plaintiff's stress "may be due to the contentiousness of this litigation."[31] It then observed, however, that "[s]he cannot recover for emotional distress caused by litigation.[32]

Measure of Damages

Although emotional distress damage awards by state courts in some employment discrimination cases—particularly in California—have been quite high,[33] federal courts have been somewhat more parsimonious in awarding emotional distress damage awards in employment cases under the Civil Rights Act of 1991.

In numerous cases, district courts or courts of appeals have ordered substantial reductions in large jury verdicts for emotional distress. For example, in *Hetzel v. County of Prince William,*[34] the Fourth Circuit reversed and remanded an award of $500,000 in emotional distress damages to a police officer found to have been terminated in retaliation for her complaints about sex and national origin discrimination. The plaintiff had offered only her own testimony that she had suffered headaches, stress, trouble reading to her daughter, and problems with her family life. She reported no physical illnesses or injuries, she sought no medical attention, and she continued to perform her job and receive favorable performance evaluations. She also failed to put on corroborating testimony

---

[29]Mister v. Illinois Cent. Gulf R.R. Co., 790 F. Supp. 1411, 1421, 61 FEP Cases 1391, 1398 (S.D. Ill. 1992).

[30]992 F. Supp. 731, 76 FEP Cases 280 (D.N.J. 1998).

[31]*Id.* at 763 n.3, 76 FEP Cases at 284 n.3.

[32]*Id.,* 76 FEP Cases at 284 n.3.

[33]*See* Bihun v. AT&T Info. Sys. Inc., 13 Cal. App. 4th 976, 16 Cal. Rptr. 2d 787, 67 FEP Cases 427 (1993) (affirming emotional distress damage award of $662,000 in sexual harassment case as not excessive).

[34]89 F.3d 169, 71 FEP Cases 520 (4th Cir. 1996).

regarding her damages. Moreover, the court noted that much of the plaintiff's claimed distress was actually caused by her erroneous belief that she was herself the victim of discrimination. The court distinguished high awards for emotional distress in other cases on the grounds that the plaintiffs in those cases were in fact the victims of discrimination, or they lost their jobs and had difficulty finding new employment, or they suffered serious and often permanent physical injuries.

In *Fitzgerald v. Mountain States Telephone & Telegraph Co.,*[35] the court reversed emotional distress damage awards in the amount of $250,000 apiece for two plaintiffs in a Section 1981 case, reasoning that such high awards were the product of "passion or prejudice." Neither plaintiff put on testimony from a treating psychologist or physician, and both continued working in their fields. One plaintiff testified merely that discriminatory remarks made during a diversity training session "left her devastated" and "stripped her dignity away," and caused her to have more frequent herpes outbreaks. The other plaintiff testified that he felt angry and insulted, had headaches, and missed more than three weeks of work. The court ordered a new trial on compensatory damages.

In *Rush v. Scott Specialty Gases Inc.,*[36] the court reduced a $1 million compensatory damages award to $100,000 in a sexual harassment case, finding that although the plaintiff presented adequate evidence that she suffered emotional injury, the damage award was excessive. Other courts have ordered similar reductions.[37]

In *Blakey v. Continental Airlines,*[38] the court reduced an emotional damage award of $500,000 to a plaintiff in a sexual harassment case to $250,000. The court observed that it may consider awards in other cases—including cases from other circuits—involving similar injuries as a "helpful guide" to whether a particular damage award is excessive.[39] It then noted that the only evidence

---

[35]68 F.3d 1257, 69 FEP Cases 163 (10th Cir. 1995).

[36]930 F. Supp. 194, 73 FEP Cases 1429 (E.D. Pa. 1996), *rev'd on other grounds,* 113 F.3d 476, 74 FEP Cases 1745 (3d Cir. 1997).

[37]*See, e.g.,* Ramirez v. New York City Off-Track Betting Corp., 112 F.3d 38, 73 FEP Cases 573 (2d Cir. 1997) ("pain and suffering" award of $1,145,625 reduced to $500,000 where defendant's actions left mentally ill plaintiff permanently disabled); Delli Santi v. CNA Ins. Co., 88 F.3d 192, 71 FEP Cases 143 (3d Cir. 1996) (affirming district court's reduction of $300,000 emotional damage award to $5,000 in retaliation case); Williams v. Pharmacia Inc., 956 F. Supp. 1457, 73 FEP Cases 294 (N.D. Ind. 1996) (reduction of $250,000 emotional damage award to $40,000 in lost promotion case); McIntosh v. Irving Trust Co., 887 F. Supp. 662, 74 FEP Cases 99 (S.D.N.Y. 1995) (reduction of $219,428 emotional damage award to $20,000 in failure to promote and wrongful termination case); Lightfoot v. Union Carbide Corp., 901 F. Supp. 166, 71 FEP Cases 269 (S.D.N.Y. 1995) (reduction of $750,000 emotional damage award to $75,000 in age discrimination case; verdict was a "material deviation from the norm"); Abrams v. Lightolier, 841 F. Supp. 584, 65 FEP Cases 1149 (D.N.J. 1994) ($100,000 "pain and suffering" award in age discrimination case reduced to $2,500; plaintiff testified only that he was "very, very upset" about having been accused of bribery by employer).

[38]992 F. Supp. 731, 76 FEP Cases 280 (D.N.J. 1998).

[39]*Id.* at 736, 76 FEP Cases at 285.

of emotional damage presented at trial was the plaintiff's own testimony and that of her psychiatric expert, who had met with her for two hours and reviewed her records for 90 minutes. Her expert testified that the plaintiff suffered some emotional distress as a result of events at work but that other events outside of work—including her volatile relationship with her boyfriend's ex-wife, who had her arrested and threatened her with physical violence—contributed to her emotional distress. Her expert also testified that most of the plaintiff's emotional problems had resolved more than three years prior to trial. The court also noted that the plaintiff was never hospitalized and she was not disabled from future employment. In fact, the court noted the plaintiff's testimony that her job as an airline pilot was inherently stressful, and that she was medically able to perform it during the entire period she was also suffering from emotional distress. The court then remarked: "This is not the kind of evidence that $500,000 awards are made of."[40] It then remitted the award to $250,000, which amount it noted was "high, but within the realm of reason."[41] In support of such an award, the court cited that fact that the plaintiff had been subjected to pornography in the workplace for at least three years, and that she received psychological counseling and psychotropic medication as a result.

In other cases, courts have affirmed emotional distress damage awards in widely varying amounts, where the damages were said to be caused by sexual harassment,[42] wrongful or discriminatory termination,[43] or wrongfully denied promotions.[44]

Preexisting Conditions and the "Eggshell Plaintiff" Rule

Much controversy has arisen over application of the "eggshell plaintiff" rule in employment cases. Evidence of preexisting mental disorders significantly clouds the issue of causation where workplace events are alleged to have produced a mental condition similar to that which was preexisting. The recent

---

[40]*Id.*, 76 FEP Cases at 284.

[41]*Id.* at 740, 76 FEP Cases at 288.

[42]*See, e.g.,* Kelly-Zurian v. Wohl Shoe Co. Inc., 22 Cal. App. 4th 397, 27 Cal. Rptr. 2d 457, 64 FEP Cases 603 (1994) ($125,000); Farpella-Crosby v. Horizon Health Care, 97 F.3d 803, 72 FEP Cases 254 (5th Cir. 1996) ($7,500); McKinnon v. Kwong Wah Restaurant, 83 F.3d 498, 70 FEP Cases 1037 (1st Cir. 1996) ($2,500).

[43]*See, e.g.,* Lussier v. Runyon, 1994 WL 129776, 3 AD Cases 223 (D. Me. 1994) ($75,000); U.S. EEOC v. AIC Sec. Investigations, Ltd., 55 F.3d 1276, 4 AD Cases 693 (7th Cir. 1995) ($50,000); Hearn v. General Elec. Co., 927 F. Supp. 1486, 71 FEP Cases 435 (M.D. Ala. 1996) ($50,000); Luciano v. Olsten Corp., 912 F. Supp. 663, 73 FEP Cases 221 (E.D.N.Y. 1996) ($11,400); Keys v. U.S. Welding, Fabrication & Mfg. Inc., 59 FEP Cases 1537 (N.D. Ohio 1992) ($2,500).

[44]*See, e.g.,* McClam v. City of Norfolk Police Dep't, 877 F. Supp. 277, 71 FEP Cases 757 (E.D. Va. 1995) ($15,000); Odima v. Westin Tucson Hotel, 53 F.3d 1484, 67 FEP Cases 1222 (9th Cir. 1995) ($10,000); McNight v. Circuit City Stores Inc., 73 FEP Cases 841 (E.D. Va. 1997) ($2,700).

trend in the case law indicates that the "eggshell plaintiff" rule will not be applied to liability issues in employment lawsuits, but it will be applied to damage issues.

For example, in *Sudtelgte v. Reno,*[45] the court declined to apply the "eggshell plaintiff" rule with respect to liability in a sexual harassment case. Reasoning that to apply a different liability threshold to abnormally sensitive plaintiffs than is applied to plaintiffs in general would be inconsistent with the "reasonable woman" standard used to determine liability for harassment,[46] the *Sudtelgte* court maintained that harassment claims "based on abnormal sensitivity, whether or not the sensitivity was simply unusual or produced by mental illness," are not viable.[47]

A similar approach was taken in *Poole v. Copland Inc.,*[48] involving a claim for intentional infliction of emotional distress allegedly resulting from various acts of sexual harassment in the workplace. The plaintiff in that case had an extensive history of prior trauma, including being sexually molested by a neighbor at age nine, a marriage to an abusive drug addict at age 16, molestation by an uncle at age 18, a two-week kidnap and rape experience also at age 18, and being beaten by her father when she was 19. Psychiatrists testified that the plaintiff suffered from a dissociative disorder as a result. The state court of appeals in *Poole* held that although the "eggshell plaintiff" rule applies to mental as well as physical injuries, where an "eggshell plaintiff" is involved, special jury instruction must be given on the issue of liability, "requiring the jury to find that the alleged conduct could reasonably be expected to injure a person of ordinary mental condition."[49] Thus, only if the harassment would injure a person of "ordinary susceptibility," maintained the *Poole* court, will it be actionable.

Where damage awards are concerned, however, the EEOC and most federal courts will apply the "eggshell plaintiff" rule. In its policy guide,[50] the EEOC states:

> The claim of emotional harm will be seriously undermined if the onset of symptoms of emotional harm preceded the discrimination. However, if a complaining party had preexisting emotional difficulties and his mental health deteriorates as a result of the discriminatory conduct, the additional harm may be attributed to the respondent. The fact that the complaining party may be unusually emotionally sensitive and incur great emotional harm from discriminatory conduct will not absolve the respondent from responsibility for the greater emotional harm. For example, suppose the Commission finds that the respondent is liable for sexual

---

[45] 63 FEP Cases 1257 (W.D. Mo. 1994).

[46] *See* Ellison v. Brady, 924 F.2d 872, 879, 54 FEP Cases 1346, 1353 (9th Cir. 1991).

[47] 63 FEP Cases at 1267.

[48] 481 S.E.2d 88, 12 IER Cases 833 (N.C. Ct. App. 1997).

[49] *Id.* at 94, 12 IER Cases at 838.

[50] Policy Guide on Compensatory and Punitive Damages Under 1991 Civil Rights Act (July 7, 1992), *reprinted in* 8 FEP Manual 405: 7091–7102.

> harassment against three female employees, one of whom is an incest victim. The incest victim incurred much greater emotional harm from the sexual harassment than did her two co-workers. The respondent is liable for the greater emotional harm that the incest victim suffered.[51]

The court in *Shea v. Icelandair*[52] followed a similar approach. In that case, the plaintiff claimed that his being demoted caused his Parkinson's disease to worsen. Noting that "[i]t is well settled that aggravation of a pre-existing condition gives rise to liability,"[53] the court permitted the plaintiff to recover damages for the worsening of the symptoms of his preexisting disease.

A more difficult situation is presented, however, where a plaintiff does not claim that the defendant's conduct exacerbated a preexisting physical or mental disorder, but rather where the existence of such a disorder is discovered by the defendant and used to challenge the plaintiff's claim that *all* of the emotional distress that he or she is suffering must be attributed to the defendant. This actually tends to be the more common circumstance, as relatively few plaintiffs will readily acknowledge that they had psychological difficulties prior to entering the defendant's workplace. Most courts in this situation will take a plaintiff's prior traumatic experiences and mental health history into account as mitigating factors in awarding emotional distress damages.

In *Jenson v. Eveleth Taconite Co.,*[54] for example, the Eighth Circuit rejected the trial court's assertion that there is "no scientifically developed psychiatric model or procedure for determining whether a particular stress caused a particular symptom or mental state,"[55] and maintained that "[t]o limit its liability through apportionment, a defendant must prove that a plaintiff's damages are divisible, and other outside factors contributed to the plaintiff's harm."[56]

In *McKinnon v. Kwong Wah Restaurant,*[57] the First Circuit, rejecting plaintiffs' argument on appeal, affirmed the district court's award of $2,500 apiece to two plaintiffs for emotional distress in a sexual harassment case. The court of appeals noted that "both plaintiffs were suffering from emotional distress caused by sources independent from their employment."[58] The court noted that one plaintiff had separated from her boyfriend after the discovery of an unplanned pregnancy and that the other had been sexually abused by her stepfather from age 5 to age 17. The court of appeals concluded that in spite of the difficulty in "distinguishing between plaintiffs' trauma caused by the

---

[51]*Id.* at 7097 (*citing* Williamson v. Handy Button Mach. Co., 817 F.2d 1290, 43 FEP Cases 1465 (7th Cir. 1987)).

[52]925 F. Supp. 1014, 70 FEP Cases 1544 (S.D.N.Y. 1996).

[53]*Id.* at 1025, 70 FEP Cases 1552.

[54]130 F.3d 1287, 75 FEP Cases 852 (8th Cir. 1997).

[55]*Id.* at 1297, 75 FEP Cases at 859.

[56]*Id.* at 1294, 75 FEP Cases at 857. The *Jenson* court also noted that plaintiffs do not bear the burden of proving that other factors did not contribute to their emotional harm. *Id.*, 75 FEP Cases at 857–58.

[57]83 F.3d 498, 70 FEP Cases 1037 (1st Cir. 1996).

[58]*Id.,* 70 FEP Cases at 1043.

defendants' harassment and that arising from other causes," the district court's damage awards were proper.[59]

In *Hurley v. Atlantic City Police Department,*[60] the court reduced the jury's award of $575,000 for emotional distress damages in a sexual harassment case to $175,000. Although the court found that the sexual harassment had caused the plaintiff to suffer "serious harm," the court also noted that the testimony of the defendant's psychological expert

> strongly suggests that the difficulties plaintiff has faced and continues to face are rooted in sources other than workplace harassment, such as a troubled childhood marked by sexual molestation, abandonment, and foster homes; physical abuse by both her husbands; and other severe personal, marital and family problems unrelated to her work environment.[61]

The fact that a plaintiff may have experienced prior traumas therefore may significantly affect the value of the plaintiff's emotional damage claim, even where liability is established. The trend among courts appears to be toward taking evidence of prior significant emotional traumas into account in determining the value of an emotional damage claim.

The Mental Examination

As pointed out in the Main Volume, the mental examination of the plaintiff ordinarily is the foundation upon which the defense of an emotional damage claim is built. The examination provides an opportunity for the defendant's mental health expert[62] to interview the plaintiff in a nonadversarial clinical setting to determine the existence and severity of any emotional injury and to gather clues as to the cause of such injury.[63] It also provides an opportunity for the examiner—or another qualified professional—to administer various forms of psychological testing. The defense examiner then integrates the findings from the mental examination with the results of the psychological testing and the information obtained in the records review to formulate opinions concerning the various psychological issues in the case.

The availability of a mental examination of the plaintiff and the conditions under which such an examination is to proceed are matters that increasingly have been the subject of dispute in employment lawsuits.

---

[59]*Id.,* 70 FEP Cases at 1043.

[60]933 F. Supp. 396, 72 FEP Cases 1828 (D.N.J. 1996).

[61]*Id.* at 424, 72 FEP Cases at 1850.

[62]In addition to examinations by psychiatrists and psychologists, at least one court has held that plaintiffs may also be compelled to undergo evaluations by vocational experts pursuant to Rule 35. *Jeffrys v. LRP Publications Inc.,* 1999 WL 79058 (E.D. Pa. 1999). For a sample brief in support of a motion to compel a plaintiff to undergo a Rule 35 mental examination, see Appendix D.

[63]Of course, the plaintiff may retain a mental health expert to conduct such an examination as well, but such an examination does not require court involvement.

Rule 35 of the Federal Rules of Civil Procedure provides that when the mental condition of a party is "in controversy," the court may order the party to submit to a mental examination by a "suitably licensed or certified examiner."[64] Such an order may be made only upon a motion establishing good cause, and the order is to specify "the time, place, manner, conditions, and scope of the examination and the person or persons by whom it is to be made."

The showing necessary for an order compelling a Rule 35 mental examination was set forth by the U.S. Supreme Court in *Schlagenhauf v. Holder.*[65] The Court in *Schlagenhauf* established that a party seeking a mental examination under Rule 35 must demonstrate both that the other party's mental condition is in controversy and that good cause exists for conducting such an examination.[66] This determination must be made on a case-by-case basis, keeping in mind that these requirements are not simply a formality and are not met by mere conclusory allegations of the pleadings, nor by mere "relevance" to the case. Rather, there must be an affirmative showing that each condition as to which the examination is sought is genuinely in controversy and that good cause exists for ordering the examination.[67] The *Schlagenhauf* Court went on to state, however, that a plaintiff who claims to have suffered a mental or physical injury places his or her mental or physical state in controversy and provides the defendant with good cause for an examination to determine the existence and extent of such asserted injury.[68]

Schlagenhauf has received varied interpretations in employment cases. Consequently, the nature of the showing that a defendant must make to meet the "in controversy" and "good cause" prerequisites for a mental examination of a plaintiff in an employment lawsuit remains unsettled in a number of respects. As will be discussed in the following section, a number of conflicting federal court decisions have come down in the past few years. Most of the conflict has been over whether the mental condition of a plaintiff who claims to have suffered emotional distress as a result of harassment or discrimination, but who does not assert a separate claim for intentional infliction of emotional distress, has been placed "in controversy" for purposes of Rule 35.

The "In Controversy" Requirement

Some courts have either explicitly or implicitly adopted the rationale of *Schlagenhauf*[69] and found that mere allegations of mental or emotional distress place a plaintiff's mental condition in controversy. For example, in *Ali v. Wang*

---

[64]Mental examinations also may proceed upon agreement of the parties. *See* FED. R. CIV. P. 35 advisory committee notes to 1970 Amendment. A court order is necessary only if the parties cannot reach an agreement.

[65]379 U.S. 104 (1964).

[66]*Id.* at 117–19.

[67]*Id.* at 118–19.

[68]*Id.* at 119.

[69]379 U.S. 104 (1964).

Laboratories,[70] the court ordered a discrimination plaintiff to undergo a mental examination in spite of the fact that he apparently was not asserting a separate claim for intentional infliction of emotional distress and he did not plan to offer expert testimony at trial. The court nonetheless held that in light of the fact that the plaintiff was seeking "substantial" emotional distress damages, the defendant should not be limited to merely cross-examining the plaintiff on his emotional distress damages. The court maintained: "The testimony of an expert is a well recognized and reasonable way" of challenging a plaintiff's claim of emotional damages, "and an examination of plaintiff by that expert is necessary for the expert to form a meaningful opinion."[71]

Similarly, a mental examination was ordered in *Smedley v. Capps, Staples, Ward, Hastings & Dodson,*[72] even though the plaintiff indicated that she would not call any mental health experts at trial. The court noted that the plaintiff planned to present evidence of her "normal" emotional distress, and it agreed with the defendants' argument that they needed a Rule 35 mental examination to refute such evidence. The court was not deterred by the fact that the plaintiff had previously dismissed her claim for intentional infliction of emotional distress.

In *Carrier Corp. v. New York State Division of Human Rights,*[73] a New York state appellate court reversed an administrative law judge's refusal to order a complainant in a sexual harassment and retaliation case to undergo a psychiatric examination. The complainant in that case was awarded $100,000 in emotional distress damages in a state administrative proceeding based largely upon the testimony of her own psychiatrist. The appellate court maintained that because of the seriousness of the emotional injuries alleged, the complainant should have been subject to a psychiatric examination to aid the defendant employer in rebutting the testimony of the complainant's psychiatrist.

Other courts, without extensive analysis, have found plaintiffs to have put their mental conditions in controversy in employment cases where they sought to recover damages for emotional injuries.[74]

In contrast, still other courts have declined to find a plaintiff's mental condition to be in controversy where the plaintiff made only simple allegations of mental or emotional distress.[75] Some of these cases, however, pre-date the

---

[70]162 F.R.D. 165, 4 AD Cases 520 (M.D. Fla. 1995).

[71]*Id.* at 168, 4 AD Cases at 522.

[72]820 F. Supp. 1227, 61 FEP Cases 1360 (N.D. Cal. 1993).

[73]224 A.D.2d 936, 637 N.Y.S.2d 877 (1996).

[74]*See, e.g.,* Ford v. Contra Costa County, 179 F.R.D. 579, 76 FEP Cases 1849 (N.D. Cal. 1998); Large v. Our Lady of Mercy Med. Ctr., 76 FEP Cases 1054 (S.D.N.Y. 1998); Jansen v. Packaging Corp. of Am., 158 F.R.D. 409, 410, 66 FEP Cases 556, 557 (N.D. Ill. 1994); Zabkowicz v. West Bend Co., 585 F. Supp. 635, 636, 35 FEP Cases 209 (E.D. Wis. 1984); Ryzlak v. McNeil Pharm. Co., 38 Fed. R. Serv. 2d 443, 444 (E.D. Pa. 1982).

[75]*See, e.g.,* Neal v. Siegel-Robert Inc., 171 F.R.D. 264, 266, 73 FEP Cases 637, 638 (E.D. Mo. 1996); Lahr v. Fulbright & Jaworski, L.L.P., 164 F.R.D. 204, 210–11 (N.D. Tex. 1996); Morton v. Haskell Co., 5 AD Cases 272, 274 (M.D. Fla. 1995); Turner v. Imperial Stores, 161 F.R.D. 89, 97 (S.D. Cal. 1995); Robinson v. Jacksonville

Civil Rights Act of 1991. For example, in *Cody v. Marriott Corp.,*[76] the court in an employment discrimination case denied the defendants' Rule 35 motion, but noted that the plaintiff did not claim to have suffered a psychiatric disorder and did not undergo psychiatric or psychological counseling as a result of the emotional distress she suffered. In *Robinson v. Jacksonville Shipyards,*[77] the court denied a Rule 35 motion in a sexual harassment case, but, significantly, the plaintiff was not seeking damages for emotional distress. She sought only back pay and declaratory and injunctive relief. In *Bridges v. Eastman Kodak Co.,*[78] a sexual harassment case, the defendants' Rule 35 motion was denied where the plaintiffs did not claim that they suffered any ongoing mental injuries and did not assert a separate claim for intentional infliction of emotional distress. The court suggested, however, that had the plaintiffs claimed ongoing mental illnesses, mental examinations would have been warranted.

Courts have offered additional rationales for finding that the mental condition of a plaintiff in employment litigation was not in controversy. Some courts maintain that "emotional distress" is not synonymous with "mental injury" as that term was used by the Supreme Court in *Schlagenhauf.*[79] Other courts point out that a party may suffer compensable "emotional distress" without having a "mental condition."[80] Still other courts have expressed a fear that allowing mental examinations whenever there is a claim of mental or emotional distress would "open the floodgates" to requests for such examinations.[81] One court concluded that "basic complaints" of emotional distress are within the understanding of the jury, making a mental examination unnecessary.[82]

"Garden Variety" Emotional Damages Claims [New Topic]

Recently, some courts have come to use the term "garden variety" to describe the types of emotional damage claims that do not warrant a Rule 35 mental examination. This term dates back to *Turner v. Imperial Stores,*[83] where the

Shipyards Inc., 118 F.R.D. 525, 531, 54 FEP Cases 83, 88 (M.D. Fla. 1988); Cody v. Marriott Corp., 103 F.R.D. 421, 422–23, 44 FEP Cases 1228, 1229 (D. Mass. 1984).

[76] 103 F.R.D. 421, 44 FEP Cases 1228 (D. Mass. 1984).

[77] 118 F.R.D. 525, 54 FEP Cases 83 (M.D. Fla. 1988).

[78] 850 F. Supp. 216 (S.D.N.Y. 1994).

[79] 379 U.S. 104 (1964). *See, e.g.,* Neal v. Siegel-Robert Inc., 171 F.R.D. 264, 266, 73 FEP Cases 637, 638 (E.D. Mo. 1996); *Turner,* 161 F.R.D. at 97.

[80] *See, e.g.,* Lahr v. Fulbright & Jaworski, L.L.P., 164 F.R.D. 204, 211 (N.D. Tex. 1996); Morton v. Haskell Co., 5 AD Cases 272, 274 (M.D. Fla. 1995).

[81] *See, e.g., Turner,* 161 F.R.D. at 97 n.4; O'Quinn v. New York Univ. Med. Ctr., 163 F.R.D. 226, 228 n.2, 68 FEP Cases 1798, 1800 n.2 (S.D.N.Y. 1995); Cody v. Marriott Corp., 103 F.R.D. 421, 422, 44 FEP Cases 1228, 1229 (D. Mass. 1984).

[82] *Neal,* 171 F.R.D. at 267, 73 FEP Cases at 638. *See also* Hardy v. ESSROC Materials Inc., 1998 WL 133306 (E.D. Pa. 1998) (motion to compel mental examination denied where it was based solely upon plaintiff's claim that discrimination caused her to feel anxious and have trouble sleeping).

[83] 161 F.R.D. 89 (S.D. Cal. 1995).

court denied the defendants' Rule 35 motion, in spite of the fact that the plaintiff was seeking more than $1 million in emotional distress damages. The court pointed out that the plaintiff (1) was not asserting a separate claim for intentional infliction of emotional distress, (2) did not claim to suffer from a specific psychiatric injury or disorder, (3) did not claim to suffer "unusually severe" emotional distress, and (4) did not plan to offer expert testimony on her claim of emotional distress. The *Turner* court held that "emotional distress" is not the same as a "mental injury" and that a mere "garden variety" claim for emotional distress is not sufficient to justify a Rule 35 mental examination.[84]

In *Fox v. Gates Corp.*,[85] the court similarly denied the defendant's motion to compel a mental examination. In noting that the plaintiff was asserting only a "garden variety" claim for emotional distress damages resulting from the defendant's refusal to hire her, the court pointed out that the plaintiff was not asserting a separate cause of action for intentional or negligent infliction of emotional distress, was not claiming to have suffered a specific psychiatric injury, and was not claiming to have suffered "unusually severe" emotional distress.[86]

In *Lahr v. Fulbright & Jaworski, L.L.P.*,[87] the court maintained that where a "garden variety" claim is involved, the actual amount of emotional distress suffered by the plaintiff is not at issue. That court explained:

> Like the personal injury claimant who sues to recover damages for mental anguish associated with an injury, a Title VII claimant may seek compensatory damages for emotional pain, suffering, inconvenience, mental anguish, and loss of enjoyment of life. . . . Because this is an assessment of the pain that in reasonable probability results from discrimination, and not that which actually resulted, the defendant in such a suit is not entitled to a compelled mental examination.[88]

The problem with this "garden variety" concept is that it may work well with respect to pain and suffering attendant to a physical injury such as a broken leg, but it is virtually impossible to measure when there is no physical injury and the harm is purely intangible. There is no "garden variety" or "standard" amount of emotional distress that automatically flows from workplace incidents. The psychological impact of a stressor such as a wrongful termination or sexual harassment may differ vastly, depending upon a variety of factors, including the frequency and severity of the stressor and the plaintiff's psychological history and functioning.

---

[84]*See also* Sabree v. Carpenters Local No. 33, 126 F.R.D. 422, 426 (D. Mass. 1989) (plaintiff making a "garden variety" claim of emotional distress did not place his mental condition at issue in the context of a request for production of documents pursuant to FED. R. CIV. P. 34).

[85]179 F.R.D. 303 (D. Colo. 1998).

[86]*Id.* at 307.

[87]164 F.R.D. 204 (N.D. Tex. 1996).

[88]*Id.* at 446 (citations omitted). In *EEOC v. Old Western Furniture Corp.*, 173 F.R.D. 444 (W.D. Tex. 1996), the court relied on this language from *Lahr* in denying the defendant's Rule 35 motion.

Courts have rejected the "garden variety" label, moreover, where the plaintiff claims to have suffered more specific types of mental or emotional distress. For example, in *Thiessen v. General Electric Capital Corp.*,[89] the court initially denied the defendant's Rule 35 motion based upon the plaintiff's general prayer in his complaint for emotional distress damages, noting that the plaintiff had only asserted a "garden variety" emotional distress claim, "one which amounted to no more than an attempt to recover for the generalized insult, hurt feelings and lingering resentment which anyone could be expected to feel if he or she were the recipient of an adverse employment action attributed to discrimination."[90] The court denied the motion without prejudice, however, and the defendant brought the motion again and submitted excerpts of the plaintiff's deposition wherein he claimed to have suffered specific ailments, including water in his lungs, congestive heart failure, and "periods of great sadness and depression." He also claimed that he had not slept well, that he had become very tired, and that he had nearly broken up with his fiancee as the result of workplace events. The court granted the renewed motion, observing that the plaintiff no longer was asserting simply a "garden variety" claim. The court also noted that the fact that the plaintiff offered not to present any expert or medical testimony at trial would not bar the defendant's motion for a mental examination.[91]

Similarly, in *Dahdal v. Thorn Americas Inc.*,[92] the plaintiff resisted the defendant's Rule 35 motion by arguing that it constituted harassment of her and by offering not to enter into evidence medical testimony at trial or the bills she paid for psychological counseling. The court rejected the argument that the motion was motivated by harassment and granted the motion in reliance on matters revealed in the plaintiff's deposition and in the records of the psychiatrist who had treated the plaintiff. Her testimony and the records indicated that the plaintiff was claiming that workplace events caused her to suffer flashbacks to sexual abuse she had suffered prior to going to work for the defendant and that as a result, she suffered severe depression and suicidal thoughts. The court found that the plaintiff had gone beyond alleging a mere "garden variety" injury and ordered her to submit to a mental examination, remarking that the defendant was entitled to pursue discovery designed to determine whether the distress the plaintiff claimed to have suffered was the result of sexual harassment and discrimination, her prior life experiences, or a combination of the two.[93]

---

[89]178 F.R.D. 568 (D. Kan. 1998).
[90]*Id.* at 569.
[91]*Id.* at 571.
[92]76 FEP Cases 88 (D. Kan. 1998).
[93]*Id.* at 89.

Factors Likely to Lead to a Finding of "In Controversy" [New Topic]

Although there is some disagreement as to what additional showing is necessary to establish that a plaintiff's mental condition is in controversy as discussed below, one or some combination of the following factors have led courts to conclude a controversy exists: (1) a separate tort claim for intentional infliction of emotional distress; (2) an allegation that the plaintiff suffers from a specific psychiatric disorder; (3) the plaintiff's plan to offer the testimony of his or her own psychiatric or psychological expert at trial; (4) allegations of continuing mental or emotional injury; (5) allegations of "severe" emotional injury; or (6) plaintiff's concession that his or her mental condition is in controversy.[94]

Separate Claim for Intentional Infliction of Emotional Distress

A plaintiff's mental condition is unquestionably placed in controversy where a separate claim of intentional or negligent infliction of emotional distress is brought.[95] The rationale for this universal rule was explained in *Lahr v. Fulbright & Jaworski, L.L.P.*[96] In *Lahr,* the plaintiff filed suit after her termination, claiming sexual harassment, retaliation, and intentional infliction of emotional distress. During discovery, the magistrate judge ordered the plaintiff to submit to a Rule 35 mental examination, finding that the plaintiff had placed her mental condition in controversy by making a claim of intentional infliction of emotional distress.

In upholding the magistrate judge's ruling, the district court explained that, unlike in most cases where the question is how much mental anguish has the plaintiff suffered as a result of the defendant's wrongful action, "[i]n an action for intentional infliction of emotional distress, the injury that forms the basis of the claim is the severe emotional distress that accompanies the Defendant's outrageous conduct."[97] Therefore, "[a] claimant for intentional infliction of emotional distress does not ask a jury to value the suffering that would ordinarily accompany a wrong. Instead, she raises mental anguish as the essence of the wrong, thereby making her mental condition an issue in the case."[98] The *Lahr* court further explained that this is precisely the type of tort

---

[94]*See* Sarko v. Penn-Del Directory Co., 170 F.R.D. 127, 131 (E.D. Pa. 1997); Turner v. Imperial Stores, 161 F.R.D. 89, 95 (S.D. Cal. 1995).

[95]*See Sarko,* 170 F.R.D. at 131; Lahr v. Fulbright & Jaworski, L.L.P., 164 F.R.D. 204, 209 (N.D. Tex. 1996); *Turner,* 161 F.R.D. at 95; Ragge v. MCA/Universal Studios, 165 F.R.D. 605, 608–09 (C.D. Cal. 1995); Hirschheimer v. Associated Minerals & Minerals Corp., 1995 WL 736901, at *2 (S.D.N.Y. Dec. 12, 1995); Curtis v. Express Inc., 868 F. Supp. 467, 469, 66 FEP Cases 449, 450 (N.D.N.Y. 1994); Bridges v. Eastman Kodak Co., 850 F. Supp. 216, 222, 64 FEP Cases 1100, 1104–05 (S.D.N.Y. 1994); Everly v. United Parcel Serv. Inc., 1991 WL 18429, at *1 (N.D. Ill. Feb. 5, 1991).

[96]164 F.R.D. 204 (N.D. Tex. 1996).

[97]*Id.* at 209.

[98]*Id.*

claim that the Supreme Court found in *Schlagenhauf*[99] would satisfy the "in controversy" requirement of Rule 35. Accordingly, "[a] plaintiff who alleges an action for intentional infliction of emotional distress asserts a mental or emotional injury, and thereby places her mental condition in controversy on the basis of the pleadings alone."[100]

Alleged Presence of a Specific Psychiatric Disorder

Courts routinely have found that a plaintiff's mental condition is in controversy when the plaintiff claims to have suffered a specific psychiatric disorder. In *Morton v. Haskell Co.,*[101] the plaintiff claimed that he had suffered a clinical depression and was discriminated against in violation of the Americans With Disabilities Act and denied leave in violation of the Family and Medical Leave Act. The court granted the defendant's motion to compel a mental examination under Rule 35. In reaching its conclusion, the court reasoned:

> The Court agrees with those cases which hold that plaintiff's "mental condition" within the meaning of Rule 35 is not necessarily placed in controversy merely because Plaintiff seeks recovery for "emotional distress." A person with no "mental condition" may still suffer emotional distress which is compensable. Plaintiff, however, has gone beyond a mere claim for emotional distress as a component for damages in the intentional infliction of emotional distress count. The crux of plaintiff's claims relate to the existence and severity of his clinical depression. Plaintiff's mental condition has thus clearly been placed in controversy since it forms the foundation for most of his claims. If plaintiff did not suffer from this mental condition, or if it was insufficiently severe, he will not prevail on the bulk of his claims. This is clearly sufficient to place plaintiff's mental condition in controversy.[102]

Similarly, in *Ziemann v. Burlington County Bridge Commission,*[103] the plaintiff claimed that she had a depressive disorder resulting in a 60 percent permanent psychiatric disability, half of which she attributed to alleged sexual harassment in the workplace. The court granted the defendant's motion to compel a psychiatric examination pursuant to Rule 35, finding that the plaintiff's mental condition was clearly placed in controversy "because [her] allegations of distinct psychological injuries comprise the almost-exclusive element of damages."[104]

Other courts also have ordered Rule 35 mental examinations without offering any significant analysis of the issue, where the plaintiff has alleged a specific psychiatric disorder.[105]

---

[99]379 U.S. 104 (1964).

[100]*Id.*

[101]5 AD Cases 272 (M.D. Fla. 1995).

[102]*Id.* at 274.

[103]155 F.R.D. 497 (D.N.J. 1994).

[104]*Id.* at 501 n.1.

[105]*See, e.g.,* Shepherd v. American Broad. Cos., 151 F.R.D. 194, 212 (D.D.C. 1993), *rev'd in part and vacated in part on other grounds,* 62 F.3d 1469 (D.C. Cir.

Plaintiff's Use of a Mental Health Expert

A plaintiff also generally is considered to have put his or her mental condition in issue by indicating that he or she will call a mental health professional to testify at trial either in the capacity of expert witness or as treating physician or therapist.[106] In *Shepherd v. American Broadcasting Cos.,*[107] two plaintiffs claimed that the defendants engaged in various racially discriminatory practices and retaliatory acts in connection with the plaintiffs' employment. The court entered a default judgment for the plaintiffs due to the defendants' misconduct during the litigation of the suit. In their proposed order of relief, both plaintiffs requested compensatory damages for emotional pain and suffering. Defendants opposed plaintiffs' claims for compensatory damages and sought a Rule 35 mental examination for each plaintiff. The court, in granting the defendants' request, found that both plaintiffs had definitely placed their mental conditions in controversy. The court's conclusion was based, in substantial part, on the fact that one of the plaintiffs had submitted the full text of her treating physician's deposition in support of her claim that she was suffering from posttraumatic stress disorder.

The court in *Ziemann v. Burlington County Bridge Commission,*[108] a sexual harassment case, also found that the plaintiff had placed her mental condition in controversy by retaining her own psychiatric expert, who was likely to testify on her behalf at trial. As the court noted, "[t]he decisions sanctioning evaluation by defense experts have generally entailed the plaintiff's introduction of psychiatric testimony at trial, which the defense is then permitted to rebut by testimony as to its own mental evaluation."[109]

In *Chaparro v. IBP Inc.,*[110] the plaintiff identified an expert witness who was expected to testify about the emotional impact of the allegedly discriminatory and retaliatory termination of her employment, as well as her treating physician, who was expected to testify about her treatment for depression. The court ordered a Rule 35 mental examination, finding that the plaintiff's intention to call an expert and her treating physician to testify on her behalf at trial indicated that she had affirmatively put her mental condition in controversy.[111]

By the same token, evidence that an expert will not be called may be used to show that a plaintiff's mental condition is not in controversy. For example,

---

1995); Little v. Edgington, 53 FEP Cases 1061 (D. Or. 1990); Kresko v. Rulli, 432 N.W.2d 764 (Minn. Ct. App. 1988); Sarko v. Penn-Del Directory Co., 170 F.R.D. 127, 131 (E.D. Pa. 1997); Turner v. Imperial Stores, 161 F.R.D. 89, 95 (S.D. Cal. 1995); Cody v. Marriott Corp., 103 F.R.D. 421, 423, 44 FEP Cases 1228, 1229 (D. Mass. 1984).

[106]*See Sarko,* 170 F.R.D. at 131; *Turner,* 161 F.R.D. at 95; Chaparo v. IBP Inc., 1994 WL 714369, at *3 (D. Kan. 1994); *Ziemann,* 155 F.R.D. at 501 n.1.

[107]151 F.R.D. 194 (D.D.C. 1993), *rev'd in part and vacated in part on other grounds,* 62 F.3d 1469 (D.C. Cir. 1995).

[108]155 F.R.D. 497 (D.N.J. 1994).

[109]*Id.* at 501 n.1.

[110]1994 WL 714369 (D. Kan. Dec. 7, 1994).

[111]*Id.* at *3.

in *Borquez v. Ozer,*[112] the Colorado Court of Appeals held that the plaintiff's general allegations of mental suffering and emotional distress in his wrongful discharge suit did not place his mental condition in controversy where he did not intend to make his mental state a matter of genuine controversy, did not intend to call a psychiatric expert witness at trial, and did not intend to present any medical evidence of his mental suffering.[113]

Allegation of Continuing Emotional Injury

Absent one of the other aforementioned factors set out in *The "In Controversy" Requirement,* above, some courts have adhered to the notion that there must be allegations of continuing mental or emotional distress or injury before a plaintiff's mental condition is considered to be in controversy.[114]

For example, in *Doyle v. Superior Court,*[115] a California appellate court held that claims of only past mental and emotional suffering were insufficient to put a plaintiff's mental condition at issue. It distinguished the California Supreme Court's decision in *Vinson v. Superior Court*[116] in that there were allegations of continuing emotional distress in *Vinson.*[117] The *Doyle* court took a very narrow view of the definition of "in controversy." It explained:

> The mental condition of a person who is suffering ongoing mental distress is clearly "in controversy" in an action seeking damages for that ongoing mental distress. The "controversy" surrounding such a person's mental condition includes not only the nature and extent of the person's current mental injury but also the actual cause of this injury. In contrast, where a plaintiff alleges that she is not suffering any current mental injury but only that she has suffered emotional distress in the past arising from the defendant's misconduct, a mental examination

---

[112]923 P.2d 166, 69 FEP Cases 1415, 11 IER Cases 496 (Colo. Ct. App. 1995), *aff'd in part and rev'd in part on other grounds,* 940 P.2d 371, 12 IER Cases 1665 (Colo. 1997).

[113]923 P.2d at 176, 69 FEP Cases at 421, 11 IER Cases at 503–04. *See also* Neal v. Siegel-Robert Inc., 171 F.R.D. 264, 267, 73 FEP Cases 637, 638 (E.D. Mo. 1996) (age discrimination plaintiff's deposition testimony that he did not intend to see a psychiatrist or psychologist was evidence that his mental condition had not been placed in controversy).

[114]*See, e.g.,* O'Quinn v. New York Univ. Med. Ctr., 163 F.R.D. 226, 228, 68 FEP Cases 1798, 1800 (S.D.N.Y. 1995); Curtis v. Express Inc., 868 F. Supp. 467, 469, 66 FEP Cases 449, 450 (N.D.N.Y. 1994); Bridges v. Eastman Kodak Co., 850 F. Supp. 216, 222, 64 FEP Cases 1100, 1104 (S.D.N.Y. 1994). *See also* Sarko v. Penn-Del Directory Co., 170 F.R.D. 127, 131 (E.D. Pa. 1997) (recognizing that courts tend to order mental examinations where "the plaintiff alleges that he suffers a severe ongoing mental injury").

[115]50 Cal. App. 4th 1878, 58 Cal. Rptr. 2d 476 (1996).

[116]43 Cal. 3d 833, 239 Cal. Rptr. 292, 44 FEP Cases 1174 (1987).

[117]*Vinson* also involved a separate claim for intentional infliction of emotional distress.

is unnecessary because such an allegation alone does not place the nature and cause of the plaintiff's current mental condition "in controversy."[118]

In placing so much emphasis on the fact that the plaintiff's *current* mental condition was not in dispute, the *Doyle* court seemed to miss the point that the plaintiff there was not suing for current emotional injuries, but rather for past emotional injuries, the causation of which the defendant disputed. Although the plaintiff's past emotional condition was in controversy, the defendant was prevented by the court's decision from defending itself in that dispute via a mental examination of the plaintiff.

One issue that arises with respect to claims of emotional injury that is not continuing is the reliability of medical or psychological opinions concerning whether or not the plaintiff suffered emotional injury in the past. At least one court has indicated its belief that a physician conducting a Rule 35 examination is able to provide a "retrospective opinion" of the plaintiff's condition during the relevant time period, although in that case, the plaintiff alleged ongoing as well as prior mental injuries.[119] In *Jenson v. Eveleth Taconite Co.,*[120] moreover, the Eighth Circuit referred to as "questionable" the lower court's finding that there is no scientifically developed psychiatric model or procedure for determining whether a particular stressor caused a particular symptom or mental state and noted that several courts "have noted the probative value of expert psychological proof regarding causation of the claimant's depression and emotional distress."[121]

Thus, for example, if a plaintiff were to claim that she was "severely depressed" following an episode of sexual harassment but is no longer depressed, a skilled forensic psychiatrist or psychologist could still elicit from the plaintiff a description of her symptoms and functioning during the period of her claimed depression, and compare such an account with the diagnostic criteria contained in the American Psychiatric Association's *Diagnostic and Statistical Manual of Mental Disorders.*[122] If such a plaintiff claimed to have been severely depressed and unable to work but did not describe having suffered a sufficient number of symptoms required for a diagnosis of depression, and if she related that she was able to care for herself and her family, apply successfully for disability benefits, and assist her attorney with the prosecution of her lawsuit, there would appear to be enough of a scientific basis for a qualified mental health expert to testify that the plaintiff did not meet the diagnostic criteria for a severe and disabling depression during the time period in question.

---

[118]50 Cal. App. 4th at 1887, 58 Cal. Rptr. at 482.

[119]Morton v. Haskell Co., 5 AD Cases 272, 274 (M.D. Fla. 1995).

[120]130 F.3d 1287 (8th Cir. 1997).

[121]*Id.* at 1297 (*citing* Karcher v. Emerson Elec. Co., 94 F.3d 502, 71 FEP Cases 1651 (8th Cir. 1996); Webb v. Hyman, 861 F. Supp. 1094 (D.D.C. 1994); Alberts v. Wickes Lumber Co., 69 FEP Cases 304 (N.D. Ill. 1995); Hurley v. Atlantic City Police Dep't, 933 F. Supp. 396 (D.N.J. 1996)).

[122](4th ed. 1994).

Accordingly, the distinction between past and current mental condition seems an artificial one, albeit one that some courts are willing to recognize. Conversely, courts routinely have found a plaintiff's mental condition to be in controversy where there were allegations of ongoing mental or emotional distress.[123]

Allegation of Severe Emotional Injury

Claims of severe emotional distress alone may be sufficient to place a plaintiff's mental condition "in controversy." For example, in *Chapparo v. IBP Inc.,*[124] the plaintiff asserted claims of employment discrimination and retaliatory discharge, alleging "grievous emotional injury." The plaintiff also indicated that her treating physician as well as an expert would testify on her behalf at trial. The defendant then moved to compel a mental examination under Rule 35, arguing that the plaintiff's claim of severe emotional distress and the designation of the two expert witnesses placed her mental condition in controversy. The court granted the motion, noting that although the mere assertion of a claim for emotional distress does not by itself put the plaintiff's mental condition in controversy, here the plaintiff had identified two experts who would testify about her emotional condition and treatment, and more important, "[b]eyond a more conventional claim of emotional distress, she has alleged her distress to be 'severe and extreme.' "[125] Although the severity of the emotional injury allegedly suffered by the plaintiff was not the only factor that the court looked at in determining whether plaintiff's mental condition had been placed in controversy, the *Chapparo* court suggested that such allegations alone may be enough to meet the "in controversy" requirement.[126]

Other courts have not made this point as strongly. In *Ali v. Wang Laboratories,*[127] the court held that the "in controversy" requirement was satisfied based on allegations of severe and ongoing emotional distress, but it did not indicate whether allegations of severe emotional distress alone would have produced the same result.[128] In *Turner v. Imperial Stores,*[129] the court observed

---

[123]*See, e.g.,* Sarko v. Penn-Del Directory Co., 170 F.R.D. 127 (E.D. Pa. 1997); Hirschheimer v. Associated Minerals & Minerals Corp., 1995 WL 736901 (S.D.N.Y. Dec. 12, 1995); Ali v. Wang Labs., 162 F.R.D. 165, 4 AD Cases 520 (M.D. Fla. 1995); Ragge v. MCA/Universal Studios, 165 F.R.D. 605 (C.D. Cal. 1995); Jansen v. Packaging Corp. of Am., 158 F.R.D. 409, 66 FEP Cases 556 (N.D. Ill. 1994); Ryzlak v. McNeil Pharm. Co., 38 Fed. R. Serv. 2d 443 (E.D. Pa. 1982).

[124]1994 WL 714369 (D. Kan. Dec. 7, 1994).

[125]*Id.* at *3.

[126]*See also* Shepherd v. American Broad. Cos., 151 F.R.D. 194, 212–13 (D.D.C. 1993), *rev'd in part and vacated in part on other grounds,* 62 F.3d 1469 (D.C. Cir. 1995); Lowe v. Philadelphia Newspapers Inc., 101 F.R.D. 296, 298–99, 44 FEP Cases 1224, 1225–26 (E.D. Pa. 1983).

[127]162 F.R.D. 165, 4 AD Cases 520 (M.D. Fla. 1995).

[128]*Id.* at 168, 4 AD Cases at 522.

[129]161 F.R.D. 89 (S.D. Cal. 1995).

that other courts have ordered Rule 35 mental examinations when the plaintiff alleged unusually severe emotional distress, but the court went on to hold that there was no claim for severe emotional distress in that particular case even though the plaintiff was seeking more than $1 million in damages for "humiliation, mental anguish, and emotional distress."[130]

Plaintiff Concedes That Mental Condition Is in Controversy

The "in controversy" requirement is easily satisfied when a plaintiff concedes that his or her mental condition has been placed at issue.[131] When this occurs, the only issue for the court is whether there is good cause to order a Rule 35 mental examination.[132] The "good cause" requirement is discussed in detail below.

The Good Cause Requirement

In addition to showing that a plaintiff's mental condition is in controversy, a defendant also must show that there exists good cause for conducting a mental examination before one will be ordered pursuant to Rule 35. The Supreme Court commented in *Schlagenhauf*[133] that in a negligence action, allegations of mental or emotional injuries, alone, are enough to demonstrate good cause. In the arena of employment litigation, a few courts have followed this reasoning and found good cause to exist based entirely upon allegations of mental or emotional distress.[134]

"Good cause" has been held to require a showing that "the party seeking the medical examination has exhausted other discovery procedures before seeking such examination."[135] This can be demonstrated through the affidavit of an

---

[130]*Id.* at 97. *But see Shepherd,* 151 F.R.D. at 212–13 (holding that plaintiffs have placed their mental conditions "in controversy" by demanding close to $2 million in compensatory damages for emotional distress).

[131]*See, e.g.,* Shirsat v. Mutual Pharm. Co., 169 F.R.D. 68, 70 (E.D. Pa. 1996) (wrongful discharge); Ferrell v. Shell Oil Co., 1995 WL 688795, at *1 (E.D. La. 1995) (sex discrimination, sexual harassment, intentional infliction of emotional distress). *See also* Sarko v. Penn-Del Directory Co., 170 F.R.D. 127, 131 (E.D. Pa. 1997) (recognizing that plaintiff's mental condition has been put in controversy where plaintiff concedes the issue); *Turner,* 161 F.R.D. at 95 (same).

[132]*Shirsat,* 169 F.R.D. at 70; *Ferrell,* 1995 WL 688795, at *1.

[133]379 U.S. 104, 119 (1964).

[134]*See, e.g.,* Jansen v. Packaging Corp. of Am., 158 F.R.D. 409, 410, 66 FEP Cases 556, 557 (N.D. Ill. 1994); Smedley v. Capps, Staples, Ward, Hastings & Dodson, 820 F. Supp. 1227, 1232, 61 FEP Cases 1360, 1364 (N.D. Cal. 1993); Zabkowicz v. West Bend Co., 585 F. Supp. 635, 636, 35 FEP Cases 209, 209 (E.D. Wis. 1984).

[135]Everly v. United Parcel Serv. Inc., 1991 WL 18429, at *1 (N.D. Ill. 1991). *Accord* Lahr v. Fulbright & Jaworski, L.L.P., 164 F.R.D. 204, 211–12 (N.D. Tex. 1996); Ragge v. MCA/Universal Studios, 165 F.R.D. 605, 609 (C.D. Cal. 1995).

expert attesting that the discovery materials available to the defendant are inadequate by themselves from a psychiatric or psychological standpoint for the expert to formulate an opinion concerning the existence, nature, and cause of the plaintiff's emotional injury.[136]

"[S]ometimes the two requirements of Rule 35 are merged,"[137] however, and the presence of some other factors beyond a mere allegation of mental or emotional distress, such as those required by some courts for a plaintiff's mental condition to be "in controversy," may also satisfy the good cause requirement. For example, a number of courts will find good cause for ordering a mental examination upon allegations of ongoing emotional distress.[138] Similarly, a separate tort claim of intentional or negligent infliction of emotional distress also may provide good cause.[139]

A common basis for finding "good cause," whether or not other discovery methods have been exhausted, is the defendant's need to rebut the plaintiff's claims for damages for mental or emotional distress. This is especially true when plaintiffs plan to offer the testimony of their own experts or treating physicians or therapists to support their claims.[140]

Even when the plaintiff does not plan to use an expert, a court may still find that the defendant has good cause for a Rule 35 mental examination, to permit it to rebut the plaintiff's claims for mental or emotional damages. As the court in *Ali v. Wang Laboratories*[141] explained:

> While plaintiff may be content to offer only his own testimony to a jury, defendant is not compelled to limit its case to mere cross examination. Since plaintiff's mental condition is in controversy and substantial damages are asserted, it is essential for defendant to have the reasonable opportunity to challenge plaintiff's claim and testimony. The testimony of an expert is a well recognized and reason-

---

[136]*See, e.g., Everly,* 1991 WL 18429, at *1; *Lahr,* 164 F.R.D. at 211–12.

[137]*Ragge,* 165 F.R.D. at 609.

[138]*See, e.g.,* Sarko v. Penn-Del Directory Co., 170 F.R.D. 127, 131 (E.D. Pa. 1997); Hirschheimer v. Associated Minerals & Minerals Corp., 1995 WL 736901, at *2 (S.D.N.Y. 1995); *Ragge,* 165 F.R.D. at 609; *Jansen,* 158 F.R.D. at 410, 66 FEP Cases at 557; Vinson v. Superior Court, 43 Cal. 3d 833, 839–40, 239 Cal. Rptr. 292, 297–98, 44 FEP Cases 1174, 1176 (1987).

[139]*See, e.g., Hirschheimer,* 1995 WL 736901, at *2.

[140]*See, e.g.,* Ferrell v. Shell Oil Co., 1995 WL 688795, at *1 (E.D. La. 1995); Morton v. Haskell Co., 5 AD Cases 272, 274 (M.D. Fla. 1995); Chaparro v. IBP Inc., 1994 WL 714369, at *3 (D. Kan. 1994); Shepherd v. American Broad. Cos., 151 F.R.D. 194, 213 (D.D.C. 1993), *rev'd in part and vacated in part on other grounds,* 62 F.3d 1469 (D.C. Cir. 1995); Lowe v. Philadelphia Newspapers Inc., 101 F.R.D. 296, 298–99, 44 FEP Cases 1224, 1226 (E.D. Pa. 1983); Ryzlak v. McNeil Pharm. Co., 38 Fed. R. Serv. 2d 443, 444 (E.D. Pa. 1982). *See also* Kresko v. Rulli, 432 N.W.2d 764, 770 (Minn. Ct. App. 1988) (not expressly addressing "good cause" but recognizing that a mental examination was appropriate where, among other things, plaintiff listed and called two expert witnesses to testify as to her psychological status).

[141]162 F.R.D. 165, 4 AD Cases 520 (M.D. Fla. 1995).

able way of doing so, and an examination of plaintiff by that expert is necessary for the expert . . . to form a meaningful opinion.[142]

Similarly, the California Supreme Court in *Vinson* observed, with respect to the plaintiff's claim for emotional distress damages in that case: "[P]laintiff cannot be allowed to make her very serious allegations without affording defendants an opportunity to put their truth to the test."[143]

Occasionally, a plaintiff will object to a Rule 35 mental examination on the grounds that a prior examination already has been conducted and that a second examination would subject the plaintiff to unnecessary harassment. Courts have found good cause to order the second examination where there was a change of circumstances warranting a new examination,[144] where the prior examination did not address all of the issues being litigated,[145] or where the prior examination was conducted by the plaintiff's psychologist or psychiatrist.[146]

Statutes of Limitations [New Topic]

In *Stoll v. Runyon*,[147] the Ninth Circuit held that the limitations period for a plaintiff to file a sexual harassment charge under Title VII would be tolled on account of the psychological injuries suffered by the plaintiff as a result of the harassment.

In *Stoll*, the plaintiff was raped by a supervisor, and was repeatedly asked by supervisors and co-workers to perform oral sex on them. Her male co-workers rubbed up against her, pressing their erect penises against her back, and followed her into the women's restroom, and her supervisor refused to allow her to go to the restroom when menstruating. The plaintiff was diagnosed with severe major depression, severe generalized anxiety disorder, and somatic pain disorder. Her psychiatrist testified that she might never recover from the abuse and might never work again. She attempted suicide four times and was on psychiatric disability leave.

The plaintiff had pursued a Title VII claim, which was heard by an administrative law judge of the Equal Employment Opportunity Commission. The judge did not award her front pay, and she appealed the ruling to the Office of Federal Operations. That agency also denied her request for front pay. Almost a year later, the plaintiff filed a handwritten pro se complaint in

---

[142]*Id.* at 168, 4 AD Cases at 522 (citations omitted).

[143]Vinson v. Superior Court, 43 Cal. 3d 833, 842, 239 Cal. Rptr. 292, 298, 44 FEP Cases 1174, 1177 (1987).

[144]*See* Ziemann v. Burlington County Bridge Comm'n, 155 F.R.D. 497, 501–02 (D.N.J. 1994).

[145]*See* Little v. Edgington, 53 FEP Cases 1061, 1062 (D. Or. 1990).

[146]*See* Shirsat v. Mutual Pharm. Co., 169 F.R.D. 68, 70 (E.D. Pa. 1996).

[147]165 F.3d 1238, 78 FEP Cases 1312 (9th Cir. 1998).

federal court under Title VII. The defendant moved to dismiss on the ground that the complaint was not filed withing the 90-day limitations period following the plaintiff's exhaustion of her administrative appeals, and the court granted the motion over the plaintiff's objection that the statute had been equitably tolled.

The Ninth Circuit reversed, noting that equitable tolling applies when the plaintiff has been prevented from timely asserting a claim by wrongful conduct by the defendant, or when extraordinary circumstances beyond the plaintiff's control have made it impossible to file a claim on time. It held that both grounds for equitable tolling had been met. The court explained that "the Post Office is not entitled to benefit from the fact that its own admittedly outrageous acts left Stoll so broken and damaged that she cannot protect her own rights."[148] It also held that the plaintiff was mentally incapacitated, which prevented her from relating effectively with her lawyer so as to have filed her lawsuit on time. Specifically, the court cited evidence that the plaintiff was unable to open her mail without suffering a panic attack and could not concentrate well enough to read. The plaintiff testified that she was unable to communicate directly with her own lawyer about matters involving the case. Instead, her lawyer would send all correspondence relating to the case to the plaintiff's psychiatrist's office, where a receptionist would open it and explain it to her. Her psychiatrist testified that the plaintiff was heavily medicated on Valium and Vicodin and was unable to understand her legal rights.

Although the facts in *Stoll* are much more egregious and extreme than those encountered in most harassment and discrimination cases, the Ninth Circuit's result suggests that some courts may find the limitations period to be tolled where the plaintiff is mentally incapacitated—particularly if the mental incapacitation flowed from the workplace events at issue.[149] Courts will have to use care, however, to ensure that the element of extreme mental incapacity present in *Stoll* is not trivialized in future cases such that every plaintiff who suffers some emotional distress from discrimination or harassment might argue for tolling.

---

[148]*Id.* at 1242, 78 FEP Cases at 1315.

[149]*But see* David v. Trugreen Ltd. Partnership, 1999 WL 288686 (N.D. Tex. 1999) (rejecting tolling argument because plaintiff's mental illness was not alleged to be caused by the workplace, and noting that the plaintiff was competent to seek legal counsel and apply for an auto loan, and was released by his doctor to return to work, during the limitations period).

CHAPTER 2

MENTAL DISORDERS COMMONLY CLAIMED IN EMPLOYMENT LITIGATION

The Concept of a Mental Disorder

The Diagnostic and Statistical Manual of Mental Disorders

In late 1994, the American Psychiatric Association released the fourth edition of its *Diagnostic and Statistical Manual of Mental Disorders*™, known as *DSM-IV*™. *DSM-IV* is to be used for the diagnosis of mental disorders after January 1, 1995. The *DSM-IV* diagnostic criteria for the mental disorders set forth in the Main Volume are as follows.

Commonly Claimed Mental Disorders

Adjustment Disorders

Exhibit 2-1S Diagnostic Criteria for Adjustment Disorder

A. The development of emotional or behavioral symptoms in response to an identifiable stressor(s) occurring within three months of the onset of the stressor(s).

B. These symptoms or behaviors are clinically significant as evidenced by either of the following:
   (1) marked distress that is in excess of what would be expected from exposure to the stressor
   (2) significant impairment in social or occupational (academic) functioning

C. The stress-related disturbance does not meet the criteria for another specific Axis I disorder and is not merely an exacerbation of a preexisting Axis I or II disorder.

D. The symptoms do not represent Bereavement.

continued

Exhibit 2-1S *Continued.*

E. Once the stressor (or its consequences) has terminated, the symptoms do not persist for more than an additional 6 months.

Specify if:

Acute: if the disturbance lasts less than 6 months
Chronic: if the disturbance lasts for 6 months or longer

Adjustment Disorders are coded based on the subtype, which is selected according to the predominant symptoms. The specific stressor(s) can be specified on Axis IV.

309.0	With Depressed Mood
309.24	With Anxiety
309.28	With Mixed Anxiety and Depressed Mood
309.3	With Disturbance of Conduct
309.4	With Mixed Disturbance of Emotions and Conduct
309.9	Unspecified

Source: Reprinted with permission from the DIAGNOSTIC AND STATISTICAL MANUAL OF MENTAL DISORDERS 626–27 (4th ed. 1994). Copyright 1994 American Psychiatric Association.

Exhibit 2-2S Types of Adjustment Disorders

- Adjustment Disorder with Depressed Mood
- Adjustment Disorder with Anxiety
- Adjustment Disorder with Mixed Anxiety and Depressed Mood
- Adjustment Disorder with Disturbance of Conduct
- Adjustment Disorder with Mixed Disturbance of Emotions and Conduct
- Adjustment Disorder Unspecified

Source: Reprinted with permission from the DIAGNOSTIC AND STATISTICAL MANUAL OF MENTAL DISORDERS 623–24 (4th ed. 1994). Copyright 1994 American Psychiatric Association.

Mood Disorders

Major Depression

Exhibit 2-3S Diagnostic Criteria for Major Depressive Disorder

Single Episode

A. Presence of a single Major Depressive Episode.

B. The Major Depressive Episode is not better accounted for by Schizoaffective Disorder and is not superimposed on Schizophrenia, Schizophreniform Disorder, Delusional Disorder, or Psychotic Disorder Not Otherwise Specified.

C. There has never been a Manic Episode, a Mixed Episode, or a Hypomanic Episode. **Note:** This exclusion does not apply if all of the manic-like, mixed-like, or hypomanic-like episodes are substance or treatment induced or are due to the direct physiological effects of a general medical condition.

Specify (for current or most recent episode):
Severity/Psychotic/Remission Specifiers
With Catatonic Features
With Melancholic Features
With Atypical Features
With Postpartum Onset

Recurrent

A. Presence of two or more Major Depressive Episodes. *Note:* To be considered separate episodes, there must be an interval of at least 2 consecutive months in which criteria are not met for a Major Depressive Episode.

B. The Major Depressive Episodes are not better accounted for by Schizoaffective Disorder and are not superimposed on Schizophrenia, Schizophreniform Disorder, Delusional Disorder, or Psychotic Disorder Not Otherwise Specified.

C. There has never been a Manic Episode, a Mixed Episode, or a Hypomanic Episode. **Note:** This exclusion does not apply if all of the manic-like, mixed-like, or hypomanic-like episodes are substance or treatment induced or are due to the direct physiological effects of a general medical condition.

Specify (for current or most recent episode):
Severity/Psychotic/Remission Specifiers
Chronic
With Catatonic Features
With Melancholic Features
With Atypical Features
With Postpartum Onset

Specify:
Longitudinal Course Specifiers (With and Without Interepisode Recovery)
With Seasonal Pattern

Source: Reprinted with permission from the DIAGNOSTIC AND STATISTICAL MANUAL OF MENTAL DISORDERS 344–45 (4th ed. 1994). Copyright 1994 American Psychiatric Association.

Dysthymia

Exhibit 2-4S Diagnostic Criteria for Dysthymic Disorder

A. Depressed mood for most of the day, for more days than not, as indicated either by subjective account or observation by others, for at least 2 years. **Note:** In children and adolescents, mood can be irritable and duration must be at least 1 year.

B. Presence, while depressed, of two (or more) of the following:
(1) poor appetite or overeating
(2) insomnia or hypersomnia
(3) low energy or fatigue

continued

Exhibit 2-4S ***Continued.***

(4) low self-esteem
(5) poor concentration or difficulty making decisions
(6) feelings of hopelessness

C. During the 2-year period (1 year for children or adolescents) of the disturbance, the person has never been without the symptoms in Criteria A and B for more than 2 months at a time.

D. No Major Depressive Episode has been present during the first 2 years of the disturbance; **i.e.,** the disturbance is not better accounted for by chronic Major Depressive Disorder, or Major Depressive Disorder, In Partial Remission.

Note: There may have been a previous Major Depressive Episode provided there was a full remission (no significant signs or symptoms for 2 months) before development of the Dysthymic Disorder. In addition, after the initial 2 years (1 year in children or adolescents) of Dysthymic Disorder, there may be superimposed episodes of Major Depressive Disorder, in which case both diagnoses may be given when the criteria are met for a Major Depressive Episode.

E. There has never been a Manic Episode, a Mixed Episode, or a Hypomanic Episode, and criteria have never been met for Cyclothymic Disorder.

F. The disturbance does not occur exclusively during the course of a chronic Psychotic Disorder, such as Schizophrenia or Delusional Disorder.

G. The symptoms are not due to the direct physiological effects of a substance (e.g., a drug of abuse, a medication) or a general medical condition (e.g., hypothyroidism).

H. The symptoms cause clinically significant distress or impairment in social, occupational, or other important areas of functioning.

Specify if:
Early Onset: if onset is before age 21 years
Late Onset: if onset is age 21 years or older

Specify (for most recent 2 years of Dysthymic Disorder):
With Atypical Features

Source: Reprinted with permission from the DIAGNOSTIC AND STATISTICAL MANUAL OF MENTAL DISORDERS 349 (4th ed. 1994). Copyright 1994 American Psychiatric Association.

Anxiety Disorders

Panic Disorder

Exhibit 2-5S Diagnostic Criteria for Panic Disorder

Without Agoraphobia

A. Both (1) and (2):
(1) recurrent unexpected Panic Attacks

(2) at least one of the attacks has been followed by 1 month or more of one (or more) of the following:
  (a) persistent concern about having additional attacks
  (b) worry about the implications of the attack or its consequences (e.g., losing control, having a heart attack, "going crazy")
  (c) a significant change in behavior related to the attacks

B. Absence of Agoraphobia.

C. The Panic Attacks are not due to the direct physiological effects of a substance (e.g., a drug of abuse, a medication) or a general medical condition (e.g., hypothyroidism).

D. The Panic Attacks are not better accounted for by another mental disorder, such as Social Phobia (e.g., occurring on exposure to feared social situations), Specific Phobia (e.g., on exposure to a specific phobic situation), Obsessive-Compulsive Disorder (e.g., on exposure to dirt in someone with an obsession about contamination), Posttraumatic Stress Disorder (e.g., in response to stimuli associated with a severe stressor), or Separation Anxiety Disorder (e.g., in response to being away from home or close relatives).

With Agoraphobia

A. Both (1) and (2):
  (1) recurrent unexpected Panic Attacks
  (2) at least one of the attacks has been followed by 1 month or more of one (or more) of the following:
    (a) persistent concern about having additional attacks
    (b) worry about the implications of the attack or its consequences (e.g., losing control, having a heart attack, "going crazy")
    (c) a significant change in behavior related to the attacks

B. The presence of Agoraphobia

C. The Panic Attacks are not due to the direct physiological effects of a substance (e.g., a drug of abuse, a medication) or a general medical condition (e.g., hypothyroidism).

D. The Panic Attacks are not better accounted for by another mental disorder, such as Social Phobia (e.g., occurring on exposure to feared social situations), Specific Phobia (e.g., on exposure to a specific phobic situation), Obsessive-Compulsive Disorder (e.g., on exposure to dirt in someone with an obsession about contamination), Posttraumatic Stress Disorder (e.g., in response to stimuli associated with a severe stressor), or Separation Anxiety Disorder (e.g., in response to being away from home or close relatives).

Source: Reprinted with permission from the DIAGNOSTIC AND STATISTICAL MANUAL OF MENTAL DISORDERS 402–03 (4th ed. 1994).

Generalized Anxiety Disorder

Exhibit 2-6S Diagnostic Criteria for Generalized Anxiety Disorder

A. Excessive anxiety and worry (apprehensive expectation), occurring more days than not for at least 6 months, about a number of events or activities (such as work or school performance).

B. The person finds it difficult to control the worry.

C. The anxiety and worry are associated with three (or more) of the following six symptoms (with at least some symptoms present for more days than not for the last 6 months). **Note:** Only one item is required in children.
   (1) restlessness or feeling keyed up or on edge
   (2) being easily fatigued
   (3) difficulty concentrating or mind going blank
   (4) irritability
   (5) muscle tension
   (6) sleep disturbance (difficulty falling asleep, or restless unsatisfying sleep)

D. The focus of the anxiety and worry is not confined to features of an Axis I disorder, e.g., the anxiety or worry is not about having a Panic Attack (as in Panic Disorder), being embarrassed in public (as in Social Phobia), being contaminated (as in Obsessive-Compulsive Disorder), being away from home or close relatives (as in Separation Anxiety Disorder), gaining weight (as in Anorexia Nervosa), having a serious illness (as in Hypochondriasis), and the anxiety and worry do not occur exclusively during Posttraumatic Stress Disorder.

E. The anxiety, worry, or physical symptoms cause clinically significant distress or impairment in social, occupational, or other important areas of functioning.

F. The disturbance is not due to the direct physiological effects of a substance (e.g., a drug of abuse, a medication) or a general medical condition (e.g., hypothyroidism) and does not occur exclusively during a Mood Disorder, a Psychotic Disorder, or a Pervasive Developmental Disorder.

Source: Reprinted with permission from the DIAGNOSTIC AND STATISTICAL MANUAL OF MENTAL DISORDERS 435–36 (4th ed. 1994). Copyright 1994 American Psychiatric Association.

Psychological Factors Affecting Physical Condition

Exhibit 2-7S Diagnostic Criteria for Psychological Factors Affecting Physical Condition

A. A general medical condition (coded on Axis III) is present.

B. Psychological factors adversely affect the general medical condition in one of the following ways:

(1) the factors have influenced the course of the general medical condition as shown by a close temporal association between the psychological factors and the development or exacerbation of, or delayed recovery from, the general medical condition
(2) the factors interfere with the treatment of the general medical condition
(3) the factors constitute additional health risks for the individual
(4) stress-related physiological responses precipitate or exacerbate symptoms of the general medical condition

Choose name based on the nature of the psychological factors (if more than one factor is present, indicate the most prominent):

- Mental Disorder Affecting . . . [*Indicate the General Medical Condition*] (e.g., an Axis I disorder such a Major Depressive Disorder delaying recovery from a myocardial infarction)
- Psychological Symptoms Affecting . . . [*Indicate the General Medical Condition*] (e.g., depressive symptoms delaying recovery from surgery; anxiety exacerbating asthma)
- Personality Traits or Coping Style Affecting . . . [*Indicate the General Medical Condition*] (e.g., pathological denial of the need for surgery in a patient with cancer; hostile, pressured behavior contributing to cardiovascular disease)
- Maladaptive Health Behaviors Affecting . . . [*Indicate the General Medical Condition*] (e.g., overeating; lack of exercise; unsafe sex)
- Stress-Related Physiological Response Affecting . . . [*Indicate the General Medical Condition*] (e.g., stress-related exacerbations of ulcer, hypertension, arrhythmia, or tension headache)
- Other or Unspecified Psychological Factors Affecting . . . [*Indicate the General Medical Condition*] (e.g., interpersonal, cultural, or religious factors)

Source: Reprinted with permission from the DIAGNOSTIC AND STATISTICAL MANUAL OF MENTAL DISORDERS 678 (4th ed. 1994). Copyright 1994 American Psychiatric Association.

Somatoform Disorders

Hypochondriasis

Exhibit 2-8S Diagnostic Criteria for Hypochondriasis

A. Preoccupation with fears of having, or the idea that one has, a serious disease based on the person's misinterpretation of bodily symptoms.

B. The preoccupation persists despite appropriate medical evaluation and reassurance.

C. The belief in Criterion A is not of delusional intensity (as in Delusional Disorder, Somatic Type) and is not restricted to a circumscribed concern about appearance (as in Body Dysmorphic Disorder).

continued

Exhibit 2-8S ***Continued.***

D. The preoccupation causes clinically significant distress or impairment in social, occupational, or other important areas of functioning.

E. The duration of the disturbance is at least 6 months.

F. The preoccupation is not better accounted for by Generalized Anxiety Disorder, Obsessive-Compulsive Disorder, Panic Disorder, a Major Depressive Episode, Separation Anxiety, or other Somatoform Disorder.

Specify if:

With Poor Insight: for most of the time during the current episode, the person does not recognize that the concern about having a serious illness is excessive or unreasonable

Source: Reprinted with permission from the DIAGNOSTIC AND STATISTICAL MANUAL OF MENTAL DISORDERS 465 (4th ed. 1994). Copyright 1994 American Psychiatric Association.

Somatoform Pain Disorder

Exhibit 2-9S Diagnostic Criteria for Somatoform Pain Disorder

A. Pain in one or more anatomical sites is the predominant focus of the clinical presentation and is of sufficient severity to warrant clinical attention.

B. The pain causes clinically significant distress or impairment in social, occupational, or other important areas of functioning.

C. Psychological factors are judged to have an important role in the onset, severity, exacerbation, or maintenance of the pain.

D. The symptom or deficit is not intentionally produced or feigned (as in Factitious Disorder or Malingering).

E. The pain is not better accounted for by a Mood, Anxiety, or Psychotic Disorder and does not meet criteria for Dyspareunia.

Code as follows:

307.80 Pain Disorder Associated With Psychological Factors: psychological factors are judged to have the major role in the onset, severity, exacerbation, or maintenance of the pain. (If a general medical condition is present, it does not have a major role in the onset, severity, exacerbation, or maintenance of the pain). This type of Pain Disorder is not diagnosed if criteria are also met for Somatization Disorder.

Specify if:

Acute: duration of less than 6 months
Chronic: duration of 6 months or longer

Note: The following is not considered to be a mental disorder and is included here to facilitate differential diagnosis.

Pain Disorder Associated With a General Medical Condition: a general medical condition has a major role in the onset, severity, exacerbation, or maintenance of the pain. (If psychological factors are present, they are not judged to have a major role in the onset, severity, exacerbation, or maintenance of the pain.) The diagnostic code for the pain is selected based on the associated general medical condition if one has been established or on the anatomical location of the pain if the underlying general medical condition is not yet clearly established—for example, low back (724.2), sciatic (724.3), pelvic (625.9), headache (784.0), facial (784.0), chest (786.50), joint (719.4), bone (733.90), abdominal (789.0), breast (611.71), renal (788.0), ear (388.70), eye (379.91), throat (784.1), tooth (525.9), and urinary (788.0).

Source: Reprinted with permission from the DIAGNOSTIC AND STATISTICAL MANUAL OF MENTAL DISORDERS 462 (4th ed. 1994). Copyright 1994 American Psychiatric Association.

Somatization Disorder

Exhibit 2-10S Diagnostic Criteria for Somatization Disorder

A. A history of many physical complaints beginning before age 30 years that occur over a period of several years and result in treatment being sought or significant impairment in social, occupational, or other important areas of functioning.

B. Each of the following criteria must have been met, with individual symptoms occurring at any time during the course of the disturbance:
   (1) *four pain symptoms:* a history of pain related to at least four different sites or functions (e.g., head, abdomen, back, joints, extremities, chest, rectum, during menstruation, during sexual intercourse, or during urination)
   (2) *two gastrointestinal symptoms:* a history of at least two gastrointestinal symptoms other than pain (e.g., nausea, bloating, vomiting other than during pregnancy, diarrhea, or intolerance of several different foods)
   (3) *one sexual symptom:* a history of at least one sexual or reproductive symptom other than pain (e.g., sexual indifference, erectile or ejaculatory dysfunction, irregular menses, excessive menstrual bleeding, vomiting throughout pregnancy)
   (4) *one pseudoneurological symptom:* a history of at least one symptom or deficit suggesting a neurological condition not limited to pain (conversion symptoms such as impaired coordination or balance, paralysis or localized weakness, difficulty swallowing or lump in throat, aphonia, urinary retention, hallucinations, loss of touch or pain sensation, double vision, blindness, deafness, seizures; dissociative symptoms such as amnesia; or loss of consciousness other than fainting)

C. Either (1) or (2):
   (1) after appropriate investigation, each of the symptoms in Criterion B cannot be fully explained by a known general medical condition or the direct effects of a substance (e.g., a drug of abuse, a medication)

continued

Exhibit 2-10S ***Continued.***

(2) when there is a related general medical condition, the physical complaints or resulting social or occupational impairment are in excess of what would be expected from the history, physical examination, or laboratory findings

D. The symptoms are not intentionally produced or feigned (as in Factitious Disorder or Malingering).

Source: Reprinted with permission from the DIAGNOSTIC AND STATISTICAL MANUAL OF MENTAL DISORDERS 449–50 (4th ed. 1994). Copyright 1994 American Psychiatric Association.

CHAPTER 3

POSTTRAUMATIC STRESS DISORDER

Criteria for Diagnosis of PTSD

The American Psychiatric Association's fourth edition of its *Diagnostic and Statistical Manual of Mental Disorders* (*DSM-IV*)[1] changed the diagnostic criteria for Posttraumatic Stress Disorder (PTSD)[2] in some significant respects. Perhaps the most significant change involved the definition of the precipitating stressor. Unlike most other mental disorders in which the exact etiology is not known, diagnosis of PTSD requires that a triggering event or stressor be identified.

The 1987 revision to the third edition of the DSM,[3] as set out in Chapter 3 of the Main Volume, defined the triggering stressor for PTSD as an event that is "outside the range of usual human experience and that would be markedly distressing to almost anyone."[4] It listed examples such as a serious threat to one's life or physical integrity; a serious threat or harm to one's children, spouse, or other close relatives and friends; the sudden destruction of one's home or community; or seeing another person being seriously injured or killed as the result of an accident or physical violence.[5]

DSM-IV, by contrast, introduced both an objective and a subjective criterion for the triggering stressor, both of which must be satisfied for a PTSD diagnosis to be valid. *DSM-IV* first requires that the person "experienced, witnessed, or was confronted with an event or events that involved actual or threatened death or serious injury, or a threat to the physical integrity of self or others."[6] Second, the person's response must have involved "intense fear, helplessness, or horror."[7]

---

[1] American Psychiatric Association, Diagnostic and Statistical Manual of Mental Disorders (4th ed. 1994) [hereinafter *DSM-IV*].

[2] In addition to changing the diagnostic criteria, *DSM-IV* changed the name of the disorder from Post-Traumatic Stress Disorder to Posttraumatic Stress Disorder.

[3] American Psychiatric Association, Diagnostic and Statistical Manual of Mental Disorders (3d ed. rev. 1987) [hereinafter *DSM-III-R*].

[4] *DSM-III-R* at 250.

[5] *Id.*

[6] *DSM-IV* at 427.

[7] *Id.* at 428.

Exhibit 3-1S Diagnostic Criteria for Posttraumatic Stress Disorder

A. The person has been exposed to a traumatic event in which both of the following were present:
   (1) the person experienced, witnessed, or was confronted with an event or events that involved actual or threatened death or serious injury, or a threat to the physical integrity of self or others
   (2) the person's response involved intense fear, helplessness, or horror. **Note:** In children, this may be expressed instead by disorganized or agitated behavior

B. The traumatic event is persistently reexperienced in one (or more) of the following ways:
   (1) recurrent and intrusive distressing recollections of the event, including images, thoughts or perceptions. **Note:** In young children, repetitive play may occur in which themes or aspects of the trauma are expressed.
   (2) recurring distressing dreams of the event. **Note:** In children, there may be frightening dreams without recognizable content.
   (3) acting or feeling as if the traumatic event were recurring (includes a sense of reliving the experience, illusions, hallucinations, and dissociative flashback episodes, including those that occur when awakening or when intoxicated). **Note:** In young children, trauma-specific reenactment may occur.
   (4) intense psychological distress at exposure to internal and external cues that symbolize or resemble an aspect of the traumatic event
   (5) physiological reactivity on exposure to internal or external cues that symbolize or resemble an aspect of the traumatic event

C. Persistent avoidance of stimuli associated with the trauma and numbing of general responsiveness (not present before the trauma), as indicated by three (or more) of the following:
   (1) efforts to avoid thoughts, feelings, or conversation associated with the trauma
   (2) efforts to avoid activities, places, or people that arouse recollections of the trauma
   (3) inability to recall an important aspect of the trauma
   (4) markedly diminished interest or participation in significant activities
   (5) feeling of detachment or estrangement from others
   (6) restricted range of affect (e.g., unable to have loving feelings)
   (7) sense of a foreshortened future (e.g., does not expect to have a career, marriage, children, or a normal life span)

D. Persistent symptoms of increased arousal (not present before the trauma), as indicated by two (or more) of the following:
   (1) difficulty falling or staying asleep
   (2) irritability or outbursts of anger
   (3) difficulty concentrating
   (4) hypervigilance
   (5) exaggerated startle response

E. Duration of the disturbance (symptoms in Criteria B, C, and D) is more than 1 month.

F. The disturbance causes clinically significant distress or impairment in social, occupational, or other important areas of functioning.

Specify if:
Acute: if duration of symptoms is less than 3 months
Chronic: if duration of symptoms is 3 months or more

Specify if:
With delayed onset: if onset of symptoms is at least 6 months after the stressor

Source: Reprinted with permission from the DIAGNOSTIC AND STATISTICAL MANUAL OF MENTAL DISORDERS 427–29 (4th ed. 1994). Copyright 1994 American Psychiatric Association.

DSM-IV lists the following examples of traumatic events that may be sufficient to trigger PTSD: military combat, violent personal assault (sexual assault, physical attack, robbery, mugging), being kidnapped, being taken hostage, terrorist attack, torture, incarceration as a prisoner of war or in a concentration camp, natural or manmade disasters, severe automobile accidents, or being diagnosed with a life-threatening illness.[8] *DSM-IV* emphasizes that "the stressor must be of an extreme (i.e., life-threatening) nature," and the manual suggests that diagnosis of an Adjustment Disorder is appropriate where the triggering stressor does not meet the severity threshold required for a diagnosis of PTSD.[9]

PTSD is one of the most misdiagnosed conditions, particularly in the forensic context. As one authority recently noted, a PTSD diagnosis may be driven by political, social, or legal agendas.[10] Another authority observes that an expert's feelings regarding the "victims rights movement" can result in misapplication of a PTSD diagnosis.[11] Even absent such an agenda, a plaintiff's counsel may seek to invoke the PTSD label to argue to the jury that his or her client's suffering as a result of a workplace incident approximates the suffering of torture victims and prisoners of war. Some clinicians have taken advantage of *DSM-IV*'s slight broadening of the diagnostic criteria for PTSD to attempt to diagnose PTSD as a result of workplace stressors such as loss of employment, nonassaultive sexual harassment, or unpleasant interactions with bosses and co-workers. This is invalid. As one authority maintains:

---

[8]*Id.* at 424.

[9]*Id.* at 427.

[10]R. Simon, *The Credible Forensic Psychiatric Evaluation in Sexual Harassment Litigation,* 26 PSYCHIATRIC ANNALS 139, 146 (1996) (hereinafter, Simon, 26 PSYCHIATRIC ANNALS).

[11]L. Gold, *Addressing Bias in the Forensic Assessment of Sexual Harassment Claims*, 26 J. AM. ACAD. PSYCHIATRY & LAW 563, 571 (1998) (hereinafter, Gold, 26 J. AM. ACAD. PSYCHIATRY & LAW).

> The most common forms of sexual harassment involve the less severe behaviors of touching, suggestive comments, and the like, as opposed to physical assault or rape. An individual would be unlikely to develop PTSD as a response to these forms of sexual harassment, although mood or other anxiety disorders could result from these experiences. Indeed, a very profound response such as PTSD to minimally severe stressors raises the issues of malingering and the individual's susceptibility to psychiatric morbidity.[12]

In the case of termination of employment, the PTSD diagnosis is sometimes predicated upon simplistic formulations such as "His job was his life, and when they took his job they took his life." Significantly, however, *DSM-IV* specifies that "being fired" is *not* a triggering stressor of sufficient severity as to justify a PTSD diagnosis, and it suggests that an Adjustment Disorder diagnosis is appropriate where PTSD-like symptoms follow a nontraumatic event such as a job termination.[13]

Similarly, a PTSD diagnosis as the result of a supervisor's making sexual advances, telling dirty jokes, or yelling at subordinates also is incorrect. There is a movement afoot to gain recognition for a type of "cumulative stressor" PTSD based on *DSM-IV*'s statement that an "event or events" may trigger PTSD. This movement tends to ignore the fact that if more than one event is to be taken into account, each of the events must themselves meet the severity threshold. Although rape may be a sufficient triggering stressor for PTSD, whether or not it occurs in the workplace, attempts to diagnose PTSD as a result of nonassaultive sexual harassment on the grounds that sexual harassment is "like" rape or upon the plaintiff's statement that the harassment "felt like rape" are similarly invalid.[14]

Another key point often overlooked is that even where a sufficiently severe triggering stressor is present, PTSD symptoms do not always result. In fact, as one authority recently observed, fewer than 25 percent of individuals exposed to typical traumatic stressors develop PTSD.[15] Moreover, a valid PTSD diagnosis requires that the symptoms of disturbance (the B, C, and D criteria) last for more than one month. *DSM-IV* introduced a new diagnosis, Acute Stress Disorder, to cover reactions to traumatic events that resolve within one month of the traumatic stressor.

PTSD in the Courts

General Principles

Although PTSD diagnoses are appearing with greater frequency in reported employment cases, few courts have directly addressed the legitimacy of such

[12]Gold, 26 J. AM. ACAD. PSYCHIATRY & LAW at 572–73.

[13]*DSM-IV* at 427.

[14]*See* P. Lees-Haley & S. Anderson, *What PTSD is* Not, CLAIMS 25 (Apr. 1995) (medical error to diagnose PTSD following sexual harassment of nonassaultive variety).

[15]Simon, 26 PSYCHIATRIC ANNALS at 146.

diagnoses. Many courts have simply admitted evidence of a plaintiff's PTSD diagnosis without comment. As the Sixth Circuit recognized in a nonemployment case, however:

> A plaintiff's claim that a particular event or series of events caused him PTSD must be subjected to the closest scrutiny. The court must demand that a plaintiff produce sufficient authority that the particular event constitutes a "recognized stressor" or a psychologically traumatic event which would produce significant symptoms of distress in almost everyone experiencing such an event.[16]

In that case, the court rejected the plaintiffs' claim that their drinking contaminated water caused them to develop PTSD, noting that such "does not constitute the type of recognizable stressor identified either by professional medical organizations or courts."[17]

If a diagnosis of PTSD is to be introduced, courts do seem to require that the clinician making the diagnosis be qualified to do so. For example, in *Jackson v. Bayou Industries,*[18] the court rejected the plaintiffs' tender of an expert witness who sought to testify that the plaintiffs suffered PTSD as a result of racial discrimination that they experienced in the workplace over a two-week period. The court held that the proffered expert, who was only a "licensed professional counselor" and possessed a masters degree in psychology, was not qualified to diagnose the plaintiffs' mental conditions. Accordingly, the court excluded the PTSD diagnosis. The *Jackson* court suggested that only a psychiatrist or licensed psychologist would be qualified to diagnose PTSD.[19]

At issue in *Harvey v. District of Columbia*[20] was the sufficiency of the plaintiff's disclosure pursuant to Federal Rule of Civil Procedure 26(a)(2)(B) of the opinions of her proffered psychological expert to the effect that the plaintiff suffered from PTSD as a result of sexual harassment. The report stated only that:

> Dr. Edwards will testify as to Plaintiff [sic] has suffered as a result of emotional distress. And upon further exploration, her testimony may included [sic] how Plaintiff suffered from being sexually assaulted while on the job and the continuous pattern of harassment by the perpetrators, her peers and other department employees and the extent of how such actions affected Plaintiff's employment. Such conduct has lead [sic] to an undermining of Ms. Harvey's work performance, self esteem, and resulted in post-traumatic stress disorder.[21]

The court characterized the foregoing report as "woefully inadequate," in that it did not contain a complete statement of all opinions to be expressed and the basis and reasons therefor as well as the data or other information

---

[16]Sterling v. Velsicol Chem. Corp., 855 F.2d 1188, 1210 (6th Cir. 1988).

[17]*Id.*

[18]1995 WL 143538 (E.D. La. 1995).

[19]For more detailed coverage of expert qualifications, see Chapter 11, "Avoiding 'Junk Science' in Employment Litigation," of this Supplement.

[20]949 F. Supp. 874, 72 FEP Cases 1074 (D.D.C. 1996).

[21]*Id.* at 877, 72 FEP Cases at 1076.

Exhibit 3-2S Diagnostic Criteria for Acute Stress Disorder

A. The person has been exposed to a traumatic event in which both of the following were present:
   (1) the person experienced, witnessed, or was confronted with an event or events that involved actual or threatened death or serious injury, or a threat to the physical integrity of self or others
   (2) the person's response involved intense fear, helplessness, or horror

B. Either while experiencing or after experiencing the distressing event, the individual has three (or more) of the following dissociative symptoms:
   (1) a subjective sense of numbing, detachment, or absence of emotional responsiveness
   (2) a reduction in awareness of his or her surroundings (e.g., "Being in a daze")
   (3) derealization
   (4) depersonalization
   (5) dissociative amnesia (i.e., inability to recall an important aspect of the trauma)

C. The traumatic event is persistently reexperienced in at least one of the following ways: recurrent images, thoughts, dreams, illusions, flashback episodes, or a sense of reliving the experience; or distress on exposure to reminders of the traumatic experience.

D. Marked avoidance of stimuli that arouse recollections of the trauma (e.g., thoughts, feelings, conversations, activities, places, people).

E. Marked symptoms of anxiety or increased arousal (e.g., difficulty sleeping, irritability, poor concentration, hypervigilance, exaggerated startle response, motor restlessness).

F. The disturbance causes clinically significant distress or impairment in social, occupational, or other important areas of functioning or impairs the individual's ability to pursue some necessary task, such as obtaining necessary assistance or mobilizing personal resources by telling family members about the traumatic event.

G. The disturbance lasts for a minimum of 2 days and a maximum of 4 weeks and occurs within 4 weeks of the traumatic event.

H. The disturbance is not due to the direct physiological effects of a substance (e.g., a drug of abuse, a medication) or a general medical condition, is not better accounted for by Brief Psychotic Disorder, and is not merely an exacerbation of a preexisting Axis I or Axis II disorder.

Source: Reprinted with permission from the DIAGNOSTIC AND STATISTICAL MANUAL OF MENTAL DISORDERS 431–32 (4th ed. 1994). Copyright 1994 American Psychiatric Association.

considered by the witness in forming the opinions.[22] Noting the delay of the defendants in objecting to the report, the court declined to disqualify the witness, but rather ordered that the plaintiff produce her for deposition. *Harvey* does indicate, however, that abbreviated or conclusory disclosures concerning PTSD (as well as other diagnoses) are not acceptable under the new federal discovery rules.

PTSD in Harassment and Discrimination Cases

PTSD diagnoses have appeared in discussions of liability and damages by a number of courts.

In *Burns v. Republic Savings Bank*,[23] the court rejected the plaintiff's psychologist's diagnosis that the plaintiff suffered PTSD as a result of perceived pay inequities and other aspects of alleged gender discrimination. The court announced: "The evidence demonstrates that post-traumatic stress disorder is not an appropriate diagnosis absent a life-threatening stress."[24]

In *Broderick v. Ruder,*[25] the court rejected the plaintiff's psychiatrist's diagnosis of PTSD in a sexual harassment case, where the harassment largely consisted of inappropriate language and misconduct of a nonassaultive variety. The court noted that the psychiatrist's "analogy relating the Buffalo Creek, West Virginia, flood and the Beverly Hills nightclub fire to plaintiff's reaction to a sexually hostile work environment is not convincing."[26]

In *Hosey v. McDonald's Corp.,*[27] the plaintiff, who was an 18-year-old high school football player as well as a part-time McDonald's employee, alleged that he was sexually harassed by his 18-year-old female floor supervisor at the restaurant. He claimed that his supervisor asked him out on numerous occasions and pinched him on his rear. He claimed he was forced to resign and began to see a psychologist, who diagnosed him as suffering from PTSD. Without directly addressing the PTSD diagnosis, the court awarded summary judgment for the employer, finding no hostile working environment and noting that "Title VII does not prohibit teenagers from asking each other for dates."[28]

In *Skidmore v. Precision Printing & Packaging Inc.*,[29] by contrast, the Fifth Circuit affirmed the plaintiff's psychiatrist's diagnosis of PTSD and depression resulting from a pattern of harassment that included a co-worker licking and kissing the plaintiff's face and neck and placing his hands around her neck as if to choke her, as well as sexual remarks, inviting her to his home for a "hot body oil massage," and asking her to leave her husband and have his child. The court noted that the plaintiff's psychiatrist had testified to "his experience,

---

[22]*Id.*, 72 FEP Cases at 1076.

[23]25 F. Supp.2d 809 (N.D. Ohio 1998).

[24]*Id.* at 822.

[25]685 F. Supp. 1269, 46 FEP Cases 1271 (D.D.C. 1988).

[26]*Id.* at 1273 n.3.

[27]71 FEP Cases 201 (D. Md. 1996).

[28]*Id.* at 203.

[29]188 F.3d 606 (5th Cir. 1999).

to the criteria by which he diagnosed Skidmore, and to standard methods of diagnosis in his field."[30]

In *Gotthardt v. National Railroad Passenger Corp.,*[31] at issue was the plaintiff's ability to collect front pay. The Ninth Circuit first noted that, in order to receive front pay, a plaintiff must show that her employer's violation of Title VII caused her loss of employment. The plaintiff's psychologist had testified at trial that the hostile workplace environment (which largely consisted of crude language and insulting epithets) caused the plaintiff to develop PTSD and rendered her unable to return to work. The Ninth Circuit refused to disturb the trial court's finding of a causal connection between the harassment and the PTSD, even though there was evidence that the plaintiff had previously received 11 months of treatment for PTSD stemming from an unrelated train accident.

In *Webb v. Hyman,*[32] the court admitted the plaintiff's psychologist's PTSD diagnosis in a sexual harassment case where the plaintiff claimed that her supervisor had locked her in a room and forcibly kissed her and stuck his tongue in her mouth, fondled her, and then accused her of stealing. The plaintiff's psychologist testified that PTSD could be based on cumulative traumatic events such as the plaintiff's supervisor's repeated sexual advances. The court did not address the propriety of such a diagnosis, but merely affirmed the jury verdict in the plaintiff's favor and noted that even the defense psychological expert admitted that the plaintiff had suffered a great deal of emotional distress from workplace events.

In *Hansel v. Public Service Co. of Colorado,*[33] the court noted the PTSD diagnoses of the plaintiff's treating psychologist and psychological expert in finding that a hostile working environment existed and in determining that an award of front pay was justified. In that case, the plaintiff had been subjected to a course of severe harassment, including being held down in a car while co-workers fondled her genitals, having her car windows broken, and having a male co-worker follow her into the women's restroom carrying a hangman's noose.

In two cases, courts have noted PTSD diagnoses in affirming jury verdicts for plaintiffs in sexual harassment cases where the harassment did not involve physical assaults. In *Oliphant v. Perkins Restaurants Operating Co.,*[34] the court affirmed a jury's verdict for the plaintiff on a cause of action under state law for outrage based upon a pattern of verbal abuse on the part of the plaintiff's supervisor. The court noted the plaintiff's psychologist's opinion that the plaintiff suffered PTSD and was "as badly damaged as if she had been physically abused," but emphasized that the plaintiff's psychologist's opinion was "unrefuted by any other testimony."[35] In *Baty v. Willamette Industries Inc.,*[36] the

---

[30]*Id.* at 618.

[31]191 F.3d 1148, 80 FEP Cases 1528 (9th Cir. 1999).

[32]861 F. Supp. 1094, 67 FEP Cases 1425 (D.D.C. 1994).

[33]778 F. Supp. 1126, 57 FEP Cases 858 (D. Colo. 1991).

[34]885 F. Supp. 1486 (D. Kan. 1995).

[35]*Id.* at 1492.

[36]985 F. Supp. 987 (D. Kan. 1997), *aff'd,* 172 F.3d 1232, 79 FEP Cases 1451 (10th Cir. 1999).

court affirmed a jury award for emotional distress damages, noting that the plaintiff's psychological expert had diagnosed PTSD as a result of sexual harassment (which consisted of foul language) and termination of employment.

In most employment cases to date in which courts have cited PTSD diagnoses in the course of finding for plaintiffs on issues of liability or damages, therefore, there has been either a record of egregious physically assaultive conduct or a failure by the defense to challenge the PTSD diagnosis. In none of the cases in which courts have mentioned PTSD diagnoses in favor of plaintiffs has there been any record of a challenge by defendants that the diagnoses are not appropriate using the current *DSM* diagnostic criteria.

PTSD in ADA Cases

Since publication of the Main Volume, an increasing number of cases have been decided in which plaintiffs claim to have suffered PTSD as a result of workplace events. However, instead of (or in addition to) seeking damages, they have sought "reasonable accommodation" under the Americans With Disabilities Act (ADA). In most such cases, the plaintiffs have been unsuccessful. For example:

- In *Muller v. Automobile Club,*[37] the court rejected the ADA claim of an employee who claimed that she could no longer work at her job after an altercation with a customer allegedly caused her to develop PTSD. The court reasoned that the plaintiff was unable to perform only her job, not all jobs, so she was not substantially limited in the major life activity of working, which is a prerequisite to ADA coverage.
- In *Larking v. Ciba Vision Corp.,*[38] the court held that the employer was not obligated to eliminate the telephone answering function from a job for an employee who was unable to field telephone calls because of panic attacks caused by PTSD. An employee must be able to perform the essential functions of a job to qualify for ADA protection (and an employer need not eliminate stressful but essential functions of a job), reasoned the *Larking* court, and answering the telephone was an essential function of the plaintiff's job.
- In *Daniels-Merritt v. Johnson,*[39] the plaintiff alleged that stressful working conditions caused her to develop PTSD and she sought reasonable accommodation in the form of working at home or working part time. The court rejected her claim. Without addressing the legitimacy of the PTSD diagnosis, the court held that the plaintiff's request to work at home or part time was not feasible because her job required extensive interpersonal contact with other employees, work with confidential documents, and on-the-job training.

The court rejected the plaintiff's claim in *Hatfield v. Quantum Chemical Corp.*[40] that he should be transferred to a new supervisor because harassment

---

[37]897 F. Supp. 1289, 5 AD Cases 97 (S.D. Cal. 1995).

[38]858 F. Supp. 1572, 3 AD Cases 715 (N.D. Ga. 1994).

[39]2 AD Cases 1719 (W.D. Mo. 1993).

[40]920 F. Supp. 108, 5 AD Cases 765 (S.D. Tex. 1996).

from his current supervisor caused him to develop PTSD. The court found that the plaintiff was not disabled within the meaning of the ADA:

> Hatfield can perform all of the activities required of a plant technician; he just does not want to do them around his supervisor. As conceded in Hatfield's response to the motion for summary judgment, his inability to work under a particular supervisor simply is not a substantial limitation on working in the same sense that a physical disability is a limitation. Hatfield, therefore, is not "disabled."[41]

Claims by plaintiffs that they suffered from PTSD as a result of work stress are thus vulnerable on a variety of grounds. First, they may not actually suffer from PTSD; a mental disorder must be validly diagnosed for ADA protection to apply. Second, if they are rendered unable to work at only their jobs, or for a particular boss, they are not considered to be "substantially limited" in any major life activity, such as is necessary for ADA coverage. Third, if the stressful aspects of their jobs are essential aspects of those jobs, the ADA does not require that an employer remove essential job functions. Finally, even if they otherwise qualify for ADA protection, modification of their jobs or transfer to another supervisor may not constitute a reasonable accommodation.[42]

Assessment Procedures for PTSD

The Georgetown Guidelines for Assessment of PTSD

In 1995, a series of proposed guidelines were issued for the diagnosis of PTSD in civil litigants.[43] These guidelines have become known as the "Georgetown Guidelines" because of the affiliation of their chief proponent, Robert I. Simon, M.D., with the Georgetown University School of Medicine. These guidelines,

---

[41]*Id.* at 768. Other cases rejecting reassignment to a new supervisor as a reasonable accommodation include *Weiler v. Household Finance Corp.,* 101 F.3d 519 (7th Cir. 1996) (plaintiff's request for an immediate transfer away from her boss after he yelled at her during a performance review rejected); and *Mancini v. General Elec. Co.,* 820 F. Supp. 141 (D. Vt. 1993) (plaintiff's claim that his supervisor caused him to suffer emotional problems that in turn caused him to be insubordinate, and that he should have been accommodated by being transferred to a new supervisor, rejected). *See also* Kerno v. Sandoz Pharms. Corp., 4 AD Cases 1195 (N.D. Ill. 1994); Adams v. Alderson, 723 F. Supp. 1531 (D.D.C. 1989).

[42]For treatment of this topic in greater detail, see J. McDonald & R. Broudy, *Job Stress and the ADA,* 23 EMPLOYEE REL. L.J. 67 (1997).

[43]R. Simon, *Toward the Development of Guidelines in the Forensic Psychiatric Examination of Posttraumatic Stress Disorder Claimants, in* POSTTRAUMATIC STRESS DISORDER IN LITIGATION 31, 33 (R. Simon ed., 1995) [hereinafter *Georgetown Guidelines*].

reprinted in Exhibit 3-3S, are designed to ensure that the diagnosis of PTSD in litigants will be accomplished through objective, scientifically valid means.

Avoidance of Idiosyncratic Definitions of PTSD

The Georgetown Guidelines condemn the use of idiosyncratic definitions of PTSD. As Simon admonishes: "Forensic examiners must be careful not to overreach in order to diagnose PTSD. . . . Credibility is severely compromised when an examiner attempts to force the diagnosis of PTSD when the criteria for this disorder clearly are not fulfilled."[44] Simon notes in another article that "[t]he diagnosis of PTSD . . . may be driven by political and social agendas," and he warns: "PTSD must not be diagnosed in order to facilitate a legal agenda."[45] Such an agenda is suggested by the recent statement by a leading feminist psychiatrist that "[p]sychiatric diagnoses vary both in the degree to which they are stigmatizing and the degree to which they blame the victim. For example, posttraumatic stress disorder is relatively less stigmatizing and less blaming of the victim, and personality disorders are more so."[46]

One means to prevent the use of the PTSD diagnosis to further a political or legal agenda is to adhere strictly to the *DSM*'s diagnostic criteria for PTSD. Simon maintains that forensic examiners should be required to follow the *DSM* diagnostic criteria in making the diagnosis of PTSD. Although noting that the *DSM* is not to be viewed as a "cookbook," it is "the best clinical diagnostic instrument we have to date for PTSD."[47] The *DSM* has been subject to extensive field trials to ensure its reliability, and as Simon observes: "[T]he laborious and painstakingly careful work done by competent researchers and clinicians working through 26 advisory committees in establishing the diagnostic criteria for psychiatric disorders gives DSM-III-R and DSM-IV substantial credibility."[48]

Difficulties arise when clinicians apply their own idiosyncratic definitions of PTSD in the litigation context. One of the purposes of the *DSM* is to provide the mental health professions with a common language with which to communicate concerning mental disorders. A diagnosis of PTSD (or virtually any other mental disorder) that does not employ this common language is meaningless. As Simon points out:

> Unfortunately, the standard criteria for the diagnosis of PTSD are ignored by a significant number of mental health practitioners who enter the legal arena. Juries and judges are frequently confused by the babel of testimony presented concerning

---

[44]*Id.* at 38.

[45]R. Simon, *The Credible Forensic Psychiatric Evaluation in Sexual Harassment Litigation,* 26 Psychiatric Annals 139, 146 (1996).

[46]M. Jensvold, *Potential for Misuse and Abuse of Psychiatry in Workplace Sexual Harassment, in* Sexual Harassment in the Workplace and Academia: Psychiatric Issues 153, 168 (D. Shrier ed., 1996).

[47]Simon, *Georgetown Guidelines* at 45.

[48]*Id.* at 46.

Exhibit 3-3S Georgetown Guidelines for Forensic Assessment of PTSD

1. In evaluating the diagnostic criteria for PTSD, the forensic examiner should be guided by official diagnostic manuals, the professional literature, and current research. Idiosyncratic definitions of PTSD must be avoided. If official diagnostic criteria are not used, the burden of proof should be on the forensic examiner to provide the scientific evidence for his or her diagnosis of PTSD.
2. In assessing the sufficiency of traumatic stressors for the diagnosis of PTSD, the forensic examiner should be guided by official diagnostic manuals, the professional literature, and current research. The possible contributions of multiple stressors to the PTSD claimant's clinical picture should be evaluated.
3. A credible forensic psychiatric evaluation of a PTSD claimant requires a thorough examination of the claimant's psychiatric and medical history, including review of prior medical, psychiatric, and other pertinent records.
4. Relying solely on the subjective reporting of symptoms by the PTSD claimant without considering additional sources of information is insufficient. As a corollary, treater and forensic roles should not be mixed in the forensic examination of a PTSD claimant.
5. Standard assessment methods should be used in evaluating the level of functional psychological impairment of PTSD claimants. Relying solely on clinical experience or on strictly subjective or idiosyncratic criteria in assessing psychological impairment should be avoided.

Source: Georgetown Guidelines, 33.

> what is and is not PTSD. Testimony that lacks a scientific basis undermines the credibility of the testifier as well as that of his or her profession. The ensuing harm done to claimants as well as defendants can be enormous.[49]

This confusion of judges and juries, which may not be unintended in all cases, is largely responsible for much of the inconsistency of the courts' view of PTSD. This is why some courts will allow testimony about diagnoses of PTSD flowing from, for example, hearing dirty jokes, experiencing co-workers' boorish behavior, or being yelled at by one's boss, while other courts, applying the *DSM-IV* criteria, properly hold that PTSD is not validly diagnosed under such circumstances. The danger in this inconsistency is that if *every* unpleasant experience can be considered to produce PTSD, then PTSD will become meaningless as a construct and those who are genuinely traumatized will have no

[49] *Id.*

means by which to relate their predicament.[50] This is one area in which some courts' propensity to "let it all in for what it's worth," or to admit a plaintiff's therapist's invalid diagnosis because the plaintiff cannot afford to hire a qualified expert who could produce a valid diagnosis,[51] is particularly dangerous to the integrity of the legal system.

Consideration of the Possibility of Multiple Stressors

As Simon maintains:

> As part of a credible forensic examination, other stressors in the claimant's life need to be considered. Most of us live in a world of multiple stressors. The forensic examiner must not be deterred by the claimant's assertions concerning the cause of psychological impairments. Comorbid disorders associated with *multiple* psychological stressors may contribute significantly to the clinical picture.[52]

Thus, although an investigation into possible alternative stressors is important in any forensic examination, such is particularly essential where PTSD is at issue, especially when relatively minor stressors are claimed to have produced PTSD. As Simon points out, "[m]inor stressors that allegedly cause PTSD must be met with commonsense skepticism."[53]

Particularly in sexual harassment cases, it is important to determine whether the plaintiff suffered any prior traumas such as childhood sexual or physical abuse, or a prior sexual assault.[54] The plaintiff may exhibit genuine symptoms of PTSD, but the PTSD may be the result of an unresolved prior trauma rather than workplace events. The base rate for PTSD in the general population has been found to be 9.2 percent.[55] Thus, it is not unreasonable to assume that 1 in 10 employees may already have PTSD symptomatology that preexists and that may be unrelated to workplace events. As two researchers recently observed: "A woman who appears to be suffering from PTSD as a result of sexual harassment may actually have a long and complex assault history, which may account for or contribute to her current symptomatology."[56]

---

[50]As Simon points out: "Defining the stressor criteria reasonably narrowly prevents trivializing the diagnosis of PTSD through unwarranted widespread use." *Id.* at 51.

[51]This is a particularly inappropriate basis for allowing plaintiffs to introduce faulty diagnoses in that the Civil Rights Act of 1991 permits the court to award a successful plaintiff expert witness fees as well as attorneys' fees. *See* 42 U.S.C. §2000e-5(k).

[52]Simon, *Georgetown Guidelines* at 57.

[53]*Id.*

[54]*See* Chapter 10, "Special Issues in Sexual Harassment Cases," of this Supplement and of the Main Volume at 355–56.

[55]Simon, *Georgetown Guidelines* at 58.

[56]B. Dansky & D. Kirkpatrick, *Effects of Sexual Harassment, in* SEXUAL HARASSMENT: THEORY, RESEARCH AND TREATMENT 152, 170 (W. O'Donohue ed., 1997).

Thorough Review of Plaintiff's Prior Psychiatric History

Simon further observes:

> It seems unnecessary to assert that a claimant's psychiatric history must be explored. Yet it is truly remarkable to observe how often psychiatric and psychological evaluations of PTSD claimants (as well as others) do not proceed beyond the claimant's allegations. It is as if the claimant's life began at the time of the alleged traumatic event. . . . No forensic psychiatric examination is credible without a thorough investigation of the claimant's past. Accordingly, attempts to restrict or constrain development of detailed historical information by either party to litigation must be vigorously resisted.[57]

This thorough review of the plaintiff's psychiatric history should take particular account of potential Axis II conditions that preceded the plaintiff's entry into the workplace. As Simon points out, many of these Axis II conditions are triggered initially by childhood sexual abuse, which produces a PTSD condition that precedes or co-exists with an Axis II condition such as Borderline Personality Disorder.[58] Such a chronic PTSD condition can not only produce the same symptomatology as PTSD triggered by more recent stressors, but it can cause a hypervigilance to sexual cues that may be the catalyst of the sexual harassment claim itself.[59]

Reliance Upon More Than the Subjective Report of the Plaintiff

Simon admonishes that "the forensic examiner must not rely solely on the subjective reporting of the claimant. Additional sources of information must be obtained."[60] This is because there are no objectively observable clinical signs or symptoms of PTSD and the possibility of malingered or embellished PTSD must always be considered.[61] Additional sources of information include review of records and interviews of third parties.

In addition, Simon stresses that a psychiatrist or psychologist should not serve as both treater and expert for the same person. This is because the treater is expected to be an ally of the plaintiff rather than a skeptic, which is not ordinarily a problem where a patient comes for help in getting better rather than for help in bolstering a legal case. In the forensic context, however, the third-party expert is unconstrained by any therapeutic relationship with the plaintiff and is free to examine the plaintiff's claims with objectivity.[62]

---

[57] Simon, *Georgetown Guidelines* at 58.

[58] *Id.* at 59–60.

[59] *See* Chapter 10, "Special Issues in Sexual Harassment Cases," of this Supplement and of the Main Volume at 355–56.

[60] Simon, *Georgetown Guidelines* at 62.

[61] *Id.* For a discussion of malingering, see Chapter 7, "Malingering," of the Main Volume.

[62] Simon, *Georgetown Guidelines* at 64–65.

Assessment of Functional Impairment

Simon emphasizes that a valid diagnosis of PTSD (as well as diagnoses of most other mental disorders) does not automatically entail a given level of functional impairment.[63] The examiner must explore to just what extent the plaintiff's functioning has been impaired. This is particularly the case with respect to the ability to work. A PTSD diagnosis does not mean that the plaintiff is necessarily disabled from working.[64]

In assessing functional impairment, the examiner should use objective criteria such as the *DSM-IV*'s Axis V Global Assessment of Functioning Scale and the American Medical Association's *Guides to Evaluation of Permanent Impairment,*[65] according to Simon. The examiner should not rely on idiosyncratic criteria or "clinical experience" in assessing impairment.

Simon also notes that there are numerous effective psychotherapeutic and psychopharmacologic treatments available for persons with PTSD, and that assessment of permanent impairment should not be attempted until an appropriate course of treatment has been completed.[66]

---

[63]*Id.* at 68.

[64]*See* Muller v. Automobile Club of S. Cal., 897 F. Supp. 1289, 5 AD Cases 97 (S.D. Cal. 1995) (plaintiff, diagnosed with PTSD after an altercation with customer, was not disabled from working).

[65]Simon, *Georgetown Guidelines* at 72–73; American Medical Association, *Guides to Evaluation of Permanent Impairment* (1993).

[66]Simon, *Georgetown Guidelines* at 72–73.

CHAPTER 4

PERSONALITY DISORDERS AND TRAITS

The Role of Personality Disorders in Workplace Harassment and Discrimination Cases

The existence of personality disorders may be relevant to both liability and damages in an employment lawsuit.

Liability

The key to understanding the genesis of many employment disputes that lead to claims of harassment and discrimination lies in an understanding of personality disorders and the ways in which they affect a person's interpersonal relationships and interpretation of the words and actions of others. Courts in employment cases are beginning to recognize the role that personality disorders play in the chain of events that precede many harassment and discrimination lawsuits. Personality disorders are relevant to the issue of employer liability in employment lawsuits in two respects.

First, personality disorders often cause interactions between people that later are alleged to have been imposed on the plaintiff by others. In this sense, a plaintiff suffering from a personality disorder may not merely be the innocent victim of another's unprovoked wrongdoing. Such a plaintiff's own irritability, perfectionism, manipulation of others, or sexually suggestive behavior is often the beginning of a chain of events that ultimately leads to a claim of wrongful termination, harassment, or discrimination. For example, an employee with a Borderline Personality Disorder may direct sexually suggestive comments or even blatantly seductive conduct toward a supervisor and then angrily accuse the supervisor of sexual harassment should he respond. Borderline personalities also tend to view others in extreme terms as either "all good" or "all bad." Thus, an employee with Borderline Personality Disorder may idolize her supervisor until he criticizes her work performance, and then react with rage and accuse her boss of misconduct.[1] Another example is a manager with a Narcissistic Personality Disorder, whose insensitivity toward others may cause subordinates to seek to avoid him or complain of mistreatment, which may ultimately lead to his failure as a manager. He will likely react with rage when demoted or terminated, blaming everyone but himself for his troubles in the ensuing litigation.

Second, personality disorders often are relevant to a plaintiff's perception of the events that led to the litigation. Individuals with personality disorders often interpret events in a distorted fashion and seek to rationalize their own unreasonable behavior. The fact that the plaintiff's perceptions may be distorted on account of a personality disorder may help to explain the diametrically opposite characterization of the very same event by plaintiff and defendant in so many employment lawsuits, particularly in "he said/she said" cases where there are no third-party witnesses to help break the credibility impasse. Unlike psychotic individuals with patently bizarre perceptions, employees with personality disorders have relatively good contact with reality. Thus, their accusations, although false, are not obviously bizarre and on the contrary may sound quite plausible.

Often, to the personality-disordered individual, "believing is seeing." For example, if on account of a personality disorder one presumes that another person is thinking in sexual terms, a variety of behaviors can be construed as sexual in nature—choice of clothing, a smile, an inadvertent touch, a compliment, any sort of effort to engage in joint activities, how close one stands, an invitation to lunch, humorous remarks, gestures, the amount of eye contact, glances, references to other relationships—the list is endless. Similarly, if one assumes that others are discriminating, this assumption becomes a self-fulfilling prophecy—one perceives discrimination to be lurking around every corner. Inattention, inadvertent slights, nonspecific discourtesy, lack of personal concern, random acts of preference, and numerous other ordinary events are consistent with such an assumption and may be construed as evidence of discrimination.

Personality-disordered individuals often construe ordinary behavior as wrongdoing and personal insult, and they selectively attend to those aspects of events that confirm their negative expectations. This is known as confirmatory bias. Following an innocuous event, the employee with distorted perceptions sincerely may become convinced that he or she was treated in an abusive or unjust manner. To make matters worse, because litigation arises after the fact, viewing events retrospectively makes them seem much simpler than they really were.

---

[1]In *Ramirez v. Kelly,* 1997 WL 223053 (N.D. Ill. 1997), the plaintiff and the defendant, who was above the plaintiff in the chain of command, had a sexual relationship. After the plaintiff found out that the defendant was married, the plaintiff sued for sexual harassment, claiming that she was raped and coerced to carry on the sexual relationship. The plaintiff was diagnosed by the defense psychiatric expert as having Borderline Personality Disorder, although the court expressed some skepticism about the psychiatrist's diagnostic methods.

The courts have begun to recognize the role that personality disorders play in the genesis of disputes involving alleged workplace harassment and discrimination. In *Lowe v. Philadelphia Newspapers Inc.,*[2] a racial harassment case, the court admitted the testimony of a psychiatrist to show that, because of a personality disorder, the plaintiff was oversensitive to ordinary criticism and perceived it as harassment. The plaintiff had attempted to have the court bifurcate the liability and damages issues of the case and exclude testimony of defense psychiatrists concerning her personality disorder from the liability phase. In denying the plaintiff's motion, the court observed that the psychiatrists' testimony was relevant to "whether the alleged harassment claimed by plaintiff is racial and is harassment at all." The court noted that one defense psychiatrist had testified on deposition that, because of her personality disorder, the plaintiff was overly sensitive and may have overreacted to events on the job. As the *Lowe* court explained:

> Testimony concerning a . . . plaintiff's mental disorder which causes him or her to perceive criticism as harassment, and to perceive racial slurs where no racial motivation is present, is highly relevant to the question whether plaintiff's perception of racial harassment is correct.[3]

A personality disorder was found to be at the root of a sexual harassment claim in *Spencer v. General Electric Co.*[4] Although the court in that case found a hostile working environment to exist based upon sexual joking and horseplay on the part of the plaintiff's supervisor and co-workers, it rejected the plaintiff's allegations of more serious misconduct, including "more than 100 sexual assaults" by her supervisor in the workplace during the workday, none of which were corroborated by third-party witnesses. The plaintiff attempted to explain the numerous inconsistencies in her story by presenting testimony from her psychiatrist that the harassing events caused her to develop a posttraumatic stress disorder that impaired her ability to recall details. The court rejected this notion and instead credited the testimony of the defense psychiatrist, which was that the plaintiff's "memory problems" resulted from "convenient selectivity rather than emotional trauma," and that the plaintiff suffered from Histrionic Personality Disorder. The court cited the characteristics of such a disorder, including "immaturity, shallowness, self-centeredness, obsession with one's personal appearance and exaggerated emotionality," and then observed that having heard hours of testimony from and about the plaintiff, the defense psychiatrist's conclusions "ring true."

In *Sudtelgte v. Reno,*[5] the court admitted extensive psychiatric testimony in a sexual harassment lawsuit concerning the fact that the plaintiff suffered

---

[2]594 F. Supp. 123, 54 FEP Cases 167 (E.D. Pa. 1984).

[3]*Id.* at 125–26, 54 FEP Cases at 169. The *Lowe* court cited *Davis v. U.S. Steel Corp.,* 539 F. Supp. 839, 54 FEP Cases 203 (E.D. Pa. 1982), in which incidents alleged by the plaintiff to be racial harassment were held to be legitimate criticism inaccurately perceived by the plaintiff because of an emotional disorder.

[4]697 F. Supp. 204, 51 FEP Cases 1696 (E.D. Va. 1988), *aff'd,* 894 F.2d 651, 51 FEP Cases 1725 (4th Cir. 1990).

[5]63 FEP Cases 1257 (W.D. Mo. 1994).

from a Paranoid Personality Disorder that adversely affected her ability to get along with supervisors and co-workers and that caused her to feel persistently "picked on." The plaintiff alleged a variety of "harassing" conduct, such as co-workers asking to borrow her car, urging her to drink beer with them, and once photographing her with her finger in her nose. Several psychiatrists and psychologists testified at the trial, all to the same general effect—that the plaintiff had numerous preexisting chronic mental problems, including a personality disorder, that interfered with her ability to get along with others and that caused her to misperceive events and the motivations of others. The *Sudtelgte* court held that although the plaintiff may have felt subjectively harassed, such was the result of her abnormal sensitivity caused by her personality disorder, and she could not show that a "reasonable woman" would have been similarly offended. The *Sudtelgte* court also noted the impact of the plaintiff's personality disorder on her credibility, observing that the plaintiff's "current perceptions of present and past events are grossly unreliable, probably because of her mental illness."[6]

The most recent and dramatic recognition to date by a court of the role of personality disorders in the genesis of harassment and discrimination claims occurred in *Pascouau v. Martin Marietta Corp.*[7] In that case, in which the plaintiff claimed co-workers called her names and passed gas in her presence,[8] the court concluded that "the conduct that could be described as harassment was not based on gender, but rather on Plaintiff's demonstrated lack of interpersonal skills." In its discussion of the facts of the case, the court described at some length the plaintiff's pre-existing psychological problems, many of which arose from the plaintiff's dysfunctional childhood. The court noted, for example, that the plaintiff still suffered symptoms of Posttraumatic Stress Disorder as a result of an incident when she was eight years old in which her mother forced her and her sister into a car at knifepoint and then drove the car off a bridge in a suicide attempt.

The defense psychiatric expert testified that the plaintiff in *Pascouau* suffered from a pre-existing mixed personality disorder with borderline and narcissistic characteristics. The *Pascouou* court explained the relevance of the plaintiff's personality disorder:

> The personality disorder is a condition, largely the product of being raised in a dysfunctional home with dysfunctional parents, in which Plaintiff did not learn how to solve problems effectively or to communicate effectively with other people. The disorder leads to the formulation of implausible perceptions and thus different kinds of conclusions about what other people's actions and behavior mean as distinguished from what a reasonable person not subject to such a disorder would perceive them to mean.

---

[6]*Id.* at 1257.

[7]994 F. Supp. 1276, 76 FEP Cases 651 (D. Colo. 1998), *aff'd in relevant part,* 185 F.3d 874 (10th Cir. 1999) (table).

[8]The *Pascouau* court remarked: "I am not going to be the first judge to relate breaking wind to sexual behavior." *Id.* at 1280, 76 FEP Cases at 655.

> Consistent with this disorder, Plaintiff makes judgments that are highly personalized and overly emotional. She sees things in black and white terms rather than shades of gray that permit allowances and generally feels whatever goes wrong is someone else's fault and she had no role in the misadventure. Persons with this disorder take no responsibility for what goes wrong in their lives.[9]

The *Pascouau* court then went on to discuss the role in the case of the symptoms of Borderline Personality Disorder exhibited by the plaintiff:

> The essence of the Plaintiff's complaints in this case is the product of Plaintiff's "splitting," a psychiatric term meaning the patient initially over-evaluates and over-values other people, and then, when the slightest thing goes wrong, demeans those people and becomes angry and upset with them. The major affective characteristic is anger or rage. Secondarily, such a person is fearful of being abandoned or not being liked and does not want to be alone. As a result, the borderline personality very often gets involved in unsuccessful intimate relationships. Depression frequently accompanies this personality disorder because the unsuccessful outcomes of interactions with other people lead to prolonged disappointment.[10]

The court credited the testimony of the defense psychiatrist, a Dr. Plezak, noting:

> When asked if Plaintiff's allegations had any role in the causes of Plaintiff's disorders, Dr. Plezak replied that the situation is reversed in that the disorders are causes of the allegations. The incidents Plaintiff related were characterized by misinterpretations of events and interactions with fellow employees that were far more intense than would be interpreted by a reasonable person.[11]

Conversely, the *Pascouau* court rejected the view of the plaintiff's psychiatrist that all of the plaintiff's emotional difficulties were the result of her experiences in the workplace, noting that "his conclusion dismisses the profuse psychiatric history of the Plaintiff which accounts for the symptoms she had displayed all her life and continued to display even at the time of trial."[12]

In *Lanni v. New Jersey,*[13] thc plaintiff brought a motion in limine to exclude the testimony of the defendant's psychiatrist, who had diagnosed the plaintiff as having a Narcissistic Personality Disorder, among other conditions. In denying the motion, the court stated that it had reviewed the psychiatrist's report, which detailed how the plaintiff's psychiatric condition might explain the plaintiff's perception that he was being mistreated at work. The court found that the psychiatrist's testimony would "not only assist the trier of fact in understanding various mental and cognitive conditions, but will also assist in sorting out issues of causation."[14]

---

[9] *Id.* at 1279, 76 FEP Cases at 653–54.
[10] *Id.*, 76 FEP Cases at 654.
[11] *Id.*, 76 FEP Cases at 654.
[12] *Id.*, 76 FEP Cases at 654.
[13] 177 F.R.D. 295 (D.N.J. 1998).
[14] *Id.* at 302.

In *Newberry v. East Texas State University,*[15] an Americans With Disabilities Act case, the plaintiff's psychiatrist testified that the plaintiff suffered from an Obsessive-Compulsive Personality Disorder. The plaintiff himself had testified that this disorder interfered with his relations with others by instilling in him a rigid perfectionism, rigidly ethical behavior, and an insistence on addressing all details of his interpersonal relationships.[16]

In other recent cases, even though no personality disorder was diagnosed, the court attributed the plaintiffs' difficulties in the workplace to their own manner of relating to others as opposed to harassment or discrimination. For example, in *Munday v. Waste Management of North America,*[17] the plaintiff complained that she was harassed based upon her gender and treated differently than male employees. Although finding that co-workers made some inappropriate comments, the court rejected the plaintiff's hostile environment claim, and then explained:

> Munday herself greatly contributed to the difficulties of which she complains by her own abrasive conduct and by her tendency to blame her problems on others and to assume little responsibility for her own errors, as well as by her general dissatisfaction with her own life.[18]

The *Munday* court went on to observe of the plaintiff: "As a result of her workplace demeanor, she appears to have herself initiated many of the perceived—and sometimes real—problems which she claims she suffered."[19]

Similarly, in *Jensvold v. Shalala,*[20] the court rejected the plaintiff's claims of gender discrimination in terms and conditions of employment. In doing so, the court remarked:

> Plaintiff's version of events remains an illusion. Her skewed perception of events, whether after-the-fact rationalizations borne of a personal sense of failure, or a contemporaneous self-fulfilling prophesy, is entirely of her own creation. Dr. Jensvold was ready to see sinister motive in any action she perceived as remotely critical of her. This is unfortunate, for she obviously had promise as a medical researcher. Instead of trying harder, she sought to lay blame on others.[21]

The courts therefore are increasingly willing to examine the plaintiff's role in the events that the plaintiff alleges give rise to the defendant's liability.

Damages

Even if a personality disorder was not a contributing factor to the workplace dispute in litigation, the existence of such a disorder still may be an important

---

[15]161 F.3d 276, 8 AD Cases 1595 (5th Cir. 1998).

[16]*Id.* at 278, 8 AD Cases at 1597.

[17]858 F. Supp. 1364, 72 FEP Cases 471 (D. Md. 1994), *rev'd in part on other grounds,* 126 F.3d 239, 74 FEP Cases 1478 (4th Cir. 1997).

[18]*Id.* at 1372, 72 FEP Cases at 477.

[19]*Id.* at 1374, 72 FEP Cases at 478.

[20]925 F. Supp. 1109, 70 FEP Cases 788 (D. Md. 1996).

[21]*Id.* at 1114, 70 FEP Cases at 792.

issue in an employment lawsuit. Where a plaintiff actually appears to be in a state of severe emotional distress but the alleged workplace cause of such distress seems somewhat trivial, a personality disorder might in fact be the cause of much of the plaintiff's distress. This is because personality disorders almost always pre-date the plaintiff's entry into the workplace and they often cause chronic psychological symptomatology that is unrelated to any specific incident. They also may produce marital discord, relationship difficulties, low self-esteem, and even suicide attempts, all of which are frequently misattributed to workplace harassment or discrimination. It is therefore critical to determine whether the emotional distress of which the plaintiff complains is truly attributable to the workplace or is instead attributable to some preexisting cause such as a personality disorder. Moreover, because personality disorders begin in adolescence or early adulthood, their symptoms would necessarily preexist employment in virtually every case and cannot possibly have been caused by the employer. Personality disorders, therefore, provide an important alternative explanation for the cause of emotional distress a plaintiff may claim to have suffered—emotional distress that in fact may be quite real.

The following is a summary of some of the psychological symptoms and other dysfunctional effects of personality disorders that may be misattributed to workplace events:[22]

- *Paranoid Personality Disorder:* Anxiety, delusional disorders, brief reactive psychosis, relationship difficulties
- *Obsessive-Compulsive Personality Disorder:* Anxiety, depression, vocational failure, relationship difficulties
- *Antisocial Personality Disorder:* Substance abuse, malingering, vocational failure, relationship difficulties, criminal activity
- *Borderline Personality Disorder:* Depression, anxiety, panic disorder, brief reactive psychosis, substance abuse, suicidal gestures, somatic disorders, dissociation, poor self-esteem, rage, relationship difficulties, vocational failure
- *Histrionic Personality Disorder:* Anxiety, depression, relationship difficulties, somatic disorders, conversion disorder
- *Narcissistic Personality Disorder:* Depression, delusional disorders, relationship difficulties, vocational failure
- *Dependent Personality Disorder:* Anxiety, depression, poor self-esteem, agoraphobia, somatic disorders

---

[22]This summary first appeared in J. McDonald & P. Lees-Haley, *Personality Disorders in the Workplace: How They May Contribute to Claims of Employment Law Violations,* 22 Employee Relations L.J. 57, 74 (1996).

CHAPTER 5

ROLE OF THE MENTAL HEALTH PROFESSIONAL IN EMPLOYMENT LITIGATION

Qualifications of Mental Health Expert Witnesses

Courts have placed the qualifications of proffered mental health expert witnesses under greater scrutiny subsequent to the U.S. Supreme Court's decision in *Daubert v. Merrill Dow Pharmaceuticals Inc.*[1] This topic is covered in more detail in Chapter 11, "Avoiding 'Junk Science' in Employment Litigation."

Retaining an Expert

Right to Choose the Examiner

Ordinarily, the parties have the right to choose their own experts. Where a Federal Rules of Civil Procedure Rule 35 mental examination is to occur, typically the defendant chooses and retains the examiner, who will then serve as the defendant's expert witness at trial. Most courts addressing this issue in the context of employment litigation have accepted the defendant's choice.[2] As the court declared in *Ragge v. MCA/Universal Studios,*[3] "only if plaintiff raises a valid objection will the Court appoint a different examiner."[4] The court in *Ragge* did not consider the plaintiff's mere unsupported allegation that the examiner was not neutral, and that he was hostile to her, to constitute a "valid objection."[5]

---

[1]509 U.S. 579 (1993).

[2]*See, e.g.,* Morton v. Haskell Co., 5 AD Cases 272, 275 (M.D. Fla. 1995); Ragge v. MCA/Universal Studios, 165 F.R.D. 605, 609 (C.D. Cal. 1995); Zabkowicz v. West Bend Co., 585 F. Supp. 635, 636, 35 FEP Cases 209 (E.D. Wis. 1984).

[3]165 F.R.D. 605 (C.D. Cal. 1995).

[4]*Id.* at 609.

[5]*Id.*

Similarly, the court in *Morton v. Haskell Co.*[6] intimated that proof that the examiner designated by the defendant will abuse the proper purpose of the examination may be legitimate grounds for rejecting the defendant's choice, but the court found no such evidence in that case.[7]

By contrast, in *Jansen v. Packaging Corp. of America,*[8] the court granted a sexual harassment plaintiff's request that an independent examiner be appointed rather than the one chosen by the defendant.[9] The court emphasized the fact that the plaintiff did not plan to use her own expert witness at trial and that instead she planned only to call upon her treating physician, with whom, by the defendant's own admission, she had refused to discuss the issues that would be probed during the mental examination. According to the court,

> [i]f the real purpose of Packaging's motion is the entirely legitimate one of seeking to obtain an independent and impartial insight into Jansen's claims of mental harm, that purpose would seem better served by assuring true independence on the part of the examiner, rather than by forcing Jansen into a battle of experts that she has not sought to join (let alone to initiate).[10]

As a result, the court ordered the parties either to agree on an examiner or to submit a list of proposed designees from which the court would choose.[11]

A related issue is whether a defendant or defendants can have the plaintiff examined by more than one examiner. One court, in ordering a Rule 35 mental examination in a gender discrimination and sexual harassment case, specifically held that the plaintiff would not be subjected to an examination by each of the defendants.[12] The court maintained that it was the defendants' obligation to come to an agreement upon the arrangements for a single mental examination of the plaintiff.[13]

Withdrawing Expert Designation [New Topic]

Occasionally a party may select and designate an expert witness and then later decide not to call that expert. This occurred in *House v. Combined Insurance Co. of America,*[14] where the defendant in a sexual harassment lawsuit designated a psychiatric expert, a Dr. Taylor, and subsequently withdrew his name. The plaintiff then sought to take Dr. Taylor's deposition and the defendant resisted. The court permitted the deposition, noting that the situation presented differed from one in which an expert has merely been consulted by a party but never

---

[6]5 AD Cases 272 (M.D. Fla. 1995).
[7]*Id.* at 275.
[8]158 F.R.D. 409, 66 FEP Cases 556 (N.D. Ill. 1994).
[9]*Id.* at 410–11, 66 FEP Cases at 557–58.
[10]*Id.* at 411, 66 FEP Cases at 558.
[11]*Id.*
[12]Ferrell v. Shell Oil Co., 1995 WL 688795, at *3 (E.D. La. 1995).
[13]*Id.*
[14]168 F.R.D. 236, 71 FEP Cases 764 (N.D. Iowa 1996).

actually designated. In such cases, the consultant-expert's conclusions would be protected from disclosure by the work product doctrine. Where, by contrast, a party designates an expert and then withdraws the designation, the *House* court ruled that it had the discretion, guided by a balancing of the probative value against prejudice to the other party, to order disclosure of the withdrawn expert's opinions. It ordered the deposition of the withdrawn expert to occur, and admonished:

> The court's holding here will serve the salutory policy of requiring parties to give some thought and care to their expert witness designations, because once those designations are made, the party will have to live with the consequence that the opposing party will likely be given the opportunity to depose the expert or even to call the expert at trial on their own behalf.[15]

Nature and Scope of the Expert's Testimony

Credibility

In *Nichols v. American National Insurance Co.,*[16] the Eighth Circuit held that expert witness testimony impugning the plaintiff's "psychiatric credibility" was inadmissible under Federal Rule of Evidence 702. In *Nichols,* a sexual harassment lawsuit, the plaintiff put on a psychologist who testified that, as a result of her interviews with the plaintiff and administration of psychological testing, she believed the plaintiff suffered from Posttraumatic Stress Disorder, dysthymic disorder, and generalized anxiety disorder as a result of events in the workplace. The defendant offered the testimony of a psychiatrist who examined the plaintiff and reviewed her medical records. That psychiatrist agreed that the plaintiff suffered from dysthymia and generalized anxiety disorder, but she felt that those conditions preceded the plaintiff's entry into the workplace. She disagreed, however, that the plaintiff suffered from PTSD, and she diagnosed a personality disorder instead.

The defense psychiatrist went on to testify that the plaintiff had "poor psychiatric credibility,"[17] defined as a poor ability to assess the cause of her own psychological state or to report her psychological symptoms accurately. In reaching this assessment, the psychiatrist relied upon the fact that the plaintiff had a history of multiple psychological stressors but focused only on the workplace as the cause of her problems and that she refused to cooperate with the examination. She also observed that the plaintiff "had difficulty interpreting social settings and a tendency to blur fantasy with reality."[18] The defense psychiatrist thus testified that the plaintiff had recall bias and her statements

[15]*Id.* at 247, 71 FEP Cases at 773.
[16]154 F.3d 875, 77 FEP Cases 1338 (8th Cir. 1998).
[17]*Id.* at 882, 77 FEP Cases at 1343.
[18]*Id.*

were affected by secondary gain and malingering. She defined "recall bias" as an individual's belief that she has not experienced certain prior symptoms even though her medical records indicate otherwise.[19] She defined "secondary gain" as the possibility that the plaintiff's complaint of psychological symptoms was motivated by the possibility of a financial award.[20] She defined "malingering" as the feigning or making up of symptoms.[21] The district court overruled the plaintiff's objections to this testimony, which the Eighth Circuit held to be erroneous.

The court of appeals maintained that the defense psychiatrist invaded the province of the jury by commenting on the plaintiff's credibility: "Weighing evidence and determining credibility are tasks exclusive to the jury, and an expert should not offer an opinion about the truthfulness of witness testimony."[22] The court declared that the defense psychiatrist's

> testimony about psychiatric credibility, malingering, recall bias, and secondary gain went beyond the permissible areas of her testimony. She used these terms to indicate that Nichols' version of the facts was inconsistent and changed over time and that it was tainted by bias and desire for financial gain. These were inferences for the jury to draw from the admissible evidence before it, and [the defense psychiatrist's] testimony impermissibly instructed the jury on how to weigh that evidence.[23]

The Fifth Circuit took a contrary approach in *Skidmore v. Precision Printing & Packaging Inc.*[24] In *Skidmore,* the defendant attacked the trial court's allowing the plaintiff's psychiatrist to testify about the plaintiff's credibility. Specifically, the psychiatrist testified that he did not think the plaintiff had lied to him or fabricated her psychiatric symptoms. The Fifth Circuit observed:

> Credibility determinations, of course, fall within the jury's province. [Citations.] Nonetheless, [the plaintiff's psychiatrist] in no way testified that Skidmore was undoubtedly telling the truth; instead, he merely opined that her symptoms and recollections appeared genuine and that he felt he had not been "duped" by her. We see no abuse of discretion in the district court allowing a psychiatrist to testify that a plaintiff seems genuinely distressed to him.[25]

---

[19] *Id.*, 77 FEP Cases at 1343.

[20] *Id.*, 77 FEP Cases at 1343.

[21] *Id.*, 77 FEP Cases at 1343.

[22] *Id.*, 77 FEP Cases at 1344.

[23] *Id.* at 883–84, 77 FEP Cases at 1344.

[24] 188 F.3d 606 (5th Cir. 1999).

[25] *Id.* at 618. *See also* Large v. Our Lady of Mercy Med. Ctr., 76 FEP Cases 1054 (S.D.N.Y. 1998) (in ordering plaintiff to undergo psychiatric examination, court notes that defense psychiatrist, after reviewing plaintiff's deposition testimony and diary entries, opined that plaintiff may be suffering from paranoia, "a fact which would be directly relevant to her credibility and the accuracy of her perceptions of the events which she relies upon as evidence of the discrimination and retaliation she alleges").

Nichols and *Skidmore* appear to be inconsistent. If a plaintiff's expert can testify that he believes the plaintiff was being honest in relating her symptoms, why should a defense psychiatrist not be allowed to testify that the plaintiff's symptoms appear fabricated? Assessment for the possibility of malingering is a standard part of every forensic psychiatric or psychological examination. Moreover, as one forensic psychiatrist with expertise in conducting evaluations of sexual harassment claimants has observed: "The question of perceptual distortion is clearly relevant in the assessment of sexual harassment claims, whether due to 'hypersensitivity' of a woman with borderline personality disorder or the impaired reality testing of a woman with an underlying psychosis."[26] *Nichols* seems to say that a defense examiner cannot report on his or her findings as to this important part of the evaluation, however.

Nichols also is troubling if it is read broadly to prohibit a defense expert from attacking the claims of causation of the plaintiff's emotional condition offered by the plaintiff's expert or even by the plaintiff herself. Suppose, for example, that a plaintiff has a history, well documented in her medical records, of being treated via therapy and antidepressant medication for chronic depression prior to coming to work for the defendant, yet the plaintiff's expert opines that discrimination or harassment by the defendant was the sole cause of the plaintiff's emotional damage, due process requires that the defendant be able to attack that opinion as faulty for ignoring the plaintiff's pre-existing condition. Suppose further that the plaintiff herself testifies that she has no history of depression prior to the workplace events in issue, even though such testimony is directly contradicted by her medical records. Certainly the plaintiff could be cross-examined about her medical records, but she might say she did not understand that she was being treated for depression. A defendant in most cases would want a mental health expert to explain to the jury the meaning and significance of the plaintiff's prior treatment, the nature of the condition being treated, and the form of treatment. The clear inference from such testimony would be that the plaintiff is either blatantly lying—or engaging in "recall bias."

Perhaps the solution is to avoid the term "psychiatric credibility." This is the approach suggested by dissenting Judge Loken in *Nichols,* wherein he noted that the district court might have cautioned the defense not to use the term psychiatric credibility because it sounds like the expert is invading the jury's province.[27] A defense expert does not need to use such a term to attack the plaintiff's expert's faulty methodology—such as just blindly accepting the plaintiff's own view as to her own history and the causation of her current condition. However, the defense expert must be able to challenge the credibility of the plaintiff's expert, and of the plaintiff herself if she gave false information to her expert, if the truth as to the causation of the plaintiff's condition is to be ascertained.

---

[26] L. Gold, *Addressing Bias in the Forensic Assessment of Sexual Harassment Claims*, 26 J. AM. ACAD. OF PSYCHIATRY & LAW 563, 570–71 (1998).

[27] 154 F.3d 875, 891, 77 FEP Cases 1338, 1351 (8th Cir. 1998).

Elements of the Expert's Testimony

Providing an Expert Opinion

Sometimes a plaintiff will not formally designate an expert but offer the testimony of her treating psychotherapist instead, and then argue that the expert disclosure rules do not apply because the psychotherapist will testify only as a percipient witness and not as an expert.

In *Murray v. Chicago Transit Authority*,[28] the court held that a Rule 26(a) expert report[29] was required where the plaintiff intended to offer the testimony of her treating psychiatrist that she suffered posttraumatic stress disorder as a result of sexual harassment and retaliation. The court noted that the Rule 26(a) report was required because the psychiatrist's testimony "inherently" concerned causation of the plaintiff's claimed emotional damages.[30]

Experts' Vulnerabilities in Court

Bias [New Topic]

An expert witness may be subject to attack as being biased, not just because he or she has been retained by a particular side in the litigation, but on account of other factors as well.

---

[28]1999 WL 49355 (N.D. Ill. 1999).

[29]Fed. R. Civ. P. 26(a) provides, in relevant part:

(2) Disclosure of Expert Testimony.

(A) In addition to the disclosures required by paragraph (1), a party shall disclose to other parties the identity of any person who may be used at trial to present evidence under Rules 702, 703, or 705 of the Federal Rules of Evidence.

(B) Except as otherwise stipulated or directed by the court, this disclosure shall, with respect to a witness who is retained or specially employed to provide expert testimony in the case or whose duties as an employee of the party regularly involve giving expert testimony, be accompanied by a written report prepared and signed by the witness. The report shall contain a complete statement of all opinions to be expressed and the basis and reasons therefor; the data or other information considered by the witness in forming the opinions; any exhibits to be used as a summary of or support for the opinions; the qualifications of the witness, including a list of all publications authored by the witness within the preceding ten years; the compensation to be paid for the study and testimony; and a listing of any other cases in which the witness has testified as an expert at trial or by deposition within the preceding four years.

(C) These disclosures shall be made at the times and in the sequence directed by the court. In the absence of other directions from the court or stipulation by the parties, the disclosures shall be made at least 90 days before the trial date or the date the case is to be ready for trial or, if the evidence is intended solely to contradict or rebut evidence on the same subject matter identified by another party under paragraph (2)(B), within 30 days after the disclosure made by the other party. The parties shall supplement these disclosures when required under subdivision (e)(1).

[30]1999 WL 49355, at *1.

Therapeutic Bias. Often, a plaintiff's treating therapist will seek to double as the plaintiff's expert witness. This results in the potential for therapeutic bias. Such bias stems from the fact that the treating therapist's orientation is very different from that of the testifying expert. As Thomas G. Gutheil, M.D., a leading forensic psychiatrist, recently observed:

> In general, these two roles—treater and expert—are considered incompatible because the clinical, legal and ethical mandates are markedly different for them. . . . [T]he treater's job is to place the patient's welfare first—to help and to heal—whereas the expert's job is, by testimony, to inform and teach the judge or jury, regardless of whether the expert's testimony helps or harms the patient. The treater's "client" is the patient; the expert's client is the court. *The very need of the treater to help the patient constitutes, from a forensic perspective, a form of bias through lack of the requisite objectivity and investment in the outcome.*[31]

Another authority observes:

> Treatment recommendations are to accept . . . patients' version of events not only as "therapeutic" or narrative truth, but as literal truth, to avoid causing "second injury." Such patient-oriented stances are incompatible with providing the more critical assessments required in a forensic examination.[32]

As Robert I. Simon, M.D., another leading forensic psychiatrist, similarly observes:

> The treater-examiner dichotomy is [a] source of bias. The treater is the natural ally of the plaintiff. The key therapeutic tasks involve the provisions of empathy, validation, and empowerment. In order to avoid re-victimization in therapy, some have recommended that therapists should assume the harassment occurred, that the patient has an adequate work record and that if a complaint was filed, some type of retaliation took place.[33]

Obviously, a clinician who commences an examination with those kinds of assumptions cannot perform an objective scientific evaluation of a plaintiff. Yet often a plaintiff's mental health expert, who happens to double as the

---

[31]T. Gutheil, The Psychiatrist in Court 27 (1998) (emphasis added). Similarly, the authors of a recent article in the *American Journal of Psychiatry* observed:

> The legal process is directed toward the resolution of disputes; psychotherapy pursues the medical goal of healing. Although these purposes need not always be antithetical and may even be congruent, the processes themselves typically create an irreconcilable role conflict. . . . To assume either role in a particular case is to compromise one's capacity to fulfill the other.

L. Strasburger, T. Gutheil & A. Brodsky, *On Wearing Two Hats: Role Conflict in Serving as Both Psychotherapist and Expert Witness*, 154 Am. J. Psychiatry 448, 449 (1997).

[32]L. Gold, *Addressing Bias in the Forensic Assessment of Sexual Harassment Claims*, 26 J. Am. Acad. of Psychiatry & Law 563, 564 (1998).

[33]R. Simon, *The Credible Forensic Psychiatric Evaluation in Sexual Harassment Litigation,* 26 Psychiatric Annals 139, 141 (1996).

plaintiff's treater, when questioned about his or her conclusion that workplace events caused the plaintiff to suffer one or more mental disorders, respond with: "Well, this is what my patient believes to be the case and I have no reason to think that my patient would lie to me." Such an approach is decidedly unscientific.

Moreover, the *Ethical Guidelines for the Practice of Forensic Psychiatry* of the American Academy of Psychiatry and the Law (AAPL) provide: "Treating psychiatrists should generally avoid agreeing to be an expert witness or to perform evaluations of their patients for legal purposes because a forensic evaluation usually requires that other people be interviewed and testimony may adversely affect the therapeutic relationship."[34]

Financial Bias. The AAPL's *Ethical Guidelines for the Practice of Forensic Psychiatry* also state that "[c]ontingency fees, because of the problems that these create in regard to honesty and efforts to obtain objectivity, should not be accepted."[35] The bias of an expert who will only be paid if the side retaining him or her wins is obvious. Yet, many plaintiff's experts who also serve as the treating clinician essentially work on a contingency fee basis when they perform therapy or other treatment for the plaintiff on a lien basis. Such liens are common in the workers' compensation context but they occur as well in civil lawsuits, particularly where the plaintiff's attorney refers the plaintiff to the clinician for treatment. An expert whose lien will likely go unsatisfied if the plaintiff fails to win a monetary award is vulnerable to being attacked as biased.

Sociopolitical Bias. As one leading forensic psychiatrist has observed, "the issue of sexual harassment arouses strong feelings in individuals with differing opinions regarding aspects of civil rights and feminism."[36] As this authority observes, extreme positions with respect to the issue of sexual harassment rooted in ideological positions will render an expert's opinion suspect:

> The position that any personal comment made by a male coworker toward a woman in the workplace is sexual harassment demonstrates unfamiliarity with the definition of sexual harassment. However, the position that sexual harassment is not a legitimate problem in the workplace and does not result in significant consequences is also an uninformed opinion, which equally reflects bias.[37]

---

[34]American Academy of Psychiatry and the Law, *Ethical Guidelines for the Practice of Forensic Psychiatry* IV (1995) (the *Guidelines* are reprinted herein as Appendix 5-2S).

[35]*Id. See also Report 18 of the Board of Trustees of the American Medical Association* (1998) ("the physician as a witness . . . should not accept compensation that is contingent upon the outcome of the litigation").

[36]L. Gold, *Addressing Bias in the Forensic Assessment of Sexual Harassment Claims*, 26 J. Am. Acad. of Psychiatry & Law 563, 565 (1998).

[37]*Id.* at 566.

Victim Bias. An expert's own history of victimization may also be a source of bias. As one authority describes this concept:

> The percentage of forensic examiners who have personal histories of victimization should roughly approximate the percentage of people who have had such experiences in the general population. Studies consistently indicate these percentages to be 5 to 10 percent of men and 20 to 25 percent of women. . . . Conscious or unconscious bias is likely to be present in forensic evaluations performed by examiners with histories of victimization. These individuals may overidentify with a claimant if they have been victims of harassment or sexual abuse.[38]

Thus, an expert's own abuse history may be a valid ground for inquiry in a sexual harassment lawsuit.

---

[38] *Id.* at 569.

APPENDIX 5-2S [New]

Ethical Guidelines for the Practice of Forensic Psychiatry* (American Academy of Psychiatry & the Law)

I. PREAMBLE

The American Academy of Psychiatry and the Law is dedicated to the highest standards of practice in forensic psychiatry. Recognizing the unique aspects of this practice which is at the interface of the professions of psychiatry and the law, the Academy presents these guidelines for the ethical practice of forensic psychiatry.

Commentary

Forensic Psychiatry is a subspecialty of psychiatry, a medical specialty. Membership in the American Psychiatric Association, or its equivalent, is a prerequisite for membership in the American Academy of Psychiatry and the Law. Hence, these guidelines supplement the Annotations Especially Applicable to Psychiatry of the American Psychiatric Association to the Principles of Medical Ethics of the American Medical Association.

The American Academy of Psychiatry and the Law endorses the Definition of Forensic Psychiatry adopted by the American Board of Forensic Psychiatry, Inc.

"Forensic Psychiatry is a subspecialty of psychiatry in which scientific and clinical expertise is applied to legal issues in legal contexts embracing civil, criminal, and correctional or legislative matters: forensic psychiatry should be practiced in accordance with guidelines and ethical principles enunciated by the profession of psychiatry." (Adopted May 20, 1985)

The forensic psychiatrist practices this subspecialty at the interface of two professions, each of which is concerned with human behavior and each of which has developed its own particular institutions, procedures, values, and vocabulary. As a consequence, the practice of forensic psychiatry entails inherent potentials for complications, conflicts, misunderstandings and abuses.

In view of these concerns, the American Academy of Psychiatry and Law provides these guidelines for the ethical practice of forensic psychiatry.

---

*Adopted May 1987; last revised 1995.

II. CONFIDENTIALITY

Respect for the individual's right of privacy and the maintenance of confidentiality are major concerns of the psychiatrist performing forensic evaluations. The psychiatrist maintains confidentiality to the extent possible given the legal context. Special attention is paid to any limitations on the usual precepts of medical confidentiality. An evaluation for forensic purposes begins with notice to the evaluee of any limitations on confidentiality. Information or reports derived from the forensic evaluation are subject to the rules of confidentiality as they apply to the evaluation, and any disclosure is restricted accordingly.

Commentary

The forensic situation often presents significant problems in regard to confidentiality. The psychiatrist must be aware of and alert to those issues of privacy and confidentiality presented by the particular forensic situation. Notice should be given as to any limitations. For example, before beginning a forensic evaluation, psychiatrists should inform the evaluee that although they are psychiatrists, they are not the evaluee's "doctor." Psychiatrists should indicate for whom they are conducting the examination and what they will do with the information obtained as a result of the examination. There is a continuing obligation to be sensitive to the fact that although a warning has been given, there may be slippage and a treatment relationship may develop in the mind of the examinee.

Psychiatrists should take precautions to assure that none of the confidential information they receive falls into the hands of unauthorized persons.

Psychiatrists should clarify with a potentially retaining attorney whether an initial screening conversation prior to a formal agreement will interdict consultation with the opposing side if the psychiatrist decides not to accept the consultation.

In a treatment situation, whether in regard to an inpatient or to an outpatient in a parole, probation, or conditional release situation, psychiatrists should be clear about any limitations on the usual principles of confidentiality in the treatment relationship and assure that these limitations are communicated to the patient. Psychiatrists should be familiar with the institutional policies in regard to confidentiality. Where no policy exists, psychiatrists should clarify these matters with the institutional authorities and develop working guidelines to define their role.

III. CONSENT

The informed consent of the subject of a forensic evaluation is obtained when possible. Where consent is not required, notice is given to the evaluee of the nature of the evaluation. If the evaluee is not competent to give consent, substituted consent is obtained in accordance with the laws of the jurisdiction.

Commentary

Consent is one of the core values of the ethical practice of medicine and psychiatry. It reflects respect for the person, a fundamental principle in the practices of medicine, psychiatry and forensic psychiatry. Obtaining informed consent is an expression of this respect.

It is important to appreciate that in particular situations, such as court ordered evaluations for competency to stand trial or involuntary commitment, consent is not required. In such a case, the psychiatrist should so inform the subject and explain that the evaluation is legally required and that if the subject refuses to participate in the evaluation, this fact will be included in any report or testimony.

With regard to any person charged with criminal acts, ethical considerations preclude forensic evaluation prior to access to, or availability of legal counsel. The only exception is an examination for the purpose of rendering emergency medical care and treatment.

Consent to treatment in a jail or prison or other criminal justice setting must be differentiated from consent to evaluation. The psychiatrists providing treatment in these settings should be familiar with the jurisdiction's rules in regard to the patient's right to refuse treatment.

IV. HONESTY AND STRIVING FOR OBJECTIVITY

Forensic psychiatrists function as experts within the legal process. Although they may be retained by one party to a dispute in a civil matter or the prosecution or defense in a criminal matter, they adhere to the principle of honesty and they strive for objectivity. Their clinical evaluation and the application of the data obtained to the legal criteria are performed in the spirit of such honesty and efforts to obtain objectivity. Their opinion reflects this honesty and efforts to attain objectivity.

Commentary

The adversarial nature of our Anglo-American legal process presents special hazards for the practicing forensic psychiatrist. Being retained by one side in a civil or criminal matter exposes the forensic psychiatrist to the potential for unintended bias and the danger of distortion of their opinion. It is the responsibility of forensic psychiatrists to minimize such hazards by carrying out his responsibilities in an honest manner striving to reach an objective opinion.

Practicing forensic psychiatrists enhance the honesty and striving for objectivity of their work by basing their forensic opinions, forensic reports, and forensic testimony on all the data available to them. They communicate the honesty and striving for objectivity of their work, efforts to obtain objectivity, and the soundness of their clinical opinion by distinguishing, to the extent possible, between verified and unverified information as well as among clinical "facts", "inferences" and "impressions."

While it is ethical to provide consultation to an adversary in a legal dispute as a testifying or reporting expert, honesty and striving for objectivity are required. The impression that psychiatrists in a forensic situation might distort their opinion in the service of the party which retained them is especially detrimental to the profession and must be assiduously avoided. Honesty, objectivity and the adequacy of the clinical evaluation may be called into question when an expert opinion is offered without a personal evaluation. While there are authorities who would bar an expert opinion in regard to an individual who has not been personally examined, it is the position of the Academy that if, after earnest effort, it is not possible to conduct a personal examination, an opinion may be rendered on the basis of other information. However, under such circumstances, it is the responsibility of the forensic psychiatrist to assure that the statement of their opinion and any reports or testimony based on those opinions, clearly indicate that there was no personal examination and the opinions expressed are thereby limited.

In custody cases, honesty and striving for objectivity require that all parties be interviewed, if possible, before an opinion is rendered. When this is not possible, or, if for any reason not done, this fact should be clearly indicated in the forensic psychiatrist's report and testimony. Where one parent has not been interviewed, even after deliberate effort, it may be inappropriate to comment on that parent's fitness as a parent. Any comment on that parent's fitness as a parent should be qualified and the data for the opinion should be clearly indicated.

Contingency fees, because of the problems that these create in regard to honesty and efforts to obtain objectivity, should not be accepted. On the other hand, retainer fees do not create problems in regard to honesty and efforts to obtain objectivity and, therefore, may be accepted.

Treating psychiatrists should generally avoid agreeing to be an expert witness or to perform evaluations of their patients for legal purposes because a forensic evaluation usually requires that other people be interviewed and testimony may adversely affect the therapeutic relationship.

V. QUALIFICATIONS

Expertise in the practice of forensic psychiatry is claimed only in areas of actual knowledge and skills, training and experience.

Commentary

As regards expert opinions, reports and testimony, the expert's qualifications should be presented accurately and precisely. As a correlate of the principle that expertise may be appropriately claimed only in areas of actual knowledge, skill, training and experience, there are areas of special expertise, such as the evaluation of children or persons of foreign cultures, or prisoners, that may require special training and expertise.

VI. PROCEDURES FOR HANDLING COMPLAINTS OF UNETHICAL CONDUCT

Complaints of unethical conduct against members of the Academy will be returned to the complainant with guidance as to where the complaint should be registered. Generally, they will be referred to the local district branch of the American Psychiatric Association (APA). If the member does not belong to the APA, the complainant will be referred to the state licensing board or to the psychiatric association in the appropriate country. If either the APA, American Academy of Child and Adolescent Psychiatry, or the psychiatric association of another country should expel or suspend a member, AAPL will also expel or suspend the member upon notification of such action, regardless of continuing membership status in other organizations. AAPL will not necessarily follow the APA or other organizations in other actions.

Commentary

It is the present policy of the American Academy of Psychiatry and Law not to adjudicate questions of unethical conduct against members or nonmembers.

General questions in regard to ethical practice in forensic psychiatry are welcomed by the Academy and should be submitted for consideration to the Committee on Ethics.

The Committee will issue opinions on general or hypothetical questions but will not issue an opinion on the ethical conduct of a specific forensic psychiatrist or about an actual case.

Should a specific complaint against a member be submitted to the Academy, it will be referred to the Chair of the Ethics Committee. The Chair will, in turn, generally direct the complainant to the ethics committee of the local district branch of the American Psychiatric Association, to the state licensing board, or to the psychiatric organization of other countries for foreign members.

The Academy, through its Committee on Ethics or in any other way suitable, will assist the local or national committee on ethics of the American Psychiatric Association, state licensing boards or ethics committees of psychiatric organizations in other countries in the adjudication of complaints of unethical conduct or the development of guidelines of ethical conduct as they relate to forensic psychiatric issues.

CHAPTER 6

THE CLINICAL EVALUATION

Scope and Purpose of the Clinical Evaluation

Scope of the Evaluation

Since publication of the Main Volume, the American Psychiatric Association (APA) has published its *Practice Guideline for Psychiatric Evaluation of Adults.*[1] Although stressing that the *Practice Guideline* is not intended to serve as a standard of care,[2] the APA[3] sets forth a systematic outline of what it considers to be the appropriate scope of a clinical psychiatric evaluation. This *Practice Guideline* may be useful in the forensic context in two respects. First, it may serve as a useful tool for educating courts and discovery referees and in overcoming attempts by plaintiffs' counsel to restrict the scope of inquiry during the mental examination of the plaintiff. The *Practice Guideline* might be cited as evidence that certain types of inquiries need to be made, not in an attempt to embarrass or harass the plaintiff, but because the psychiatric profession, in its considered judgment, holds that such inquiries ordinarily must be made for a valid evaluation to occur. Second, the *Practice Guideline* supplies some general principles for conducting a psychiatric evaluation that might be used to impeach an opposing expert who took shortcuts or left out important areas of inquiry.

The *Practice Guideline* divides the clinical evaluation process into a series of "domains," or areas of inquiry, as follows:

- The first two domains are the reason for the evaluation and the history of the present illness. This essentially involves the examiner eliciting from the patient

---

[1]American Psychiatric Association, *Practice Guideline for Psychiatric Evaluation of Adults,* in Practice Guidelines (1996) (hereinafter *Practice Guideline*).

[2]*Id.* at ix.

[3]Although the *Practice Guideline* is published by the APA, a wide variety of other medical and mental health organizations had input into its drafting, including the American Psychological Association, the American Medical Association, the American Nurses Association, the American Psychoanalytic Association, and the American Academy of Psychiatry and the Law. *Id.* at 31.

a description of the symptoms suffered and their history, including the patient's description of any precipitating or aggravating factors.[4]

- The next domain is the past psychiatric history. This includes "a chronological summary of all past episodes of mental illness and treatment, including psychiatric syndromes not formally diagnosed at the time, previously established diagnoses, treatments offered, and responses to treatment."[5] This history also should include prior episodes of serious emotional distress or functional impairment even though no formal treatment was procured. The *Practice Guideline* suggests that the patient be asked about "the past use of psychotropic drugs prescribed by a nonpsychiatric physician, prior suicide attempts or other self-destructive behavior. . . ."[6] The *Practice Guideline* suggests that past medical records might be consulted to obtain relevant data.[7]
- The next domain involves a general medical history. This should include an inquiry into "known general medical illnesses (e.g., hospitalizations, procedures, treatments, and medications) and undiagnosed health problems that have caused the patient major distress or functional impairment." It also should include inquiry into any episodes of important physical injury or trauma, as well as a sexual and reproductive history.[8]
- The next domain involves a history of the patient's substance use. This is to include both illegal and legal substances, such as alcohol, caffeine, and nicotine.[9]
- The next domain is an inquiry into the patient's psychosocial and development history, also known as the "personal history." This includes obtaining information about the person's formal education, religious, and cultural influences; contacts with the criminal justice system; sexual history; marriage and parenting; as well as "any history of physical, emotional, sexual, or other abuse or trauma."[10]
- The next two domains are a social history and an occupational history. The social history involves a consideration of relationships, familial and otherwise, that may serve as stressors or provide support. The occupational history involves a consideration of jobs held, reasons for job changes, and whether any of those jobs involved unusual amounts of stress.[11]
- Next is a family history, which explores the existence of medical or psychiatric illness in close relatives, including mood disorders, psychosis, suicide, and substance abuse.[12]
- Next is a review of symptoms, such as sleep, appetite, pain and discomfort, fatigue, and the like, and a mental status examination, which is not so much a separate area of inquiry as a "systematic collection of data based on observation of the patient's behavior during the interview" and at other times while in the

---

[4]*Id.* at 14.
[5]*Id.*
[6]*Id.* at 15.
[7]*Id.* at 14.
[8]*Id.* at 15.
[9]*Id.*
[10]*Id.* at 15–16.
[11]*Id.* at 16.
[12]*Id.*

examiner's view.[13] Here, a functional assessment of the patient's ability to carry out activities of everyday living is usually conducted,[14] and depending upon the circumstances, a physical examination also may be conducted.[15]

The *Practice Guideline* advises that "the psychiatrist should always consider using collateral sources of information," such as records of prior medical and/or psychiatric treatment. It stresses that "[c]ollateral information is particularly important for patients with impaired insight,"[16] which, it could be argued, might include most plaintiffs seeking to recover substantial damages for emotional distress.

The APA is not alone in maintaining that a comprehensive inquiry is necessary for a valid psychiatric evaluation to occur. Robert I. Simon, M.D.,[17] Director of the Program in Psychiatry and Law at Georgetown University, similarly observes:

> Whether the examiner is retained by the plaintiff or defense attorney, it should be obvious that he or she must perform a complete psychiatric evaluation of the examinee. Nevertheless, some forensic reports do not contain any past psychiatric history of the examinee. It is as if the life of the examinee began with the litigation. Particularly in sexual harassment litigation, the prior history of the examinee is extremely important in the evaluation of psychic injury claims. . . . The longitudinal perspective of child and adolescent development and psychopathology is critical in making correct diagnosis and treatment assessments.[18]

Dr. Simon maintains that collateral sources of information should be obtained. These include employment, school, military, medical, psychiatric, and criminal records. He notes: "Because many claimants report subjective psychological symptoms, corroboration from other sources is essential."[19] The psychiatric evaluation that does not involve such a breadth of inquiry may be vulnerable to attack on cross-examination.

Conduct of the Evaluation

Conditions Placed Upon the Examination

The conditions under which a Federal Rules of Civil Procedure Rule 35 mental examination will be conducted are increasingly a focus of litigation.

---

[13]*Id.* at 17–18.

[14]*Id.* at 19.

[15]*Id.* at 17. Physical examinations are not common during forensic mental examinations.

[16]*Id.* at 21.

[17]See discussion of the *Georgetown Guidelines for Assessment of PTSD* in Chapter 3, "Posttraumatic Stress Disorder," of this Supplement.

[18]R. Simon, *The Credible Forensic Psychiatric Evaluation in Sexual Harassment Litigation,* 26 Psychiatric Annals 139, 142 (1996).

[19]*Id.*

Presence of Third Parties

In employment cases, plaintiffs ordered to submit to a Rule 35 mental examination often will request the presence of a third party. The trial court typically has broad discretion in deciding whether to allow a third-party observer.

Concerning the presence of third parties, one leading forensic psychiatrist has observed:

> The presence of third parties is fraught with difficulties. Sometimes, such "observers" are converted into witnesses that are used against the examiner, usually criticizing the method of the examination. When the claimant's attorney is present, the claimant's psychological symptoms may appear worse, even if the attorney does not directly interfere with the examination. The attorney's presence highlights the adversarial context of the examination, usually contributing to additional anxiety and a focus on symptomatology by the claimant. The presence of supportive family members and friends may cause the claimant to appear less symptomatic than previously reported. Emotional support can have a very quieting and soothing influence on the claimant.[20]

In an early case, the California Supreme Court echoed many of the same concerns. In *Edwards v. Superior Court,*[21] the court refused to allow the plaintiff's attorney to attend the plaintiff's mental examination. The plaintiff had argued that her attorney's presence was necessary to protect her from improper questioning, to make the examination a more comfortable experience for her, and to ensure accurate reporting. The court rejected all three arguments. Concerning the plaintiff's claim that she needed counsel to protect her from improper questions, the court remarked:

> The analyst in a psychiatric examination seeks by careful direction of areas of inquiry to probe, possibly very deeply, into the psyche, measuring stress, seeking origins, tracing aberrations, and attempting to form a professional judgment or interpretation of the examinee's mental condition. Given such techniques and purposes we do not think that an attorney, no matter how well intentioned, can fairly and objectively monitor such an examination. Psychiatry is a discipline requiring highly specialized skills. Further, while properly objecting to a question on legal grounds, counsel does not necessarily possess the ability to define the psychiatric relevance of elicited answers. Many questions which would be legally objectionable, if posed in a courtroom, might be very relevant in the formulation of a sound psychiatric judgment.[22]

---

[20] *Id.*

[21] 16 Cal. 3d 905, 130 Cal. Rptr. 14 (1976).

[22] 16 Cal. 3d at 911, 130 Cal. Rptr. at 17. In *Tirado v. Erosa,* 158 F.R.D. 294 (S.D.N.Y. 1994), the court similarly rejected the plaintiff's argument that the presence of her counsel and a stenographer was necessary due to the sensitive nature of the allegations in the case (unconsented sexual touching). It observed:

> Plaintiff also asserts that the subject matter is especially sensitive, but this consideration cuts both ways. On the one hand, plaintiff might not feel comfortable discussing intimate matters with defendants' psychiatric expert, but on the other it is not clear that having four people in the room rather than two will improve

In answer to the plaintiff's argument that her counsel's presence was necessary for her comfort and emotional support, the *Edwards* court expressed its concern that the presence of others during the examination would be "distracting, if not disrupting," and noted that an examination must proceed free of such disruptions if it is to be valid.[23] Finally, the *Edwards* court held that a verbatim account of all of the questions and answers at a mental examination is not necessarily desirable, as it might cause the examinee to react defensively and inhibit the "free, open and objective communication essential to an effective psychiatric examination."[24]

A majority of courts in employment cases have disallowed the presence of plaintiff's counsel during the Rule 35 mental examination absent compelling reasons to find otherwise.[25] Justifications advanced for this view include the need (1) to conduct the examination without the distractions of a third person in order to obtain a valid psychiatric profile;[26] (2) to provide the defendant with a "level playing field" because the plaintiff's physician would have examined the plaintiff without the presence of the defendant's attorney; (3) to prevent a more adversarial atmosphere during such examinations than is already unavoidably present; (4) to avoid the possible conflict of interests created by the fact that the presence of the plaintiff's attorney during the examination makes the attorney a potential witness at trial; and (5) the lack of other less obtrusive devices to protect the interests of the plaintiff.[27]

On the other hand, a minority of courts have allowed plaintiffs' attorneys to be present during Rule 35 mental examinations, reasoning that plaintiffs' interest in protecting themselves from unsupervised interrogation by an agent of their opponents outweighs defendants' interests in making the most effective

---

> this situation. Plaintiff has made no showing that the presence of her male attorney and a complete stranger (male or female) taking down every word would make her any more comfortable.

Id. at 296.

[23]16 Cal. 3d at 911, 130 Cal. Rptr. at 18.

[24]*Id.* at 911–12, 130 Cal. Rptr. at 18.

[25]*See, e.g.,* Breda v. Wolf Camera Inc., 78 FEP Cases 433, 435 (S.D. Ga. 1998); Haensel v. Chrysler Corp., 1997 WL 537995 (E.D. La. 1997); Ferrell v. Shell Oil Co., 1995 WL 688795, at *2 (E.D. La. 1995); Hirschheimer v. Associated Minerals & Minerals Corp., 1995 WL 736901, at *3 (S.D.N.Y. 1995); Vinson v. Superior Court, 43 Cal. 3d 833, 239 Cal. Rptr. 292, 44 FEP Cases 1174 (Cal. 1987); Lowe v. Philadelphia Newspapers Inc., 101 F.R.D. 296, 299, 44 FEP Cases 1224, 1226 (E.D. Pa. 1983). *See also* Wheat v. Biesecker, 125 F.R.D. 479, 480 (N.D. Ind. 1989) (noting that majority rule is that plaintiff's attorney may not attend a Rule 35 examination).

[26]In *Tirado v. Erosa,* 158 F.R.D. 294, 295 (S.D.N.Y. 1994), the court, in denying the plaintiff's request to have her attorney and a stenographer present during her mental examination, cited an affidavit submitted by the examiner stating that the presence of third parties "could impede the effectiveness of my examination, as well as potentially hinder my ability to fully and fairly evaluate whether, and the extent to which, a mental illness and/or emotional disturbance may or may not exist."

[27]*See Ferrell,* 1995 WL 688795 at *2; *Hirschheimer,* 1995 WL 736901 at *3; *Vinson,* 43 Cal. 3d at 845–46, 239 Cal. Rptr. at 300–02, 44 FEP Cases at 1179–80.

use of their experts.[28] Some states also specifically authorize the presence of counsel during a mental examination in their state versions of Rule 35.[29]

For reasons similar to those given for prohibiting the presence of the plaintiff's attorney, most courts have prohibited other third parties from being present during a Rule 35 mental examination.[30] A few courts, however, have allowed the plaintiff's treating physician or psychotherapist to be present.[31]

Tape Recording the Examination

There is a split of authority regarding whether the mental examination may be tape recorded. Some courts prohibit the practice for many of the same reasons that the presence of the plaintiff's attorney has been disallowed.[32] One denied the plaintiff's request for tape recording, maintaining that the presence of a tape recorder "may invalidate the results of the examination, as it may consciously or unconsciously influence plaintiff to exaggerate or diminish her reactions to the examination."[33] Other courts permit tape recording, which, according to one court, is a less obtrusive means of preserving evidence of abuse by the examining physician.[34] California has a statute expressly permitting a plaintiff (as well as

---

[28]Zabkowicz v. West Bend Co., 585 F. Supp. 635, 636, 35 FEP Cases 209, 209–10 (E.D. Wis. 1984). *See also* Vreeland v. Ethan Allen Inc., 151 F.R.D. 551, 551–52 (S.D.N.Y. 1993) (upholding a magistrate's ruling that allowed the presence of the plaintiff's attorney).

[29]*See, e.g.,* ARIZ. R. CIV. P. 35(a) (1997); 735 ILL. COMP. STAT. ANN. 5/2-1003 (West 1997); MICH. CT. R. 2.311(a) (1997).

[30]*See, e.g.,* Haensel v. Chrysler Corp., 1997 WL 537995 (E.D. La. 1997) (psychologist and attorney); Hlinko v. Virgin Atlantic Airways, 1997 WL 68560 (S.D.N.Y. 1997) (female nurse); Gavenda v. Orleans County, 174 F.R.D. 272 (W.D.N.Y. 1996) (court reporter); Shirsat v. Mutual Pharm. Co., 169 F.R.D. 68, 70–71 (E.D. Pa. 1996) (third-party observers in general and court reporters in particular); Ali v. Wang Labs., 162 F.R.D. 165, 168, 4 AD Cases 520, 523 (M.D. Fla. 1995) (wife and court reporter); Ragge v. MCA/Universal Studios, 165 F.R.D. 605, 609–10 (C.D. Cal. 1995) (third-party observers in general); Galieti v. State Mut. Auto. Ins. Co., 154 F.R.D. 262, 263–65 (D. Colo. 1994) (third-party observers in general). *See also* Lahr v. Fulbright & Jaworski, L.L.P., 164 F.R.D. 204, 212 n.5 (N.D. Tex. 1996) (crediting the magistrate's finding that the presence of an observer would disrupt the examination).

[31]*See, e.g.,* Morton v. Haskell Co., 1995 WL 819182, at *3, 5 AD Cases 272, 275 (M.D. Fla. 1995); Lowe v. Philadelphia Newspapers Inc., 101 F.R.D. 296, 299, 44 FEP Cases 1224, 1226–27 (E.D. Pa. 1983). *See also Zabkowicz,* 585 F. Supp. at 636, 35 FEP Cases at 209–10 (allowing the presence of any third-party observer).

[32]*See, e.g., Shirsat,* 169 F.R.D. at 70; *Hirschheimer,* 1995 WL 736901, at *4; *Ali,* 4 AD Cases at 523.

[33]Hertenstein v. Kimberly Home Health Care Inc., 80 FEP Cases 355, 363, (D. Kan. 1999).

[34]Vinson v. Superior Court, 43 Cal. 3d 833, 845–46, 239 Cal. Rptr. 292, 300–02, 44 FEP Cases 1174, 1179 (1987). *See also* Gavenda v. Orleans County, 174 F.R.D. 272 (W.D.N.Y. 1996) (permitting tape recording of examination); *Zabkowicz,* 585 F. Supp. at 636, 35 FEP Cases at 209–10 (allowing the use of a tape recording device or the presence of any third-party observer to protect the plaintiff from "unsupervised interrogation").

the examiner) to audiotape the mental examination.[35] As a matter of practice, if the plaintiff audiotapes the examination, the examiner should audiotape it as well.

Duration of the Examination

A frequent issue surrounding Rule 35 mental examinations is the amount of time to be allowed for the examination. A properly conducted mental examination, including the administration of psychological testing,[36] should last for the better part of a day. Some courts have approved of this.[37] Other courts have either approved or specifically ordered a maximum of three hours to conduct the examination plus the time needed to administer any psychological tests.[38] In *Shepherd v. American Broadcasting Cos.,*[39] the court limited the psychiatric examinations of the race discrimination plaintiffs to five hours each, with no mention of psychological testing.[40] Further, in *Morton v. Haskell Co.,*[41] the court rejected the plaintiff's request to limit the mental examination to one hour, reasoning that there was "no basis to conclude that a one-hour examination will necessarily fit the circumstances of this case."[42] Notably, the court in that case did not impose any time restrictions for the examination.[43]

Restrictions on the Scope of the Examination

Rule 35 and most of its state counterparts require the party seeking a mental examination to specify the scope of the examination. In employment litigation,

---

[35]CAL. CODE OF CIV. PROC. §2032(g)(2).

[36]*See* §2032(d), *infra.*

[37]Ragge v. MCA/Universal Studios, 165 F.R.D. 605, 610 (C.D. Cal. 1995) (ordered seven hours total including time needed for psychological tests); Chaparro v. IBP Inc., 1994 WL 714369 at *4 (D. Kan., 1994) (approved one day or two half-day sessions if the defendant pays for the plaintiff's expenses incurred because the examination was not conducted in a single day).

[38]*See, e.g.,* Hirschheimer v. Associated Minerals & Minerals Corp., 1995 WL 736901 at *5 (S.D.N.Y. 1995) (ordered maximum of two 90-minute sessions in addition to the time needed to administer the Minnesota Multiphasic Personality Inventory-2 (MMPI-2)); Burger v. Litton Indus. Inc., 1995 WL 363741 at *2, 68 FEP Cases 737, 739 (S.D.N.Y. 1995) (ordered maximum of three hours for the examination plus the time necessary to administer the MMPI-2, which is approximately four hours); Lowe v. Philadelphia Newspapers Inc., 101 F.R.D. 296, 300, 44 FEP Cases 1224, 1228 (E.D. Pa. 1983) (ordered no more than two sessions lasting 90 minutes each); Ryzlak v. McNeil Pharm. Co., 38 Fed. R. Serv. 2d 443, 444 (E.D. Pa. 1982) (approved two 90-minute sessions).

[39]151 F.R.D. 194 (D.D.C. 1993), *rev'd in part and vacated in part on other grounds,* 62 F.3d 1469 (D.C. Cir. 1995).

[40]*Id.* at 215.

[41]5 AD Cases 272 (M.D. Fla. 1995).

[42]*Id.* at 275.

[43]*See also* Gavenda v. Orleans County, 174 F.R.D. 272 (W.D.N.Y. 1996) (court refused to place time limit on examination).

defendants naturally desire wide latitude in the scope of the examination to determine both the extent and the cause of the plaintiff's alleged mental or emotional distress or injury. Plaintiffs, on the other hand, want to limit the scope of the examination as much as possible.

From a clinical standpoint, the examiner must have wide latitude to conduct a thorough inquiry of the plaintiff's family and educational background, employment history, prior traumatic events (including sexual abuse), prior medical and psychiatric treatment, marital and relational history, and possible alternative sources of distress. These areas are essential to the formation of an informed psychiatric or psychological assessment of the plaintiff, whether conducted by plaintiff's or defendant's expert.

Yet, with increasing frequency, plaintiffs and their attorneys attempt to restrict the defense examiner's areas of inquiry on privacy or relevancy grounds, often seeking to shield from disclosure other significant traumas or life events that might bring into question the validity of the assertion that the employer is wholly to blame for the plaintiff's psychological condition. Prior sexual trauma is an area frequently sought to be shielded from inquiry,[44] as well as prior mental health treatment, prior or concurrent medical conditions, family dysfunction, and developmental difficulties. As a leading forensic psychiatrist observes, however,

> [p]articularly in sexual harassment litigation, the prior history of the examinee is extremely important in the evaluation of psychic injury claims. . . . The longitudinal perspective of child and adolescent development and psychopathology is critical in making correct diagnosis and treatment assessments.[45]

There are not as of yet many reported cases concerning the proper scope of the Rule 35 mental examination. The issue was recently addressed in *Sarko v. Penn-Del Directory Co.*[46] In *Sarko,* the plaintiff alleged that her employer discriminated against her by failing to accommodate her clinical depression, which she claimed had a long-term impact on her mental state.[47] The court held that the defendant was entitled to conduct a mental examination because the plaintiff's allegation placed her current mental condition in controversy, but it specifically limited the scope of the examination to the long-term impact that the depression had on the plaintiff's current mental state.[48]

In other cases addressing the issue, the scope of the examination has not been so severely limited. For example, in *Morton v. Haskell Co.,*[49] the plaintiff

---

[44]*See* Knoettgen v. Superior Court, 224 Cal. App. 3d 11, 273 Cal. Rptr. 636 (1990) (prohibiting discovery into plaintiff's prior sexual abuse in sexual harassment case). This subject is addressed in more detail in Chapter 10, "Special Issues in Sexual Harassment Cases," of this Supplement.

[45]R. Simon, *The Credible Forensic Psychiatric Evaluation in Sexual Harassment Litigation,* 26 Psychiatric Annals 139, 142 (1996).

[46]170 F.R.D. 127 (E.D. Pa. 1997).

[47]*Id.* at 131.

[48]*Id.*

[49]5 AD Cases 272 (M.D. Fla. 1995).

also claimed that the employer discriminated against him on account of his clinical depression. In that case, the court refused to limit the examination to the year of the alleged adverse employment action, concluding that such a limitation was unwarranted, particularly in light of the plaintiff's own allegation that he had suffered a continuing history of clinical depression.[50] Similarly, in a gender discrimination and sexual harassment case, the court permitted the defendant's examiner a broad range of inquiry:

> The scope of the examination will be: a full history of plaintiff's entire mental history and its causes; all psychological problems and/or damages that she may have experienced in the past, is currently experiencing or may continue to experience in the future; and the extent of and causes of any such problems.[51]

In *Hertenstein v. Kimberly Home Health Care Inc.,*[52] the court refused the plaintiff's request to forbid the examiner from questioning her about her sexual history, explaining:

> This is a sexual harassment case. [The plaintiff's psychological expert] has opined that alleged actions or inactions of defendant proximately caused the emotional distress of plaintiff. To validly assess her emotional state, the examiner must have leave to make relevant inquiries. To prohibit inquiry into private sexual activities may unreasonably restrict exploring the history of plaintiff relevant to this case.[53]

More law is likely to develop in this area as litigants jockey to delimit the scope of the Rule 35 mental examination in a manner most beneficial to their cases. Although litigants and courts sometimes lose sight of the fact, any significant restriction on the scope of an examiner's inquiry during a Rule 35 mental examination may render the whole exercise clinically useless.

Other Conditions [New Topic]

Plaintiffs occasionally argue that other conditions should be imposed upon their participation in a mental examination. For example, in *Hertenstein v. Kimberly Home Health Care Inc.,*[54] the plaintiff's psychologist claimed that the plaintiff had suffered major depressive disorder and posttraumatic stress disorder as a result of sexual harassment and that to avoid triggering a suicide episode, the plaintiff's mental examination would have to be handled with special care. Specifically, she recommended that the plaintiff's mental examination occur in a "nonthreatening" location such as her attorney's office, that the plaintiff have a person of her choosing present during the examination, that an audio recording be made, that the plaintiff be allowed to take breaks and make phone

---

[50] *Id.* at 275.

[51] Ferrell v. Shell Oil Co., 1995 WL 688795 at *2 (E.D. La. 1995).

[52] 80 FEP Cases 355 (D. Kan. 1999).

[53] *Id.* at 359.

[54] 80 FEP Cases 355 (D. Kan. 1999).

calls whenever she desired, and that the examiner give assurances that the examination be conducted in as "sensitive, nonthreatening [and] nonoverbearing manner as possible."[55] The defendant's examiner submitted an affidavit stating: "I would not undertake a psychiatric evaluation with these restrictions because they are contrary to good clinical or medicolegal psychiatric practice and would absolutely preclude my completion of the task requested by counsel."[56] The court rejected all of the plaintiff's proposed conditions. It declined to infer that the defense examiner's office was a "threatening" environment just because the defense retained the examiner. It found that a "need to reduce stress" was an insufficient reason to allow taking breaks at will during the examination, which was scheduled for two hours. The court declined to order the examiner to conduct the examination in any particular fashion, noting that the examiner already had acknowledged his duty to interview the plaintiff in an ethical and professional manner. The court also rejected the plaintiff's request that the examiner reveal the questions to be asked in advance of the examination.

Similarly, in *Hlinko v. Virgin Atlantic Airways,*[57] the plaintiff's psychiatrist recommended that the plaintiff's mental examination occur at her attorney's office because the plaintiff suffered from "post-traumatic symptoms including phobic avoidance of working with and being alone with men."[58] The court rejected that proposal, noting that it was "unreasonable and would unduly interfere with the expert's evaluation."[59]

---

[55]*Id.* at 358.

[56]*Id.*

[57]1997 WL 68560 (S.D.N.Y. 1997).

[58]*Id.* at *1.

[59]*Id.* at *2.

CHAPTER 7

MALINGERING

There have been no changes or developments in the law since publication of the Main Volume.

CHAPTER 8

PSYCHOLOGICAL TESTING

Legal Issues Relating to Testing

Standardized psychological testing instruments commonly are administered in the course of Federal Rules of Civil Procedure Rule 35 mental examinations in employment lawsuits. Properly administered and interpreted, these instruments can provide assistance to the expert in determining the existence and severity of a psychological injury. They also can enhance the credibility of the expert's opinion in the eyes of the factfinder, as they can be used to bring an element of objectivity to the diagnosis of mental illness—a process that is largely unfamiliar to most lay people. Certain test instruments can provide valuable clues to a plaintiff's long-term character and functioning, and some tests even can help detect malingering (i.e., the fabrication or exaggeration of symptoms) on the part of the plaintiff. Plaintiffs are challenging the use of psychological tests during the Rule 35 mental examination with increasing frequency, however.

Obtaining Both a Psychiatric Examination and Psychological Testing [New Topic]

Some plaintiffs have argued that a defendant should not be able to subject them to psychological testing in addition to a psychiatric examination. In one case, *Burger v. Litton Industries Inc.,*[1] the court allowed an examination only by the defendant's psychiatrist, rather than by both a psychiatrist and a psychologist as originally proposed by the defendant. In other cases, however, courts have permitted psychological testing in addition to a psychiatric examination.

In *Ziemann v. Burlington County Bridge Commission,*[2] the court reasoned that the use of multiple examiners was appropriate because psychiatry and

[1]68 FEP Cases 737, 739 (S.D.N.Y. 1995).
[2]155 F.R.D. 497 (D.N.J. 1994).

psychology are different disciplines, focusing on "different areas of thought and behavior."[3] In *Jackson v. Entergy Operations Inc.*,[4] the plaintiff in a sexual harassment case unsuccessfully objected to having to undergo psychological testing in addition to a psychiatric examination. En route to overruling her objection, the court noted that Rule 35 does not limit the number of examinations a party may be required to undergo. It also observed that "psychological testing is a routine component of a complete psychiatric examination," providing sufficient basis to order such testing.[5]

In *Jaqua v. Furr's/Bishop's Cafeterias, L.P.*,[6] the court rejected the plaintiff's argument that the defendant improperly subjected him to psychological testing where the defense psychiatric expert retained a psychologist to interpret psychological testing administered by the plaintiff's own psychologist. The court maintained that reviewing psychological tests obtained by someone else is not the same as performing one's own psychological testing. It also pointed out that it would have allowed the defense to conduct its own psychological testing of the plaintiff had such a request been made.

In *Chiperas v. Rubin,*[7] the court rejected the plaintiff's request that the defendant's expert not be permitted to administer psychological tests that previously had been administered to her. The court observed: "I would be loath to interfere with a conscientious determination by a medical professional that a test should be repeated to reach a sound scientific conclusion."[8]

Limitations on Tests That May Be Used

Some courts require that psychological tests conducted during a mental examination be shown to be reliable and offer probative evidence.[9] Other courts require that such tests be limited to those generally recognized in the mental health professions.[10] The Minnesota Multiphasic Personality Inventory-2 (MMPI-2), for example, is one test that is generally accepted and commonly used by mental health professionals.

Results of the MMPI have been admitted into evidence by many state and federal courts,[11] and both the MMPI and MMPI-2 have been the subject of

---

[3]*Id.* at 502.

[4]76 FEP Cases 85 (E.D. La. 1998).

[5]*Id.* at 87.

[6]175 F.R.D. 688, 75 FEP Cases 737 (D. Kan. 1997).

[7]1998 WL 765126 (D.D.C. 1998).

[8]*Id.* at *4.

[9]*See, e.g.,* Lahr v. Fulbright & Jaworski, L.L.P., 164 F.R.D. 204, 212 (N.D. Tex. 1996).

[10]*See, e.g.,* Ragge v. MCA/Universal Studios, 165 F.R.D. 605, 609 (C.D. Cal. 1995); Chaparro v. IBP Inc., 1994 WL 714369 at *4 (D. Kan. 1994).

[11]For a general discussion of the admissibility of the MMPI, as well as a listing of federal and state cases in which MMPI test results were admitted, see K. POPE ET AL., THE MMPI, MMPI-2 AND MMPI-A IN COURT 39–46 & Appendix E (1993).

extensive validation studies. In employment litigation, the MMPI-2 also is routinely allowed during Rule 35 mental examinations.[12] For example, in *Burger v. Litton Industries,*[13] over the plaintiff's claim that such amounted to "harassment," the court ordered the plaintiff in an age and sex discrimination case to take the MMPI-2, which it described as a "generally accepted and commonly used test to obtain a psychological profile and history of the subject."[14] Similarly, in *Hirschheimer v. Associated Minerals & Minerals Corp.,*[15] the court ordered the plaintiff in an age and disability discrimination lawsuit to take the MMPI-2, observing that even if, as the plaintiff argued, it provides only a "snap-shot" of the plaintiff's personality at the time the test is taken, "it is still useful as part of a psychological examination."[16] Courts have ordered psychological testing as part of the Rule 35 mental examination in other cases as well.[17]

In *Breda v. Wolf Camera Inc.,*[18] the plaintiff moved for a protective order seeking to prevent the defendant's psychologist from performing psychological testing on her. Specifically, she sought to avoid the MMPI-2 and the Rorschach Ink Blot test, arguing that the tests were overly invasive and unreliable. The court rejected her request. It observed that "[e]ven a cursory scan of the caselaw reveals that both the MMPI-2 and Rorschach are acceptable diagnostic indicators in a mental examination."[19] With respect to the plaintiff's argument that the Rorschach is not sufficiently accurate to be reliable, the court noted that such an argument should be brought in a challenge to admissibility under *Daubert v. Merrill Dow Pharmaceuticals Inc.,*[20] not in an attempt to prevent discovery.

Only one court has refused to allow such an administration of the MMPI-2. In a peculiar opinion in which the court referred to psychological tests as "mind control" devices, the court in *Usher v. Lakewood Usher Engineering & Manufacturing Co.*[21] denied the defendant's motion to have the plaintiff undergo a battery of psychological tests, including the MMPI-2, during the Rule 35 mental examination. The *Usher* court did not provide any extensive analysis in support of its decision; it indicated merely that it felt that the questions on some of the tests were intrusive and of limited relevance to the issues in the litigation. At this point, however, the *Usher* decision is in the distinct minority.

---

[12] *See, e.g.,* Shirsat v. Mutual Pharms. Co., 169 F.R.D. 68, 71–72 (E.D. Pa. 1996); Hirschheimer v. Associated Minerals & Minerals Corp., 1995 WL 736901, at *4–5 (S.D.N.Y. 1995); Burger v. Litton Indus. Inc., 68 FEP Cases 737, 739 (S.D.N.Y. 1995).

[13] 68 FEP Cases 737 (S.D.N.Y. 1995).

[14] *Id.* at 739.

[15] 1995 WL 736901 (S.D.N.Y. 1995).

[16] *Id.* at *4.

[17] *See, e.g.,* Workman v. Carolina Freight Carriers Corp., 65 FEP Cases 1209 (M.D. Ala. 1994); Chaparro v. IBP Inc., 1994 WL 714369 (D. Kan. 1994).

[18] 78 FEP Cases 433 (S.D. Ga. 1998).

[19] *Id.* at 434.

[20] 509 U.S. 579 (1993). For a complete examination of the applicability of *Daubert* in employment cases, see Chapter 11 of this Supplement.

[21] 158 F.R.D. 411, 66 FEP Cases 558 (N.D. Ill. 1994).

A variety of other tests frequently appear in employment litigation, even though they probably should not be used because they tend to be unreliable. For example, the Beck Depression Inventory (BDI) is a 21-item pencil and paper inventory created for the assessment of the severity of depression. Although this instrument can be quite useful in other clinical contexts, it can be easily manipulated by the subject in a forensic setting because it asks obviously leading questions. It essentially asks: "How depressed are you?" Accordingly, reliance upon the BDI as a basis for diagnosis of a mental disorder, or for the opinion that the patient is disabled, is scientific error.[22] Also, the BDI addresses only the seven-day period preceding its administration. It thus is not a valid instrument for describing a plaintiff's condition over a period of months or years.

Some psychological tests are projective in nature, in that they gauge the subject's reaction to certain ambiguous stimuli. These instruments include Human Figure Drawings, the Thematic Apperception Test, Sentence Completion Tests, and the Rorschach Ink Blot Test. Examiners using these procedures have plaintiffs draw pictures of houses or people or trees, or make up sentences and stories, or describe what they see in a series of ink blots. The scientific validity of many of these instruments in the forensic context is doubtful, if not nonexistent.

Obligation to Disclose Identity of Tests in Advance

An issue that is becoming more frequently litigated is whether the defense examiner must identify the psychological tests to be administered during the Rule 35 mental examination in advance of the examination. The obvious problem with advance disclosure is that the testing process becomes compromised; it cannot be known whether the plaintiff rehearsed the answers in advance, with the aid of counsel and/or therapist.[23]

The few cases decided to date are in conflict. In *Ragge v. MCA/Universal Studios,*[24] for example, the court refused to order the defense examiner to disclose in advance the specific psychological tests to be administered. An opposite conclusion was reached by the court in *Hirschheimer v. ASOMA Corp.,*[25] which limited the use of testing during the Rule 35 mental examination to the one test, the MMPI-2, that had been identified previously by the defense. The court commented: "[R]equiring Mr. Hirschheimer to undergo unidentified testing would deprive him of the opportunity to seek an order precluding those tests that may be irrelevant to this litigation."[26]

---

[22]*See* P. Lees-Haley, The Last-Minute Guide to Psychological and Neuropsychological Testing 9–11 (1993).

[23]Psychologists are ethically bound to maintain the integrity and security of psychological tests. *See* Ethical Principle No. 8, American Psychological Association, Casebook on Ethical Principles of Psychologists 109 (1987).

[24]165 F.R.D. 605 (C.D. Cal. 1995).

[25]1995 WL 736901 (S.D.N.Y. 1995).

[26]*Id.* at *4.

Refusal to Release Test Data [New Topic]

With greater frequency, plaintiffs' experts and treating psychologists are refusing to release psychological testing data in discovery, arguing that such release would amount to an ethical violation for the plaintiff's psychologist. In *Chiperas v. Rubin,*[27] the defendant subpoenaed the plaintiff's psychologist for a deposition and requested that she produce raw test data and test results relating to her administration of psychological testing to the plaintiff. The plaintiff moved to quash the subpoena, arguing that it would be a breach of ethics for the psychologist to release the test data to anyone other than another psychologist.

The *Chiperas* court acknowledged that two ethical principles affecting psychologists might apply. The first, Ethical Principle No. 8 of the American Psychological Association, provides:

> Psychologists make every effort to maintain the security of tests and other assessment techniques within the limits of legal mandates. They strive to ensure the appropriate use of assessment techniques by others.[28]

The second, contained in the APA's Standards for Education and Psychological Testing, states:

> Responsibility for test use should be assumed by or delegated only to those individuals who have the training and experience necessary to handle this responsibility in a professional and technically adequate manner.[29]

The *Chiperas* court sidestepped the ethical issue by holding that the plaintiff had no standing to move to quash a subpoena unless the plaintiff claims some personal right or privilege with regard to the documents sought. The court went on to note that the plaintiff could not claim any doctor-patient privilege in the data as he planned to offer the psychologist as a witness in support of his emotional damage claim.[30] The court further observed, however, that the plaintiff's objection had become moot as the defendant's psychiatrist had affiliated with a psychologist, so the plaintiff's psychologist could give the information directly to the defendant's psychologist.

The practical solution highlighted in *Chiperas* to this purported ethical problem may work when the defense has retained a psychologist, but what if the defense retains a psychiatrist instead? Even if the defense retains a psychologist, it is usually necessary for defense counsel to have access to psychological testing information for purposes of deposing the plaintiff's expert or for trial preparation. Suppose the plaintiff's psychologist testifies that she relied upon the MMPI-2 she administered to the plaintiff in formulating her opinion that the plaintiff suffers from depression caused by workplace events, yet the validity

---

[27] 1998 WL 765126 (D.D.C. 1998).

[28] American Psychological Association, Casebook on Ethical Principles of Psychologists 109 (1987).

[29] 1998 WL 765126, at *1.

[30] *Id.* at *2.

scales on the MMPI-2 indicate that the tests results are invalid.[31] Such information would be essential to an attack on her credibility, yet if she were to refuse to produce her test data and results under a claim of ethics, the defense would be deprived of this crucial information.[32]

The holding of the *Chiperas* court appears to be the better approach—i.e., that if a plaintiff plans to call his psychologist to testify at trial and that psychologist plans to rely on testing data, the plaintiff has waived any right to prevent the disclosure of that data. It should also be noted that neither of the ethical canons cited by the *Chiperas* court prohibit the disclosure of test data to non-psychologists. Rather, Ethical Principle No. 8 provides that psychologists are to maintain test security "within the limits of legal mandates." The legal principle of due process would seem to be a sufficient "legal mandate" to require disclosure of test data if a plaintiff plans to use it at trial. Furthermore, the concern expressed in the APA's Standards for Education and Psychological Testing that test data be handled in "a professional and technically adequate manner" may be met by a protective order limiting the dissemination of the data to opposing counsel and their experts and limiting the use to purposes related to the litigation. Such an order would ordinarily protect the plaintiff's right to privacy, the psychologist's interest in test security, and the defendant's due process right to challenge the evidence posed against it.

Use of MMPI Code Types in Litigation

One manner of interpretation of MMPI-2 results is in terms of "code types." A code type represents the highest and second-highest T scores on the MMPI-2's clinical scales. These code types may provide valuable insight into a plaintiff's personality style as it affects his or her ability to get along with others and to accurately perceive the actions and motivations of others. For example, one common code type produced by plaintiffs in discrimination lawsuits is the "2-6/6-2" code type. Such a code type would indicate that the plaintiff scored highest on scale 2 (depression) and scale 6 (paranoia). One authority on the MMPI describes this profile as depicting a "resentful martyr" who is prone to litigiousness.[33] Another authority on MMPI interpretation describes this code-type as follows:

> Touchy, moody, depressed, and oversensitive to criticism, these persons have a strong underlying anger and most often a long history of interpersonal difficulties.

---

[31]See discussion of MMPI validity scales at p. 260 of the Main Volume.

[32]Of course, the same problem would be presented if a defense psychologist attempted to avoid disclosing test results to plaintiff's counsel. *See* Breda v. Wolf Camera Inc., 78 FEP Cases 433 (S.D. Ga. 1998) (ordering defendant's psychologist to disclose psychological testing data on plaintiff to plaintiff's counsel).

[33]A. Caldwell, Forensic Questions and Answers on the MMPI/MMPI-2 41 (1997).

> Paranoid trends are usually evident. They read malevolent meaning into neutral situations, and jump to conclusions based on insufficient data. Resentfulness, agitation, fatigue, and aggressiveness are usually marked. Often these persons adopt a "chip on the shoulder" attitude in an attempt to reject others before they are rejected, or as a means to avoid becoming dependent.[34]

As such a description might provide a factfinder with a glimpse of the plaintiff's interpersonal style in the workplace, the MMPI-2's code types can be highly useful in employment litigation.

---

[34] A. Friedman et al., Psychological Assessment with the MMPI 167 (1989).

CHAPTER 9

PHARMACOLOGY ISSUES

There have been no changes or developments in the law since publication of the Main Volume.

CHAPTER 10

SPECIAL ISSUES IN SEXUAL HARASSMENT CASES

Obstacles to the Objective Assessment of Sexual Harassment Claims

Privacy Claims

With the dramatic increase in the number of sexual harassment claims litigated over the past decade has come a new source of controversy over the discoverability and admissibility of evidence of the plaintiff's prior sexual experiences. On the extremes of this controversy lie one view that to inquire into such topics is unfairly "blaming the victim" and subjecting the plaintiff to only further harassment, and the opposite view that if the plaintiff possesses "loose morals" such evidence should get to the jury to undercut the credibility of the plaintiff's claim that she was offended by harassment in the workplace.

In between these extremes, however, lies an issue that cannot so easily be dismissed if notions of due process and litigation as a search for truth are to be taken seriously. A sexual harassment plaintiff's sexual conduct with others, particularly with persons in or connected with the workplace, is often quite relevant to the central issues in a harassment lawsuit of whether the plaintiff was subjectively offended by—or, put differently, whether she welcomed—the conduct alleged to be harassment.[1] A plaintiff's intimate relationship with a spouse or lover also may become relevant to a harassment plaintiff's claim for damages—especially if she claims that workplace events disrupted her personal relationships or caused her to shun intimacy.

Equally important, whether the plaintiff suffered prior sexual *abuse* is crucially relevant to the plaintiff's claim for emotional distress damages, as

---

[1]In *Henson v. City of Dundee,* 682 F.2d 897 (11th Cir. 1982), the court maintained that sexual harassment must be *unwelcome* (that is, the employee did not solicit or incite it) to be actionable. This principle was endorsed by the Supreme Court in *Meritor Savings Bank v. Vinson,* 477 U.S. 57, 68 (1986). See discussion at pp. 335–36 of the Main Volume.

the plaintiff may well be in a state of genuine emotional turmoil that is not entirely attributable to events at work, but rather to the unresolved psychological effects of childhood sexual abuse or prior sexual assault as an adult. As one plaintiff's attorney recently conceded,

> many victims of sexual harassment have been sexually harassed or abused earlier in life. This history will probably be in the clinician's medical records and may be admitted to show that the past harassment or abuse contributed to, or caused, the plaintiff's emotional distress.
>
> Revealing this history can be devastating to a plaintiff and extremely prejudicial to a case.[2]

Unresolved effects of prior sexual abuse may even have caused a sexual harassment plaintiff to have been hypersensitive to sexual cues in the workplace (and thus to have responded other than as a nonhypersensitive, "reasonable woman" would have responded),[3] or even to have "welcomed" the conduct now characterized as harassment.

It is not as simple, therefore, as just decreeing that evidence of a plaintiff's prior sexual experiences either always should or always should not be considered in a sexual harassment lawsuit. It is necessary to strike a balance between the plaintiff's right to privacy and the defendant's right to a fair trial. Congress attempted such a balance in its recent amendment of Rule 412 of the Federal Rules of Evidence (FRE), but much uncertainty remains as this new area of the law continues to develop.

Amendments to Rule 412 of the Federal Rules of Evidence

The original version of FRE 412, enacted by Congress in 1978, limited the admissibility of a victim's past sexual behavior or conduct, but it applied only in criminal prosecutions for rape and similar sexual offenses. Its prohibition against the introduction of evidence of a victim's sexual history and conduct was not applicable to civil cases. The Rule's legislative history stated that its purpose was to protect rape victims from needless inquiries into their prior sexual conduct, particularly when such conduct might have little or no bearing on or relevance to the offense for which the defendant was being tried.[4] Rule 412, as originally enacted, was a legislative attempt to balance a rape victim's interest in protecting her private life from needless public exposure against the defendant's interest in being able to present a defense by offering relevant evidence that might prove exculpatory.

As civil claims for sexual harassment became more popular, a movement began to amend Rule 412 to provide some protections for sexual harassment plaintiffs analogous to those protections the Rule provided to rape victims. This

---

[2]E. Simon, *Experts in Employment Cases,* TRIAL 48, 49 (Oct. 1997).

[3]See discussion at p. 336 of the Main Volume.

[4]*See* 124 CONG. REC. H11,944 (daily ed. Oct. 10, 1978).

drive to amend Rule 412 to include civil actions involving sexual misconduct originated in Congress in 1991.[5] Additionally, the Advisory Committee on Evidence of the Judicial Conference of the United States began considering amending Rule 412 shortly thereafter.[6]

The ultimate adoption of the amended Rule 412 involved some controversy. The Supreme Court declined to forward to Congress the amendments to Rule 412 proposed by the Judicial Conference. As discussed below, the amendments generally restricted use of evidence of a victim's sexual history. In a letter to the Chairman of the Executive Committee of the Judicial Conference, Chief Justice Rehnquist noted that some members of the Supreme Court were of the view that the amendments to Rule 412 exceeded the Court's authority under the Rules Enabling Act, which forbids the enactment of rules that "abridge, enlarge or modify any substantive right."[7] The Supreme Court was concerned, according to the Chief Justice, that the amended Rule 412 might encroach upon the right of defendants in sexual harassment cases, recognized in *Meritor Savings Bank v. Vinson,*[8] to introduce evidence of a plaintiff's "sexually provocative speech or dress." In spite of the Supreme Court's objections, however, Congress enacted the amendments to Rule 412 into law on December 1, 1994, as part of the Violent Crime Control and Enforcement Act of 1994. Full text of amended Rule 412 is reprinted in Appendix A. Parts of amended Rule 412 are quoted and discussed below.

The amended Rule 412 begins with a general prohibition against the admission of evidence of a victim's sexual history:

> **(a) Evidence generally inadmissible.—**The following evidence is not admissible in any civil or criminal proceeding involving alleged sexual misconduct except as provided in subdivisions (b) and (c):
>
> (1) Evidence offered to prove that any alleged victim engaged in other sexual behavior.
>
> (2) Evidence offered to prove any alleged victim's sexual predisposition.

Rule 412(b) then goes on to state some exceptions to this general prohibition. Rule 412(b)(1) sets forth exceptions that apply to criminal cases. Rule 412(b)(2) sets forth the exception that applies to civil cases:

> In a civil case, evidence offered to prove the sexual behavior or sexual predisposition of any alleged victim is admissible if it is otherwise admissible under these rules and its probative value substantially outweighs the danger of harm to any victim and of unfair prejudice to any party. Evidence of an alleged victim's reputation is admissible only if it has been placed in controversy by the alleged victim.

---

[5]*See* 137 CONG. REC. S9,610 (daily ed. July 10, 1991) (proposal to amend Rule 412 as part of the Violence Against Women Act of 1991).

[6]Minutes of the Advisory Committee on the Federal Rules of Criminal Procedure (Apr. 23–24, 1992).

[7]*Supreme Court's Amendments to Fed. R. Ev. 412 Deletes "Rape Shield" Rule in Civil Cases,* 2 EMPL. DISC. REP. (BNA) 624 (May 18, 1994).

[8]477 U.S. 57 (1986).

The amended Rule 412 also mandates a specific procedure for the introduction of evidence of the victim's sexual history:

> **(c) Procedure to determine admissibility—**
> (1) A party intending to offer evidence under subdivision (b) must—(A) file a written motion at least 14 days before trial specifically describing the evidence and stating the purpose for which it is offered unless the court, for good cause requires a different time for filing or permits filing during trial; and (B) serve the motion on all parties and notify the alleged victim or, when appropriate, the alleged victim's guardian or representative.
> (2) Before admitting evidence under this rule the court must conduct a hearing in camera and afford the victim and parties a right to attend and be heard. The motion, related papers, and the record of the hearing must be sealed and remain under seal unless the court orders otherwise.

The Notes of the Advisory Committee of the Judicial Conference of the United States that drafted the amendments to Rule 412 are rather extensive and provide further gloss on the meaning of the amendments. For example, the Advisory Committee Notes make it clear that Rule 412 is to apply to sexual harassment lawsuits as well as other civil claims for sexual misconduct. The Committee goes on to state that a balancing test was adopted for civil cases because "[g]reater flexibility is needed to accommodate evolving causes of action such as claims for sexual harassment." The Committee explains the test it adopted:

> This test for admitting evidence offered to prove sexual behavior or sexual propensity in civil cases differs in three respects from the general rule governing admissibility set forth in Rule 403. First, it Reverses [sic] that [sic] usual procedure spelled out in Rule 403 by shifting the burden to the proponent to demonstrate admissibility rather than making the opponent justify exclusion of the evidence. Second, the standard expressed in subdivision (b)(2) is more stringent than in the original rule; it raises the threshold for admission by requiring that the probative value of the evidence *substantially* outweigh the specified dangers. Finally, the Rule 412 test puts "harm to the victim" on the scale in addition to prejudice to the parties.[9]

Consideration of the application of Rule 412 requires that a distinction be drawn between *volitional* sexual conduct and *nonvolitional* sexual conduct. Although Rule 412 does not explicitly draw such a distinction, it implicitly does so by placing restrictions only on evidence that an alleged victim "*engaged in*" other sexual behavior.[10] Moreover, case law to date suggests that the rule should apply to conduct in which the plaintiff was a voluntary participant, but not to prior incidents in which the plaintiff was an unwilling victim of assault or abuse.

---

[9]Advisory Committee Notes to Amendment of Fed. R. Evid. 412 (1994). For the text of the amended rule, see Appendix A.

[10]Fed. R. Evid. 412(a)(1).

Application of Rule 412 to Volitional Conduct

A variety of issues have arisen concerning the application of the new Rule 412 to prior volitional sexual conduct on the part of a sexual harassment plaintiff. These include just what kinds of "sexual behavior" are covered by the Rule, application of Rule 412 to the "welcomeness" issue, application of the Rule to damages issues, whether Rule 412 applies at the discovery stage, and to what extent it applies to third-party witnesses.

What Sexual Behavior Is Covered?

The Advisory Committee Notes to the 1994 Amendments to Rule 412 assert that "sexual behavior connotes all activities that involve actual physical conduct, i.e., sexual intercourse or sexual contact."[11] The Notes then cite illustrative examples from prior case law such as use of contraceptives,[12] birth of an illegitimate child,[13] and evidence of venereal disease.[14] The Notes go on to state: "In addition, the word 'behavior' should be construed to include activities of the mind, such as fantasies or dreams."[15]

The courts to date, however, have not applied Rule 412 in quite so broad a fashion. In *Judd v. Rodman,*[16] the plaintiff claimed that the defendant wrongfully transmitted genital herpes to her. After the jury issued a verdict against her, the plaintiff on appeal invoked Rule 412 to attack the district court's admission of evidence of her breast augmentation surgery, her prior sexual history, and her career as a nude dancer. Noting that the plaintiff failed to preserve an objection under Rule 412 to the admission of her breast augmentation surgery, the Eleventh Circuit sidestepped the issue of whether Rule 412 applied to such evidence. The plaintiff then argued that her prior sexual history should have been excluded under Rule 412 because its probative value failed to outweigh substantially the unfair prejudice toward her. The Eleventh Circuit rejected this argument, finding that the plaintiff's sexual history was highly relevant:

> A central issue in this case . . . is whether Judd contracted genital herpes from Rodman. Expert testimony revealed that the herpes virus can be dormant for long periods of time and the infected person can be asymptomatic. Consequently, evidence of prior sexual relationships and the type of protection used during sexual intercourse was highly relevant to Rodman's liability. The court did not abuse its discretion in admitting evidence of Judd's prior sexual history.[17]

---

[11]See *supra* note 9.

[12]United States v. Galloway, 937 F.2d 542 (10th Cir. 1991). *See also* Alberts v. Wickes Lumber Co., 1995 WL 117886 (N.D. Ill. 1995).

[13]United States v. One Feather, 702 F.2d 736 (8th Cir. 1983).

[14]State v. Carmichael, 727 P.2d 918 (Kan. 1986).

[15]See *supra* note 9.

[16]105 F.3d 1339 (11th Cir. 1997).

[17]*Id.* at 1343.

Finally, the Eleventh Circuit affirmed the district court's admission of the plaintiff's employment as a nude dancer. The plaintiff had challenged admission of this evidence, too, under Rule 412. As the court explained:

> Judd testified that she felt "dirty" after she contracted herpes. The court determined that Judd's employment as a nude dancer before and after she contracted herpes was probative as to damages for emotional distress because it suggested an absence of change in her body image following the herpes infection.[18]

Thus, even if activities such as nude dancing are considered "sexual behavior," they may still be admissible under Rule 412.

Other courts also have read Rule 412 somewhat narrowly. In *Janopoulos v. Harvey L. Walner & Associates,*[19] the plaintiff filed a motion in limine under Rule 412 to exclude mention of her marital history at the trial of her sexual harassment claim. The court held that Rule 412 did not apply because one's marital history is not the kind of "sexual behavior" contemplated by the Rule, but the court excluded the plaintiff's marital history nonetheless under FRE 401 and 402 as being irrelevant to any issue at trial. Similarly, in *Adams v. Goodyear Tire & Rubber Co.,*[20] the court held that Rule 412 did not apply to references in a defendant's summary judgment motion papers to the fact that the plaintiff was divorced and that her ex-husband and her current boyfriend physically abused her.

In *Barta v. City & County of Honolulu,*[21] the court in a sexual harassment lawsuit declined to apply Rule 412 to discovery of the identity of the plaintiff's social acquaintances, including those with whom she may have gone on dates. The court recognized that such individuals may have information relevant to defenses or damages. The court drew the line, however, at discovery into whether the plaintiff had sexual relations with those acquaintances.[22] *Barta* thus makes it clear that although Rule 412 will protect a plaintiff's privacy as to her intimate sexual affairs, it cannot be invoked so broadly as to prevent a defendant from conducting discovery of spouses and past or present lovers as to other relevant issues in the case merely on the ground that the plaintiff may have had sexual relations with them.

Application of Rule 412 to the "Welcomeness" Issue

In *Meritor Savings Bank v. Vinson,*[23] the Supreme Court maintained that sexual conduct in the workplace must be "unwelcome" to be actionable as sexual harassment. Previously, in *Henson v. City of Dundee,*[24] the Eleventh Circuit defined "unwelcome" sexual conduct as that which is not "solicited or incited"

---

[18] *Id.*
[19] 1995 WL 107170 (N.D. Ill. 1995).
[20] 184 F.R.D. 369 (D. Kan. 1998).
[21] 169 F.R.D. 132 (D. Haw. 1996).
[22] *Id.* at 137.
[23] 477 U.S. 57, 68 (1986).
[24] 682 F.2d 897, 903 (11th Cir. 1982).

by the plaintiff. Thus, the plaintiff's role in the events that culminated in the claim of harassment is often a central issue in a sexual harassment lawsuit. Even evidence of the plaintiff's dress and personal thoughts may be relevant to the issue of welcomeness, in the *Vinson* Court's view.[25] As one commentator has observed: "*Henson* and *Meritor* thus establish that the plaintiff's invitation to or provocation of the alleged harassment is of central if not determinative importance to the disposition of her claim."[26]

Welcomeness can be a difficult concept with which to contend, however. The *Vinson* Court could be no more precise than to say that the "totality of the circumstances" must be considered when considering welcomeness.[27] Sometimes, welcomeness evidence may be straightforward, such as where a plaintiff dresses provocatively or initiates sexual banter with co-workers and then complains of harassment when co-workers respond. More often, however, welcomeness issues are considerably more subtle, and their resolution often requires an understanding of the context of the relationship of the parties involved. For example, welcomeness issues often arise where the plaintiff and the accused harasser once were involved in a consensual relationship, or where the plaintiff willingly participated in sexual joking and horseplay in an effort to "fit in."

Yet, as Chief Justice Rehnquist predicted when the Supreme Court declined to forward the amended Rule 412 to Congress,[28] Rule 412 may have a direct impact on the admissibility of evidence of welcomeness. The Advisory Committee Notes are somewhat ambiguous in this regard. At one point they warn: "[U]nless the (b)(2) exception is satisfied, evidence such as that relating to the alleged victim's mode of dress, speech, or life-style will not be admissible."[29] At another point, however, they point out that the term "*other* sexual behavior" is used "to suggest some flexibility in admitting evidence 'intrinsic' to the alleged sexual misconduct."[30] As welcomeness is undoubtedly "intrinsic" to a claim of sexual harassment, such flexibility would appear to be warranted.

In *Socks-Brunot v. Hirschvogel Inc.*,[31] the court explicitly held that Rule 412 is applicable to evidence of "welcomeness" sought to be admitted at trial and it awarded a new trial to the plaintiff based on the defendant's failure to comply with Rule 412's requirements prior to introducing evidence of the plaintiff's role in the creation of the hostile work environment she alleged. In that case, the plaintiff alleged that her supervisor made repeated comments about the size of her breasts, asked her what size condoms she used, asked her to sit on his lap, said he thought she could not go without sex for more than

---

[25]477 U.S. at 68–69.

[26]P. Monnin, *Proving Welcomeness: The Admissibility of Evidence of Sexual History in Sexual Harassment Claims Under the 1994 Amendments to Federal Rule of Evidence 412,* 48 VAND. L. REV. 1155, 1166–67 (1995).

[27]477 U.S. at 69.

[28]See *supra* note 7, and accompanying text.

[29]See *supra* note 9.

[30]See *supra* note 9.

[31]184 F.R.D. 113 (S.D. Ohio 1999).

a few days, said her lipstick made her look like a whore, and told her that a co-worker wanted to have sex with her. He also allegedly asked her to bring him a videotape of her delivering her son so he could "see another side" of her. The defendant, for its part, put on evidence that the plaintiff spoke to co-workers about an affair she had with a prior supervisor, that she discussed oral sex with a female co-worker, that a co-worker observed the plaintiff flirting with the alleged harasser, and that the plaintiff liberally used profanity at work. In a pretrial hearing, the court held that Rule 412 would not govern introduction of evidence of welcomeness.

Following the trial, however, the *Socks-Brunot* court reversed itself and held that the defendant's evidence of welcomeness should have been sifted through the screening process required by Rule 412 before being submitted to the jury. The court rejected the defendant's argument that welcomeness evidence is not the kind of evidence of "sexual behavior" or "sexual predisposition" covered by Rule 412. Moreover, the court noted that it would have excluded under Rule 412 most of the evidence of welcomeness offered by the defendant at trial. For example, the court noted that the plaintiff's discussion of her affair with a prior supervisor was irrelevant because there was no evidence that she discussed the affair with the alleged harasser. Similarly, the court noted that the alleged harasser was not a part of the plaintiff's discussion of oral sex. The court indicated that it likely would exclude evidence of the plaintiff's flirting with the alleged harasser because he never claimed the plaintiff was flirtatious. Finally, as to the plaintiff's use of profanity, the court noted that the plaintiff was not complaining that her supervisor used profanity in her presence but rather that he directed sexually explicit and degrading comments toward her.

A court took a more liberal approach in a case involving the plaintiff's own blatant sexual antics in the workplace in *Sublette v. Glidden Co.*[32] In that case alleging a hostile work environment, the plaintiff sought to exclude under Rule 412 and the defendant sought to admit evidence of the plaintiff's wearing a sign saying "Best Blow Jobs on the # 8 line," her offering to give oral sex to a co-worker, her ripping her t-shirt to expose her breasts, her wetting her t-shirt and standing in front of a large fan to show off her breasts, her touching male employees on their thighs and buttocks, her allowing a male co-worker to place his hand print in paint on her buttocks, and her discussions with co-workers of her intimate relations with her husband. The court remarked that it had "little difficulty" in finding such evidence to be relevant to welcomeness.[33]

Similarly, in *Fedio v. Circuit City Stores Inc.*,[34] another hostile environment case wherein the plaintiff alleged that sexual propositions and crude comments were made to her, the court admitted evidence of the plaintiff's own conversations in the workplace about sex. Specifically, the court admitted testimony that the plaintiff told co-workers that she was going to wear a finger ring until she "got laid" and that she subsequently removed the ring. It also admitted

[32]1998 WL 964189 (E.D. Pa. 1998).

[33]*Id.* at *3.

[34]1998 WL 966000 (E.D. Pa. 1998).

testimony that she told co-workers that she had kept a delivery driver waiting outside her apartment while she had sexual intercourse with her roommate. The court also admitted testimony that the plaintiff had been the victim of a date rape before she came to work for the defendant. The court maintained that the evidence was "highly probative of how little Plaintiff would be offended by [a supervisor's] sexual innuendoes when she in fact felt comfortable publicizing information regarding her sex life."[35] The court further observed: "Plaintiff volunteered to her co-workers information regarding her sexual proclivities. To allow an alleged victim to publicly flaunt her sexual behaviors and yet remain protected by Rule 412 would be tantamount to a complete disregard of the rule's purpose."[36]

Between these extremes, and although the cases are not uniform, the rule that seems to be emerging from the developing case law is that evidence of a plaintiff's sexual conduct with individuals subsequently alleged to be her harassers ordinarily will not be barred by Rule 412, while evidence of a plaintiff's sexual activities with persons unconnected with the workplace will be excluded.[37] The application of Rule 412 to evidence of a plaintiff's actions with respect to others in the workplace who are not accused harassers remains unsettled. For example:

- In *Herchenroeder v. Johns Hopkins University,*[38] the court permitted questioning of the plaintiff[39] as to whether she and her accused harasser had ever discussed having sexual relations.[40]
- In *Rodriguez-Hernandez v. Miranda-Velez,*[41] the First Circuit affirmed the district court's allowing the defendant to introduce evidence of the plaintiff's flirtatious behavior toward the defendant, and that the plaintiff's relationship with a man outside the workplace was interfering with her work. Also affirmed were the district court's exclusion of evidence attacking the plaintiff's moral character, characterizing her as promiscuous, and revealing that her boyfriend was married.

---

[35] *Id.* at *6.

[36] *Id.*

[37] This rule is supported by the statement in the Advisory Committee Notes that in a sexual harassment case, "while some evidence of the alleged victim's sexual behavior and/or predisposition in the workplace may perhaps be relevant, non-workplace conduct will usually be irrelevant." The Advisory Committee then cited *Burns v. McGregor Electronic Industries Inc.,* 989 F.2d 959, 962–63, 61 FEP Cases 592, 594–95 (8th Cir. 1993) (holding that plaintiff's posing nude for magazine outside work hours is irrelevant to issue of welcomeness).

[38] 171 F.R.D. 179 (D. Md. 1997).

[39] The court directed that this questioning be done in the form of written interrogatories and that the plaintiff's answers be subject to a confidentiality agreement/protective order. *Id.* at 182.

[40] *Id.* at 180. The plaintiff had previously testified, without objection, that she had not actually had sexual relations with the accused.

[41] 132 F.3d 848, 75 FEP Cases 1228 (1st Cir. 1998).

- In *Sheffield v. Hilltop Sand & Gravel Co.,*[42] the court permitted the accused harasser to testify that the plaintiff participated in sexually provocative discussions and activities in the workplace.[43] It barred introduction of evidence that the plaintiff used "vulgar language" in the workplace and discussed with co-workers her sexual relationship with her husband, however. Although noting that such evidence "might be relevant," the court excluded it as a sanction against defendants for their failure to file their Rule 412 motion under seal as required by Rule 412(c).[44]
- In *Barta v. City & County of Honolulu,*[45] the court ruled that discovery into evidence of the plaintiff's sexual conduct with the named defendants, while on duty, would be permitted under Rule 412 as evidence of possible welcomeness.[46] It barred discovery, however, of the plaintiff's sexual activities off-duty and outside the workplace with co-workers who were not defendants in the lawsuit.[47]
- In *Excel Corporation v. Bosley,*[48] the Eighth Circuit affirmed the district court's exclusion of evidence of sexual relations that occurred between the plaintiff and her alleged harasser (who was also her ex-husband) during the same period as the alleged workplace harassment (which largely consisted of degrading sexual epithets and threats to kill her boyfriend). Part of the defendant's proffer was the testimony of a psychologist who treated both the plaintiff and her ex-husband, who indicated that the plaintiff had acknowledged sending her ex-husband "mixed signals." While the court of appeal found that the district court did not "manifestly err" in excluding the evidence, it emphasized not only that the sexual activity occurred outside of the workplace and that the corporate employer was not aware of it when it addressed the plaintiff's complaint of harassment.
- In *Truong v. Smith,*[49] the court barred discovery of plaintiff's extramarital affairs, but noted that "evidence that a sexual assault victim has engaged in consensual sexual relations with the defendant in the past under similar conditions may have some logical relevance to the question of consent to the act charged."[50]
- In *Ratts v. Board of County Commissioners,*[51] the court permitted deposition questioning of the plaintiff concerning her sexual activities with one of the defendants occurring prior to the period during which that defendant allegedly sexually harassed her, but it blocked questioning about her sexual activities with individuals other than the defendant.

---

[42]895 F. Supp. 105, 68 FEP Cases 930 (E.D. Va. 1995).

[43]895 F. Supp. at 109.

[44]*Id. But see* Fedio v. Circuit City Stores Inc., 1998 WL 966000 (E.D. Pa. 1998) (admitting evidence of plaintiff's sexual history and conduct even though defendant did not comply with Rule 412's procedural requirements).

[45]169 F.R.D. 132 (D. Haw. 1996).

[46]*Id.* at 135.

[47]*Id.* at 136.

[48]165 F.3d 635, 78 FEP Cases 1844 (8th Cir. 1999).

[49]183 F.R.D. 273 (D. Colo. 1998).

[50]*Id.* at 275.

[51]1999 WL 965705 (D. Kan. 1999).

- In *Sanchez v. Zabihi,*[52] the court permitted a broader range of discovery under Rule 412 relating to a welcomeness defense. It permitted questioning of the plaintiff as to whether she had made any romantic or sexual advances toward a co-worker, had been the subject of any romantic or sexual advances by a co-worker, or had a romantic or sexual relationship with any co-worker (except her spouse) within the three years prior to the alleged incidents of sexual harassment.[53]
- In contrast, in *Howard v. Historic Tours of America,*[54] the court prohibited discovery of plaintiffs' sexual affairs with non-harassing co-workers, which the defendants had sought to offer as evidence of welcomeness. The court remarked: "[I]t is absurd to think that any man in 1997 can be justified in believing that a woman who engages in [extramarital sex] is so degraded morally that she will welcome his sexual advances without protest."[55]
- Finally, in the most permissive reading of Rule 412 to date, the court in *Holt v. Welch Allyn Inc.*[56] permitted discovery of photographs showing the plaintiff at a party with a male exotic dancer. The court noted testimony by a co-worker that the plaintiff had seen the photographs in the workplace and was not offended, and upheld the magistrate judge's ruling that the plaintiff's behavior in the workplace "may be relevant to whether or not those co-workers perceived their workplace behavior toward her to be 'unwanted harassment.' "[57]

Application of Rule 412 to Emotional Damages Issues

In *Alberts v. Wickes Lumber Co.,*[58] Rule 412 was applied in a number of respects to damages issues. The plaintiff claimed that she had been sexually assaulted by a co-worker. Although the court excluded evidence of whether or not the plaintiff was using birth control on the night of the alleged assault, it permitted discovery into whether the plaintiff kept contraceptives in the glove compartment of her car. This evidence was allowed because the alleged assailant testified that, a few weeks after the alleged assault, the plaintiff invited him into her car, which was parked in the garage of her home, and while showing him the car's stereo system, opened the glove compartment to reveal contraceptives. The court observed about this evidence:

> Proof of this evidence would allow the defendants a strong argument to the jury that the plaintiff . . . could not possibly have been as traumatized as she now claims to be by the experience she had with this very same person just a few

---

[52]166 F.R.D. 500, 71 FEP Cases 835 (D.N.M. 1996).

[53]166 F.R.D. at 502, 71 FEP Cases 835, 836. The *Zabihi* court also required that this information be obtained via interrogatory and be maintained under seal by defendants' counsel.

[54]177 F.R.D. 48 (D.D.C. 1997).

[55]*Id.* at 52.

[56]3 WH Cases 2d 1622 (N.D.N.Y. 1997).

[57]*Id.* at 1628.

[58]1995 WL 117886 (N.D. Ill. 1995).

> weeks before. A person so traumatized would not place herself in such a position. The behavior is not what one would expect if the plaintiff's claims of emotional trauma are true.[59]

The court went on to point out that the plaintiff claimed that the sexual assault and harassment by the assailant caused her to suffer lasting emotional impairment, yet for her later to invite her alleged assailant into the front seat of her car alone with her in the presence of condoms "could very well be significant evidence tending to rebut her claim of severe emotional trauma."[60] *Alberts* thus suggests that a plaintiff's sexual conduct with an alleged harasser subsequent to the alleged harassment may be admissible under Rule 412.

The next issue addressed in *Alberts* was the ability of the defendant to ask the plaintiff about affairs she had with men other than the alleged harasser, in order to show that the plaintiff's emotional distress was caused by bad relationships with these other men rather than by the defendant. Although the court foreclosed such an inquiry under Rule 412, it did so *not* because such an inquiry is inherently impermissible, but because the defendant had failed to lay a sufficient predicate. The court noted that the defendant had sought to justify such questioning by arguing that the plaintiff had failed to tell her psychologist (who would testify as to her emotional distress) about these relationships, but it pointed out that the defendant had not questioned the psychologist on deposition about whether such information would be useful to him or would in any way change his opinion or alter his analysis of the plaintiff's emotional damages.[61] *Alberts* suggests, therefore, that, upon a proper showing, discovery of a plaintiff's other romantic relationships, particularly bad ones, may be permissible under Rule 412 as evidence of alternate causation of emotional distress. As the *Alberts* court suggests, an admission from the plaintiff's psychological expert that such information may be relevant to his analysis is one way to lay the predicate for such discovery. Another way might be testimony from the defendant's psychological expert to the same effect.

Finally, the court in *Alberts* permitted questioning of a sexual harassment plaintiff about the specifics of her claim that the harassment caused her to experience problems in achieving sexual intimacy. The court first noted that "it is doubtful that this conduct falls under the prohibition of Rule 412" because that Rule prohibits only evidence offered to prove that a plaintiff engaged in other sexual behavior, yet the plaintiff in *Alberts* testified that she did not—and indeed could not—engage in other sexual behavior.[62] Even if Rule 412 were to apply, reasoned the court, the evidence would be admissible. The court explained:

> [H]ere it is the plaintiff who has, by her pleadings, injected into the very heart of her damages claim her inability to engage in intimate sexual relationships

---

[59] *Id.* at *3.
[60] *Id.* at *4.
[61] *Id.*
[62] *Id.* at *5.

> after the complained of occurrence. To allow [the plaintiff] to use these alleged experiences as evidence of her damages, but at the same time deny [the defendant] the opportunity to prove that these claims are not true, would be to turn the rape "shield" law into a sword solely for the plaintiff's benefit. If [the plaintiff] chooses to base her case for damages on her inability to engage in sexual behavior subsequent to the date of the alleged offense, then Rule 412 cannot be deemed to bar [the defendant] from mounting a defense against such a claim by the most direct and traditional of methods, i.e., proof that such a claim is simply not true.[63]

Similarly, in *Sublette v. Glidden Co.*,[64] the court denied the plaintiff's motion to exclude evidence that, after she left her job with the defendant (and then left a similar job with another employer), she took a job massaging men at a health club. The court held that the evidence was relevant to counter the plaintiff's claim that she suffered such severe emotional damage from sexual harassment by the defendant that she was unable to work around men.

These authorities thus can be cited to prevent a plaintiff from claiming that sexual harassment (or some other workplace incident) negatively affected her sex life and then hiding behind Rule 412 when the defendant attempts to test that claim.

Applicability of Rule 412 in Discovery

The Advisory Committee Notes to the 1994 Amendments to Rule 412 provide that the procedures set forth in subdivision (c) of that Rule "do not apply to discovery of a victim's past sexual conduct or predisposition in civil cases, which will continue to be governed by Fed. R. Civ. P. 26,"[65] which requires only "relevance" as a prerequisite to discovery. The Notes go on to suggest that courts should issue appropriate orders under Rule 26(c) to "protect the victim against unwarranted inquiries and to ensure confidentiality."[66] The Notes to Rule 412 thus suggest a different standard for discovery of information covered by Rule 412 than for its admissibility. In the Advisory Committee's view, a protective order should issue "unless the party seeking discovery makes a showing that the evidence sought to be discovered would be relevant under the facts and theories of a particular case, and cannot be obtained except through discovery."[67] Accordingly, only "relevance" need be shown for discoverability; not that the "probative value substantially outweighs the danger of harm to any victim and of unfair prejudice to any party," as is required by Rule 412(b)(2) for admissibility.

Some courts have held that Rule 412 does not apply at all in discovery. For example, in *Holt v. Welch Allyn Inc.*,[68] the defendant sought production of

---

[63] *Id.*

[64] 1998 WL 964189 (E.D. Pa. 1998).

[65] Advisory Committee Notes to Amendment of FED. R. EVID. 412 (1994).

[66] *Id.*

[67] *Id.*

[68] 3 WH Cases 2d 1622 (N.D.N.Y. 1997).

a photograph of one of the plaintiffs at a party where a male exotic dancer performed. The plaintiffs cited Rule 412 in their attempt to bar the discovery, but the court remarked that the plaintiffs "have . . . overstated the protections of Rule 412."[69] The court pointed out that the photograph had been taken to the workplace and passed around, about which the plaintiff did not seem offended. The court felt that the photograph "may be relevant to show the perception of [plaintiff's] co-workers regarding her workplace behavior," although it also noted that the admissibility of the photograph at trial is "a matter for another day."[70]

In *Ramirez v. Nabil's Inc.*,[71] the court similarly declined to apply Rule 412 to discovery, noting that the Rule is "a rule of admissibility." In a sexual harassment case, the defendant sought production of medical records pertaining to psychiatric treatment received by two of the plaintiffs when they were adolescents. While those plaintiffs did not expressly indicate that the treatment involved sexual matters, they raised Rule 412 in an attempt to bar the discovery. The court applied Federal Rule of Civil Procedure 26 instead and ordered the records produced. It stated that the discovery sought appeared "reasonably calculated to lead to the discovery of admissible evidence regarding the claims of emotional distress by Cook and Boden and possibly the sexual propensities of Cook."[72] Thus, the ruling in *Ramirez* suggests that evidence of prior sexual abuse may be discoverable as to potential sexual propensities of a plaintiff as well as to possible alternative causation of damages.

Other courts that have addressed the issue have held that Rule 412's principles must at least guide courts in determining what is discoverable under Rule 26. In *Barta v. City & County of Honolulu,*[73] the court noted that Rule 412 "must inform the discovery process." Accordingly, a court "must impose certain restrictions on discovery to preclude inquiry into areas which will clearly fail to satisfy the balancing test of Rule 412(b)(2), although the trial judge will render the decisions on what evidence is ultimately admitted."[74]

In *Giron v. Corrections Corp. of America,*[75] a Section 1983 action by a former prison inmate alleging that a guard had raped her, the court, citing *Barta,* applied Rule 412 to bar discovery of the plaintiff's prior sexual partners. The defendant had sought the identity of those persons purportedly in an attempt to learn what pre-existing psychological and medical conditions the plaintiff might have had. The court ruled that such information would be outside the expertise of a plaintiff's prior sexual partners. The court did, however, order

[69]*Id.* at 1628.

[70]*Id.*

[71]1995 WL 609415 (D. Kan. 1995).

[72]*Id.* at *3.

[73]169 F.R.D. 132, 135 (D. Haw. 1996).

[74]*Id. See also* Herchenroeder v. Johns Hopkins Univ., 171 F.R.D. 179, 182 (D. Md. 1997) (court must look to both Rule 26 and Rule 412 in discovery); Sanchez v. Zabihi, 166 F.R.D. 500, 502, 71 FEP Cases 835 (D.N.M. 1996) (Rule 412 "is applicable and has significance" in discovery).

[75]981 F. Supp. 1406 (D.N.M. 1997).

the plaintiff to provide information regarding prior sexual contacts that were "violent or damaging to her in any way," and it specifically rejected a proposed time limitation of five years preceding the event at issue in the litigation.[76] The court reasoned that evidence of prior sexual abuse might be relevant to the causation of plaintiff's emotional damages.

In *Truong v. Smith*,[77] a sexual assault case brought by a nurse against a doctor under the Violence Against Women Act, the court applied Rule 412 to the defendant's attempt to discover the plaintiff's history of extramarital affairs, which he argued were relevant to his defenses of a consensual relationship and the initiation of contact by the plaintiff. The court denied the discovery, noting that Rule 412 prohibits use of a plaintiff's past sexual behavior to attack her credibility. The court explained:

> While evidence that a sexual assault victim has engaged in consensual sexual relations with the defendant in the past under similar circumstances may have some logical relevance to the question of consent to the act charged, and evidence of prior sexual activity with the defendant under dissimilar circumstances may also have some logical relevance, . . . "(w)hen both identity of persons and similarity of circumstances are removed, proative value all but disappears."[78]

Applicability of Rule 412 to Nonparty Witnesses

In spite of the fact that the language of Rule 412 itself indicates that it applies only to alleged victims of sexual misconduct, the Committee Notes state that Rule 412 extends to "pattern" witnesses "whose testimony about other instances of sexual misconduct by the person accused is otherwise admissible."[79] This seems to mean that Rule 412 would apply to the sexual history of nonparty witnesses who testify that they also were harassed by the defendant, although at least two courts have taken somewhat contrary approaches.

In *Biggs v. Nicewonger Co.*,[80] the plaintiff filed a Rule 412 motion to exclude evidence regarding "any alleged victim's sexual predisposition," apparently referring to evidence concerning the types of clothing worn by another female employee expected to testify that she, too, had been sexually harassed

---

[76]*Id.* at 1408. As to each such encounter, the plaintiff was ordered to

> describe the manner and type of each sexual contact; the date and location of each sexual contact; all persons present during the contact; how the event occurred; the type of medical treatment received[;] the name, address and phone number of each treating physician; address of each hospital at which treatment was received; the other person who participated in the sexual contact and committed the abuse, touching or injury[;] and if such event was reported to a government agency, . . . identify that agency.

Id.

[77]183 F.R.D. 273 (D. Colo. 1998).

[78]*Id.* at 275 (quoting Ordover, *Admissibility of Patterns of Similar Sexual Conduct: The Unlamented Death of Character for Chastity*, 63 CORNELL L. REV. 90, 106 (1977)).

[79]See *supra* note 9.

[80]897 F. Supp. 483, 68 FEP Cases 1771 (D. Or. 1995).

while in the defendant's employ. The defendant opposed the motion, arguing that if the plaintiff raised the issue of the co-worker's harassment, the defendant should be permitted to demonstrate that it took corrective action, which included counseling the co-worker about her inappropriate style of dress. Although the court withheld ruling until such point as the plaintiff might attempt to introduce the alleged harassment of the co-worker, it noted that "evidence of the responses to and the actions taken by [the employer] to the complaints of [the co-worker] is relevant evidence."[81]

In *Stalnaker v. K-Mart Corp.,*[82] the court declined to apply Rule 412 to nonparty witnesses who might testify that the alleged harasser also harassed them. Although holding that Rule 412 did not apply because the witnesses were not themselves victims of alleged sexual misconduct, the court barred inquiries to the nonparty witnesses about their sexual activities unconnected to the workplace. The court did allow discovery, however, into the witnesses' "voluntary romantic or sexual activities with [the alleged harasser] to the extent they show any conduct on his part to encourage, solicit, or influence any employee of defendant to engage or continue in such activities."[83]

On the other hand, in *Burger v. Litton Industries Inc.,*[84] the court applied Rule 412 to a nonparty witness who was being deposed by the plaintiff. The witness testified to the sexual activity of others while she worked at Litton and to being sexually harassed by the plaintiff's supervisor. On cross-examination, the defendant's counsel asked the witness whether she had a sexual relationship with any other Litton employee while she worked at Litton. Noting that Rule 412 places the burden on the defendant to prove that the probative value of the evidence sought to be admitted *substantially* outweighs the invasion of privacy engendered by the admission of such evidence, the court determined that the value of the nonparty witness's answers to questions about her sexual conduct were substantially outweighed by the invasion of her privacy, and thus barred the questioning.

Applicability of Rule 412 to Prior Sexual Abuse

Most of the cases interpreting Rule 412 have involved *volitional* sexual conduct on the part of the plaintiff (i.e., consensual sexual relationships). Also of extreme significance in sexual harassment cases, however, is the existence of any prior *nonvolitional* sexual experiences in the plaintiff's lifetime (i.e., sexual abuse or assault). Molestation as a child or sexual assault as an adult can have a profound and lasting impact on the psychological condition of the victim.

---

[81]897 F. Supp. at 484, 68 FEP Cases at 1772.
[82]71 FEP Cases 705 (D. Kan. 1996).
[83]*Id.* at 707.
[84]1995 WL 476712 (S.D.N.Y. 1995).

Importance of Evidence of Prior Sexual Abuse in Sexual Harassment Cases

The existence and impact of a plaintiff's prior sexual abuse is an important issue in sexual harassment litigation. One commentator—a plaintiff's lawyer—recently observed that, although approximately 25 percent of all adult women in the United States were sexually abused as children, "there is strong evidence that the percentage is higher among sexual harassment plaintiffs."[85] The commentator actually discusses ways in which a plaintiff's childhood sexual abuse might be exploited to her tactical advantage in a sexual harassment lawsuit.[86] As another authority has observed:

> Encountering a history of childhood sexual abuse in a plaintiff should constitute a red flag for the forensic psychiatrist: the possibility that the plaintiff has been instrumental in the events of which she complains must be carefully considered.[87]

Prior sexual abuse may bear upon any or all of the following issues in litigation: (1) alternative causation of damages, (2) the plaintiff's credibility, (3) the "reasonable woman" or "reasonable person" standard, and (4) the defense of "welcomeness."[88]

Alternative Causation of Damages

As explained in the Main Volume, prior sexual abuse can cause a whole range of chronic psychopathology later in life that the abuse victim may misattribute to more contemporary events, such as workplace harassment or discrimination. Thus, although a sexual harassment plaintiff may exhibit genuine symptoms of depression or other types of emotional distress and attribute those symptoms to workplace events, it must be determined whether an alternative explanation of the causation of those symptoms is more plausible.

For example, there is substantial medical evidence indicating that childhood sexual abuse causes depressive symptoms in adult life.[89] Moreover, it is

---

[85] L. Bloom, *Gretel Fights Back: Representing Sexual Harassment Plaintiffs Who Were Sexually Abused as Children*, 12 BERKELEY WOMEN'S L.J. 1, 2–3 (1997).

[86] *Id.* at 16–18.

[87] S. Feldman-Schorrig, *Need for Expansion of Forensic Psychiatrists' Role in Sexual Harassment Cases,* 23 BULL. AM. ACAD. PSYCHIATRY & L. 513, 517 (1995).

[88] This topic is treated in considerable detail in Chapter 10 of the Main Volume and in J. McDonald & S. Feldman-Schorrig, *The Relevance of Childhood Sexual Abuse in Sexual Harassment Cases,* 20 EMPLOYEE REL. L.J. 221 (1994).

[89] *See, e.g.,* D. Schetky, *A Review of the Literature on the Long-Term Effects of Childhood Sexual Abuse,* in INCEST-RELATED SYNDROMES OF ADULT PSYCHOPATHOLOGY 41 (R. Kluft ed. 1990) ("Depression, low self-esteem, and feelings of being damaged are commonly reported among adults who experienced childhood sexual abuse"); C. Fine, *The Cognitive Sequelae of Incest,* in INCEST-RELATED SYNDROMES OF ADULT PSYCHOPATHOLOGY 163 (R. Kluft, ed. 1990) ("Feelings of depression and anxiety are by far the more common emotions described by these victims"); J. Gunderson, *Borderline Personality Disorder,* in COMPREHENSIVE TEXTBOOK OF PSYCHIATRY 1390 (H. Kaplan & B. Sadock eds., 5th ed. 1989) ("unipolar depressions of variable

commonly accepted within the psychiatric community today that childhood sexual abuse may cause a Borderline Personality Disorder to develop,[90] and many borderlines (i.e., individuals with such disorders) are chronically depressed. As one authority puts it, the borderline patient's "[r]epeated interpersonal, vocational, and academic failures lead to states of demoralization with overtones of anger, which sooner or later become clinically indistinguishable from chronic depression."[91] Therefore, where a sexual harassment claimant complains of depression, there is at least the possibility that the depression is a feature of a personality disorder and not the result of the alleged harassment.

Similarly, some plaintiffs in sexual harassment cases will claim that their depression over events in the workplace caused them to attempt suicide. Prior childhood sexual abuse on the part of the plaintiff is relevant because studies have linked childhood sexual abuse to subsequent suicidal behavior.[92] It is therefore necessary to determine whether suicidal behavior on the part of a plaintiff in a sexual harassment case is accurately attributable to workplace events or instead is just one episode of a chronic pattern of such behavior with its origins in trauma suffered in childhood.

A sexual harassment plaintiff also may claim that workplace events disrupted her marriage or other intimate relationships. Chronic chaos in personal relationships, however, is a common characteristic of victims of childhood sexual abuse and persons with Borderline Personality Disorder.[93] As one commentator observes:

---

severity are very characteristic of borderline patients"); G. GABBARD, PSYCHODYNAMIC PSYCHIATRY IN CLINICAL PRACTICE 339 (1990) ("The clinical observation that many patients with borderline personality disorder also have an Axis I diagnosis of major depression has been increasingly substantiated by research").

[90]*See* J. PARIS, BORDERLINE PERSONALITY DISORDER: ETIOLOGY AND TREATMENT 7 (1993) ("The evidence that borderline patients have a high rate of physical abuse, childhood sexual abuse, and other traumatic experiences during childhood has been reported from so many sources and samples by now that it is overwhelming"). *See also* S. Ogata et al., *Childhood Sexual and Physical Abuse in Adult Patients With Borderline Personality Disorder,* 147 AM. J. PSYCHIATRY 1008 (1990); M. Zanarini et al., *Childhood Experiences of Borderline Patients,* 30 COMPREHENSIVE PSYCHIATRY 18 (1989). A general discussion of Borderline Personality Disorder appears at pp. 110–16 of the Main Volume.

[91]J. KROLL, THE CHALLENGE OF THE BORDERLINE PATIENT 62 (1988).

[92]*See, e.g.,* A. Wagner & M. Linehan, *Relationship Between Childhood Sexual Abuse and Topography of Parasuicide Among Women With Borderline Personality Disorder,* 8 J. PERSONALITY DISORDERS 1, 2 (1994); D. Schetky, *A Review of the Literature on the Long-Term Effects of Childhood Sexual Abuse,* in INCEST-RELATED SYNDROMES OF ADULT PSYCHOPATHOLOGY 42 (R. Kluft ed., 1990); J. Briere & N. Zaidi, *Sexual Abuse Histories and Sequelae in Female Psychiatric Emergency Room Patients,* 146 AM. J. PSYCHIATRY 1602, 1604–05 (1989).

[93]*See* AMERICAN PSYCHIATRIC ASSOCIATION, DIAGNOSTIC AND STATISTICAL MANUAL OF MENTAL DISORDERS 650 (4th ed. 1994) (hereinafter *DSM-IV*) ("The essential feature of Borderline Personality Disorder is a pervasive pattern of instability of interpersonal relationships. . . .").

> Even years after the abuse, the attitudes of victims in relationships were masked by an inability to trust, by a fear of commitment and at the same time a tendency to cling to the partner, and by a passive helpless behavior as an expression of persistent emotional deficit. . . . Nearly half of the patients were living in a mostly unhappy relationship (marriage or companionship) or alone with an illegitimate child.[94]

Marital or relationship problems following a workplace incident may thus be just one example of a long history of such problems, which may well have occurred regardless of workplace events.

In *Giron v. Corrections Corp. of America*,[95] a sexual assault case brought under Section 1983, the court permitted discovery into prior incidents of sexual abuse involving the plaintiff. It reasoned that such incidents might be relevant to the issue of causation regarding plaintiff's emotional damages claim.

Impact on Plaintiff's Credibility

Although different jurisdictions take varying approaches to the issue, use of evidence of a mental condition may be permitted as a means of attacking a witness's credibility. As one California court explained:

> A witness may be cross-examined about her mental condition or emotional stability to the extent it may affect her powers of perception, memory or recollection, or communication. Expert psychiatric testimony may be admissible to impeach the credibility of a . . . witness where the witness' mental or emotional condition may affect the ability of the witness to tell the truth.[96]

Prior sexual trauma may affect a plaintiff's credibility in a number of respects. Some of these are discussed in the Main Volume.[97] There are others as well, as discussed below.

BORDERLINE RAGE One feature of Borderline Personality Disorder is rage. Individuals with a Borderline Personality Disorder often will have rapid mood shifts, in which they overreact emotionally to perceived slights by others, especially those upon whom the borderline previously depended. The anger may be interpreted as unresolved resentment that a victim of childhood sexual abuse feels toward her father or other male figure who abused her, but it is directed at whomever in her present life might serve as a convenient target.

---

[94] R. Kinzl & L. Bibl, *Sexual Abuse of Girls: Aspects of the Genesis of Mental Disorders and Therapeutic Implications,* 83 ACTA PSYCHIATRICA ET NEOROLOGICA SCANDINAVICA 429 (1991).

[95] 981 F. Supp. 1406 (D.N.M. 1997).

[96] People v. Herring, 20 Cal. App. 4th 1066, 1072, 25 Cal. Rptr. 2d 213 (1993) (citation omitted). *But see* Doyle v. Superior Court, 50 Cal. App. 4th 1878, 58 Cal. Rptr. 2d 476 (1996) (mental examinations are not authorized for purpose of testing a person's credibility).

[97] *See* Main Volume at pp. 376–82.

Borderlines are especially sensitive to rejection. They react with rage against whomever they perceive as having somehow rejected them, and they often look for ways in which to obtain revenge. This helps to explain why a borderline, who previously acted friendly and flirtatious with supervisors and co-workers and who may have even initiated sexually related conversations in the workplace, might suddenly change her mind and angrily accuse her colleagues of "harassing" her.

Borderline rage may even manifest itself in the filing of false accusations in a lawsuit. As one authority has observed, "the patient with borderline personality disorder may express rage in a vengeful manner by filing a specious suit."[98]

Dissociation Even absent conscious lying, childhood sexual abuse may still affect a sexual harassment plaintiff's credibility in that many victims of such abuse suffer from a type of psychopathology known as dissociation. Dissociation refers to a disruption in the usually integrated functions of consciousness, memory, identity, or perception of the environment. Dissociation protects the ego by keeping traumatic experiences from conscious awareness; in effect, "splitting off" affect and memory from the self.[99]

Incest victims may exhibit a variety of dissociative symptoms, including cognitive distortions such as misassuming causality, distortions of self-perception, time distortion, and dichotomous thinking (in which a person or situation is viewed as "all good" or "all bad").[100] Most significantly, however, dissociative disorders often are characterized by memory dysfunctions, including difficulty in determining whether a given memory reflects an actual event or information acquired through a nonexperiential source (e.g., reading or hearing about the event).[101] Persons with dissociative disorders also often have difficulty distinguishing between fantasy and reality. As one leading authority on dissociative disorders has observed: "The individual may report that memories have a dreamlike quality and at times cannot be distinguished from fantasy, so that the person becomes unsure of whether or not something actually occurred."[102] The fact that a dissociative personality might have such difficulty in being an accurate historian has significant implications for the credibility of such a person when in the role of a plaintiff in a sexual harassment lawsuit. Evidence of dissociative disorders may be uncovered by a thorough review of a plaintiff's history of mental health treatment. Multiple Personality Disorder is considered

---

[98]*See* T. Gutheil, *Borderline Personality Disorder, Boundary Violations and Patient-Therapist Sex: Medicolegal Pitfalls,* 146 Am. J. Psychiatry 597, 598 (1989).

[99]D. Sandberg et al., *Sexual Abuse and Revictimization: Mastery, Dysfunctional Learning, and Dissociation,* in Dissociation: Clinical and Theoretical Perspectives 257 (S. Lynn & J. Rhue eds., 1994).

[100]F. Putnam, *Dissociative Disorders in Children and Adolescents,* in Dissociation: Clinical and Theoretical Perspectives 175–89 (S. Lynn & J. Rhue eds., 1994).

[101]*Id.* at 176.

[102]F. Putnam, Diagnosis and Treatment of Multiple Personality Disorder 15 (1989).

an extreme form of dissociative disorder, so any evidence in a plaintiff's mental health history of diagnosis or treatment of multiple personalities would likely be evidence of a dissociative disorder. There is also a testing instrument known as the "Dissociative Experiences Scale" (DES), which is used to detect and measure a subject's dissociative experiences. An effort should be made to determine whether a plaintiff was administered the DES, and the answer sheet should be obtained, as many of the questions on the instrument gauge the extent of the subject's contact with reality.[103]

The "Reasonable Woman" vs. the Hypersensitive Woman

Not all "harassment" of a sexual nature is actionable. The Supreme Court, in *Harris v. Forklift Systems Inc.,*[104] decreed that to violate Title VII, harassing conduct must be "severe or pervasive enough to create an *objectively* hostile or abusive work environment."[105] The Ninth Circuit provided a precursor to this notion in *Ellison v. Brady,*[106] when it stated:

> In order to shield employers from having to accommodate the idiosyncratic concerns of the rare hyper-sensitive employee, we hold that a female plaintiff states a prima facie case of hostile environment sexual harassment when she alleges conduct which a reasonable woman would consider sufficiently severe or pervasive to alter the conditions of employment and create an abusive working environment.[107]

Thus, if a sexual harassment plaintiff is a "hypersensitive" individual who, because of her psychological history or makeup is offended by workplace conduct that a "reasonable" woman (or person of the same gender as the plaintiff) of normal sensitivity would not find offensive, such a plaintiff cannot prevail on a sexual harassment claim.[108]

Considerable evidence has been developed in the field of psychiatry suggesting that women with a history of childhood sexual abuse display clinical symptoms that are consistent with a type of posttraumatic stress disorder that becomes chronic and integrated into the victim's personality structure. Memory of the original stressor may be partially or completely repressed, but fear and

---

[103]In one sexual harassment lawsuit tried by this author, the plaintiff had been administered the DES. Her answer to one question read:

> 18. Some people sometimes feel that they become so involved in a fantasy or daydream that it feels as though it were really happening to them.
>
> Percentage of the time this happens to you: *90*

Obviously, this portion of the test became an important trial exhibit.

[104]114 S. Ct. 367 (1993).

[105]*Id.* at 370 (emphasis added).

[106]924 F.2d 872, 54 FEP Cases 1346 (1991).

[107]*Id.* at 879, 54 FEP Cases at 1350.

[108]*See* Zabkowicz v. West Bend Co., 589 F. Supp. 780, 784, 35 FEP Cases 10 (E.D. Wis. 1984) ("Title VII does not serve as a vehicle for vindicating the petty slights suffered by the hypersensitive").

hypervigilance resulting from the original trauma usually persist.[109] As one authority has pointed out, "[t]he most benign touch to someone who has been sexually abused can be experienced as sexual assault."[110]

This fear and hypervigilance may be manifest as a form of hypersensitivity to perceived sexual cues in the workplace. As the author of one study of the characteristics of sexually abused women observes, "a woman who has been [victimized] is likely to have a heightened response to harassing remarks at work." She states: "What is trivial to one person may trigger PTSD [Post-Traumatic Stress Disorder] or a stress-response syndrome in another."[111] As one leading authority on trauma observes: "Chronic physiologic hyperarousal to stimuli reminiscent of the trauma is a cardinal feature of the trauma response, well documented in a large variety of traumatized individuals, including victims of child abuse."[112]

For example, one woman, with no history of victimization, may not be troubled by a sexual proposition of a co-worker, and in fact may laugh it off or even find it flattering. Another woman, with a prior history of sexual abuse, would be more likely to react to the same proposition with anger or fear. It is essential, therefore, to know whether a sexual harassment plaintiff was the victim of childhood sexual abuse to determine whether her response to the workplace events at issue was the response of a hypersensitive person or, by contrast, the response of a reasonable person.

This point was highlighted by the court in *Blankenship v. Parke Care Centers Inc.*[113] With respect to the subjective and objective tests set forth by the Supreme Court in *Harris v. Forklift Systems Inc*,[114] the court observed: "Factors to be considered in making both the objective and subjective evaluations include the nature of the alleged harassment, *the alleged victim's background and experience,* the atmosphere of the workplace and the plaintiff's reasonable expectations regarding the workplace."[115] En route to awarding summary judgment for the defendant, the court noted that both plaintiffs were only 17 years old and had each been the victim of childhood sexual abuse. It stated:

> The Court believes that Plaintiffs' youth, their relative inexperience in dealing with issues in any workplace environment, and their history of sexual victimization

[109]J. Herman et al., *Long-Term Effects of Incestuous Abuse in Childhood,* 143 AM. J. PSYCHIATRY 1293, 1293 (1986).

[110]S. Feldman-Schorrig, *Need for Expansion of Forensic Psychiatrists' Role in Sexual Harassment Cases,* 23 BULL. AM. ACAD. PSYCHIATRY & L. 513, 519 (1995).

[111]J. Hamilton, *Emotional Consequences of Victimization and Discrimination in "Special Populations" of Women,* 12 PSYCHIATR. CLINICS N. AM. 35, 42 (1989).

[112]B. Van der Kolk, *The Compulsion to Repeat the Trauma,* 12 PSYCHIATR. CLINICS N. AM. 389, 395 (1989).

[113]913 F. Supp. 1045 (S.D. Ohio 1995), *aff'd,* 123 F.3d 868, 75 FEP Cases 1351 (6th Cir. 1997), *cert. denied,* 118 S.Ct. 1039, 77 FEP Cases 64 (1998).

[114]510 U.S. 17, 63 FEP Cases 225 (1993).

[115]913 F. Supp. at 1051 (emphasis added).

> are all relevant factors to be considered in gauging their likely subjective reaction to the sexually-charged conduct of an over-40 male co-worker.[116]

The court concluded that "although the facts herein weigh in favor of concluding that these particular Plaintiffs subjectively would perceive the alleged conduct to affect the conditions of their employment, the likely reaction of a hypothetical reasonable person is less clear."[117]

The court also took into account the plaintiff's psychological history (although it did not apparently involve childhood sexual abuse) in applying the "reasonable person" test in *Sudtelgte v. Reno.*[118] In that case, the court admitted psychiatric testimony in a sexual harassment lawsuit concerning the fact that the plaintiff suffered from a paranoid personality disorder that adversely affected her ability to get along with supervisors and co-workers and that caused her to feel persistently "picked on." The court held that although the plaintiff may have felt subjectively harassed, such was the result of her abnormal sensitivity caused by her personality disorder and she could not show that a "reasonable woman" would have been similarly offended.

Repetition Compulsion and the "Welcomeness" Defense

As noted previously, in *Meritor Savings Bank v. Vinson,*[119] the Supreme Court maintained that sexual conduct in the workplace must be "unwelcome" to be actionable. In *Henson v. City of Dundee,*[120] the court defined "unwelcome" sexual conduct as that which is not "solicited or incited" by the plaintiff. Thus, even though a plaintiff may have regarded workplace conduct of a sexual nature as undesirable or offensive, if she consciously or even unconsciously incited the conduct, her harassment claim may not be viable.

Women who have histories of sexual abuse and/or who have a Borderline Personality Disorder may interact with others in eroticized or seductive ways. In the workplace, such a woman may behave in a sexually provocative manner with supervisors or co-workers. This is in part attributable to the fact that, because of her history of abuse, such a woman may expect abuse, set herself up for it, and then find her worst fears confirmed. As one authority has observed:

> Most sexual harassment cases of the "hostile environment" type involve a complex relationship between two individuals, the plaintiff and the defendant; that relationship must of necessity be carefully analyzed.[121]

With respect to the relevance of an abuse history to sexual harassment claims, this authority notes:

---

[116] *Id.* at 1055.

[117] *Id.*

[118] 63 FEP Cases 1257 (W.D. Mo. 1994).

[119] 477 U.S. 57, 68, 40 FEP Cases 1822, 1827 (1986).

[120] 682 F.2d 897, 903, 29 FEP Cases 787, 792 (11th Cir. 1982).

[121] S. Feldman-Schorrig, *Need for Expansion of Forensic Psychiatrists' Role in Sexual Harassment Cases,* 23 BULL. AM. ACAD. PSYCHIATRY & L. 513, 517 (1995).

> Not only does a history of childhood sexual abuse make a woman particularly vulnerable to various forms of revictimization such as sexual harassment in adult life, but it may also affect her personality so that she *provokes* behavior that, in retrospect, she will probably perceive as abusive.[122]

This is what is known as "repetition compulsion,"[123] and in a sexual harassment lawsuit it is relevant to the issue of whether the plaintiff, by her words or actions, "welcomed" the conduct of which she later complained.

"Repetition compulsion" often causes a person to seek out or create situations in which she will be victimized. As a leading expert has observed:

> It is the playing out of these themes of victimization that produces in large part the intense and unstable interpersonal relationships so characteristic of the borderline. *I would stress again that the victimization is seen mainly in the borderlines' ability to get others to do things to them, or upon them. . . .* Their abilities to get others to do things to them are often dramatic and obvious.[124]

This commentator explains how a woman with a Borderline Personality Disorder might instigate sexual conduct in the workplace that might then become the basis of a sexual harassment complaint:

> The borderline performs an initial action to which others respond. The response may be predictable and within proportion to the seriousness of the initiating act, but often it is unpredictable and excessive, except in the sense that, predictably, others will take over and things may happen to the borderline to reinforce the victimization theme. In essence, the situation escalates rapidly. Often it is no longer the borderline who is out of control; it is the others. The borderline is then the indignant and hapless recipient of others' anger, irrationality, or inept attempts to help or rescue, or worse, the true victim of another's aggressiveness. Often the borderline need do no more than initiate a series of actions; sometimes, when the tempest begins to settle down, the borderline may provoke a little more, in order to heat the situation up again. . . .[125]

Evidence of a sexual harassment plaintiff's history of prior sexual abuse, therefore, may assist a qualified mental health expert to demonstrate to the factfinder how and why a plaintiff might have contributed significantly to the chain of events that ultimately led to the filing of the harassment claim.

Admissibility of Evidence of Prior Sexual Abuse

Numerous courts have considered a plaintiff's history of childhood sexual abuse as an alternative cause of emotional distress.[126] In *McCleland v. Montgomery*

---

[122]*Id.* (emphasis in original).

[123]This concept is discussed in the Main Volume at pp. 345–46.

[124]J. Kroll, The Challenge of the Borderline Patient 46 (1988) (emphasis added).

[125]*Id.* at 50–51.

[126]*See, e.g.,* McKinnon v. Kwong Wah Restaurant, 83 F.3d 498, 70 FEP Cases 1037 (1st Cir. 1996) (affirming award of $2,500 in emotional distress damages to

Ward & Co.,[127] the court admitted evidence of the plaintiffs' prior childhood and adolescent abuse, including sexual abuse, as evidence of a potential alternative cause for their emotional injuries. The court rejected the plaintiffs' motion in limine to exclude such evidence, in spite of the plaintiffs' argument that because they were not seeking damages for aggravation of preexisting mental or psychological conditions, any evidence of their prior childhood and adolescent sexual abuse was irrelevant and prejudicial.

The court in *McCleland* found that Rule 412 did *not* apply to childhood sexual abuse because the defendant did not seek to introduce the prior abuse as evidence of the plaintiffs' sexual behavior or predisposition.[128] Nonetheless, the court noted, even if Rule 412 were to be applicable, the probative value of the evidence substantially outweighed the danger of harm or undue prejudice.[129] The court noted, among other things, that while the plaintiffs received extensive psychological treatment, their focus during that treatment was on their childhood abuse; neither mentioned to their therapists that they were being sexually harassed at work.[130]

In *Delaney v. City of Hampton*,[131] the court granted the defendant's Rule 412 motion to admit evidence of the plaintiff's history of prior sexual abuse as a potential alternative cause of her emotional damages. The plaintiff alleged that as a result of sexual harassment she suffered Posttraumatic Stress Disorder requiring numerous hospitalizations and long-term psychiatric treatment. The court noted that the defendant's experts planned to testify that the plaintiff's prior sexual abuse contributed to the plaintiff's psychiatric problems.

These cases demonstrate that Rule 412 will not necessarily bar the admission of evidence of the plaintiff's prior sexual abuse in a sexual harassment case.[132] An argument can be made that because Rule 412(a)(1) addresses evidence that the plaintiff "engaged in"[133] other sexual behavior, it does not apply to prior sexual experiences in which the plaintiff was an unwilling participant.[134]

---

sexual harassment plaintiff, noting the relevance of plaintiff's having been sexually abused by her stepfather from age 5 to age 17); Hurley v. Atlantic City Police Dep't, 933 F. Supp. 396, 72 FEP Cases 1828 (D.N.J. 1996) (in reducing jury award of $575,000 for emotional distress to $175,000, noting plaintiff's history of childhood molestation and two abusive marriages). *See also* Giron v. Corrections Corp. of Am., 981 F. Supp. 1406 (D.N.M. 1997) (permitting discovery of prior sexual abuse; noting possible relevance regarding causation of emotional damages).

[127] 1995 WL 571324 (N.D. Ill. 1995).

[128] *Id.* at *4 n.1.

[129] *Id.*

[130] *Id.* at *2.

[131] 999 F. Supp. 794 (E.D. Va.), *aff'd,* 135 F.3d 769 (4th Cir. 1998) (table).

[132] *But see* Knoettgen v. Superior Court, 224 Cal. App. 3d 11, 273 Cal. Rptr. 636 (1990) (barring deposition questioning of a plaintiff concerning her history of childhood sexual abuse under California counterpart to Rule 412).

[133] BLACK'S LAW DICTIONARY (5th ed.) defines "engage" as "[t]o employ or involve one's self; to take part in; to embark on."

[134] The court made just this distinction in Giron v. Corrections Corp. of Am., 981 F. Supp. 1406 (D.N.M. 1997). *See also* Fedio v. Circuit City Stores Inc., 1998 WL

In any event, it must be kept in mind that Rule 412 is *not* an absolute prohibition upon the discovery and admissibility of evidence of a plaintiff's sexual behavior or predisposition. Rather, it is a balancing test. This means that important evidence of a plaintiff's history of sexual abuse may be available upon an adequate showing to the court of its extreme relevance to the issues in a sexual harassment lawsuit.

Role of Childhood Sexual Abuse in Sexual Harassment Cases

Psychodynamic Processes

Factitious Disorder

A factitious disorder involves the intentional production or feigning of symptoms for the purpose of assuming the role of patient or victim.[135] It is distinguished from malingering, wherein symptoms are feigned for the purpose of secondary gain, such as financial compensation or avoiding legal responsibility. The possibility that a sexual harassment claim might be the product of a desire to assume a victim role is one to be considered.[136]

Borderline Personality Disorder

As one authority recently observed:

> The constellation of personality traits, coping patterns, and responses associated with borderline personality disorder are not infrequently found in women claiming sexual harassment. These are women who often have difficulty assessing the trustworthiness of others and who may be slow to recognize and deal effectively with critical early boundary violations. They are often inappropriate or provocative themselves in ways that they do not recognize. . . .
>
> Further complicating these assessments, women with such histories tend to have more severe reactions to less severe forms of victimization, particularly sexual victimization. For these women, even mild forms of sexual harassment may precipitate severe symptoms, including those of PTSD, even if their earlier coping responses have been adequate or good.[137]

966000 (E.D. Pa. 1998) (admitting evidence, over Rule 412 objection, that plaintiff was the victim of a date rape prior to becoming employed by the defendant).

[135] AMERICAN PSYCHIATRIC ASSOCIATION, DIAGNOSTIC AND STATISTICAL MANUAL OF MENTAL DISORDERS 471 (4th ed. 1994).

[136] S. Feldman-Schorrig, *Factitious Sexual Harassment,* 24 BULL. AM. ACAD. PSYCHIATRY & L. 387 (1996).

[137] L. Gold, *Addressing Bias in the Forensic Assessment of Sexual Harassment Claims*, 26 J. AMER. ACAD. OF PSYCHIATRY & L. 563, 570 (1998).

CHAPTER 11

AVOIDING "JUNK SCIENCE" IN EMPLOYMENT LITIGATION

The testimony of psychiatric or psychological experts on emotional distress damages issues has become a prominent part of most employment lawsuits in recent years. Although expert testimony is not necessarily a prerequisite for the recovery of emotional distress damages,[1] emotional damage claims are often buttressed by testimony offered by a psychiatrist, psychologist, or other mental health professional concerning the nature and extent of the plaintiff's psychological injuries. Mental and emotional injury is a difficult phenomenon to detect and measure with precision, however, and many "expert" opinions offered in support of such injury claims amount to little more than unsubstantiated conjecture, or "junk science."[2] Recent developments in the law of evidence provide a means to prevent an opponent's introduction of "junk science" into the emotional damages aspect of employment litigation, however.

The *Daubert* Standard

In 1993, the U.S. Supreme Court established a new standard for the admissibility of scientific evidence in federal court cases. In *Daubert v. Merrill Dow Pharmaceuticals Inc.,*[3] the Court rejected the "*Frye*" rule,[4] which had required that scientific evidence be "generally accepted" as reliable in the relevant scientific community as a prerequisite to its admissibility into evidence. Although the standard adopted by the *Daubert* Court—and based on Federal Rule of Evidence

---

[1]See discussion in Chapter 1, "The Legal Context," of this Supplement and of the Main Volume.

[2]This term was popularized in P. HUBER, GALILEO'S REVENGE: JUNK SCIENCE IN THE COURTROOM (1991).

[3]509 U.S. 579 (1993).

[4]The rule was first announced in *Frye v. United States*, 293 F. 1013 (D.C. Cir. 1923).

702—superficially appears more permissive than the *Frye* rule, it actually provides trial judges with an important tool to prevent the introduction of conjecture and "junk science" under the guise of expert scientific testimony. *Daubert* involved the attempt by a plaintiff in a products liability case to introduce expert testimony that the drug at issue, Benedictin, could cause birth defects. The district court ruled such testimony inadmissible because all prior published studies had concluded that Benedictin did *not* cause birth defects. The court reasoned that the lack of published studies supporting the plaintiff's experts' position indicated that their position was not generally accepted within the scientific community. The court of appeals affirmed.

The Supreme Court reversed, holding that the proper standard for admissibility is contained in Federal Rule of Evidence 702, which superseded *Frye*, and which provides:

> If scientific, technical, or other specialized knowledge will assist the trier of fact to understand the evidence or to determine a fact in issue, a witness qualified as an expert by knowledge, skill, experience, training or education, may testify thereto in the form of an opinion or otherwise.[5]

Whether a proffered expert's theory or test is generally accepted within the relevant scientific community is one factor to be considered by the court in applying Rule 702, according to *Daubert*, but it is no longer the only criterion. The *Daubert* Court read Rule 702 to require that an expert's testimony must amount to "scientific knowledge" to be admissible. It went on to specify that "scientific" implies a grounding in the methods and procedures of science, and "knowledge" means "more than subjective belief or unsupported speculation."[6]

The *Daubert* Court further maintained that in cases involving scientific evidence, evidentiary reliability (for the purposes of admissibility under Rule 702) will be based on scientific validity. Scientific validity, according to the *Daubert* Court, means that the theory or technique that is at the root of the expert's opinion can be tested. Moreover, there must be a valid scientific connection to the pertinent inquiry as a precondition to admissibility.[7]

Daubert thus requires that when faced with the proffer of expert scientific testimony, the trial judge must determine (1) whether the proffered testimony is scientifically valid, and (2) whether it will assist the trier of fact to understand or determine a fact in issue.[8] As the *Daubert* Court put it: "This entails a preliminary assessment of whether the testimony is scientifically valid and of whether the reasoning and methodology properly can be applied to the facts in issue."[9] These preliminary matters must be established by a preponderance of the evidence prior to the introduction of such expert testimony before the jury.[10]

---

[5]FED. R. EVID. 702.

[6]509 U.S. at 589–90.

[7]*Id.* at 591–92.

[8]*Id.* at 592.

[9]*Id.* at 592–93.

[10]In *General Electric Co. v. Joiner*, 118 S. Ct. 512 (1997), the Supreme Court held that an abuse of discretion standard applies to this determination by the district court.

As one commentator has observed:

> Before *Daubert*, the trial judge had to ask: What do the relevant scientists think about this? The judge had to decide: "Has the proponent of this evidence shown me that scientists agree with her?" After *Daubert*, the trial judge has to decide: "Is this good science?"[11]

Daubert thus places the trial judge in the role of "gatekeeper" charged with verifying the scientific validity of expert testimony before such testimony is permitted to reach the jury.

This gatekeeper role of the trial court is designed to prevent juries from being swayed by "expert" testimony that may sound quite impressive but that may be scientifically meaningless. Although the Supreme Court in *Daubert* vested trial judges with this new gatekeeper role, it did not provide them with much detailed guidance on how to perform this new function. The *Daubert* Court provided a nonexclusive list of factors for trial courts to consider—whether the expert's methodology can be tested, whether it has been subject to peer review and publication, the known or potential rate of error of the methodology, and whether a methodology is "generally accepted" within the relevant scientific community[12]—but it did not provide a mandate as to which of these factors is most important or whether any or all of them must be satisfied in every case.

More detailed guidance is provided to trial courts and advocates in the Ninth Circuit's decision on remand in *Daubert*,[13] authored by Judge Alex Kozinski. Judge Kozinski begins by summarizing the trial court's task under *Daubert*:

> First, we must determine nothing less than whether the experts' testimony reflects "scientific knowledge," whether their findings are "derived by the scientific method," and whether their work product amounts to "good science." Second, we must ensure that the proposed expert testimony is "relevant to the task at hand," i.e., that it logically advances a material aspect of the proposing party's case.[14]

Judge Kozinski began by debunking the notion that expert testimony is necessarily scientific just because it may come from a scientist. He observed: "[S]omething doesn't become 'scientific knowledge' just because it's uttered

---

[11]G. Fenner, *The Daubert Handbook: The Case, Its Essential Dilemma, and Its Progeny*, 29 Creighton L. Rev. 939, 948 (Apr. 1996). This commentator further observes:

> The irony of the federal judge crafting the edifice of scientific evidence in the courtroom is that, in my experience, a chief reason many of us went to law school is that the other choices all seemed to involve science: we fled science; we fled any profession that uses numbers in any more complex way than as volume, page, or section references.

Id. at 954 (footnote omitted).

[12]509 U.S. at 593–94.

[13]43 F.3d 1311 (9th Cir.), *cert. denied*, 516 U.S. 869 (1995).

[14]*Id.* at 1315 (citations omitted).

by a scientist; nor can an expert's self-serving assertion that his conclusions were 'derived by the scientific method' be deemed conclusive."[15] The court's task, then, "is to analyze not what the experts say, but what basis they have for saying it."[16] As Judge Kozinski explains:

> [T]he expert's bald assurance of validity is not enough. Rather, the party presenting the expert must show that the expert's findings are based on sound science, and this will require some objective, independent validation of the expert's methodology.[17]

According to Judge Kozinski, "one very significant fact to be considered" by a court in determining whether expert testimony will be admissible is "whether the experts are proposing to testify about matters growing naturally and directly out of research they have conducted independent of the litigation, or whether they have developed their opinions expressly for purposes of testifying."[18] He concludes: "That the testimony proffered by an expert is based directly on legitimate, preexisting research unrelated to the litigation provides the most persuasive basis for concluding that the opinions he expresses were 'derived by the scientific method.' "[19]

Of course, particularly in employment cases involving claims of emotional injury, most experts' testimony will not be based wholly upon prior research conducted by that expert. Such testimony will still be admissible, however, provided that the proffering party comes forward with "other objective, verifiable evidence that the testimony is based on 'scientifically valid principles.' "[20] One means of showing this, according to the Ninth Circuit, is by proof that the research and analysis supporting the proffered conclusions have been subject to normal scientific scrutiny through peer review and publication.[21]

In the absence of prior research or publication in peer-reviewed journals, the proponent of expert scientific testimony may attempt to satisfy its burden through the testimony of its own experts, but, according to the Ninth Circuit,

> [f]or such a showing to be sufficient, the experts must explain precisely how they went about reaching their conclusions and point to some objective source—a learned treatise, the policy statement of a professional association, a published article in a reputable scientific journal or the like—to show that they have followed the scientific method, as it is practiced by (at least) a recognized minority of scientists in their field.[22]

Thus, the proponent of expert testimony must "explain the expert's methodology and demonstrate in some objectively verifiable way that the expert has

---

[15]*Id.* at 1315–16.
[16]*Id.* at 1316.
[17]*Id.*
[18]*Id.* at 1317.
[19]*Id.*
[20]*Id.* at 1317–18.
[21]*Id.* at 1318.
[22]*Id.* at 1319.

both chosen a reliable scientific method and followed it faithfully."[23] The opposing party must then be afforded the opportunity to challenge the showing. This could be done by presenting evidence (including expert testimony) that the opposing expert either employed unsound methodology or "failed to assiduously follow an otherwise sound protocol."[24] The court must then hold an in limine hearing outside the presence of the jury to consider the conflicting evidence and to make findings about the soundness and reliability of the methodology employed by the proffered experts.[25]

Applying these standards to the evidence before it, the Ninth Circuit in *Daubert* held that the plaintiffs' expert testimony was inadmissible. The court observed that "plaintiffs rely entirely on the experts' unadorned assertion that the methodology they employed comports with standard scientific procedures." It continued: "We've been presented with only the experts' qualifications, their conclusions and their assurances of reliability. Under *Daubert*, that's not enough."[26]

The Ninth Circuit's decision on remand in *Daubert* therefore provides important guidance on the admissibility of expert psychiatric or psychological testimony in employment cases, testimony that is often lacking in scientific basis.[27] A useful comparison may be drawn between the testimony of one of the proffered experts in *Daubert* (that Benedictin caused the plaintiffs' birth defects) with the testimony of many experts in employment cases (that being fired or harassed caused the plaintiff to suffer severe psychiatric injury). As the Ninth Circuit in *Daubert* observed:

> Dr. Palmer asserts only that Benedictin is a teratogen and that he has examined the plaintiffs' medical records, which apparently reveal the timing of their mothers' ingestion of the drug. Dr. Palmer offers no tested or testable theory to explain how, from this limited information, he was able to eliminate all other potential causes of birth defects, nor does he explain how he alone can state as a fact that Benedictin caused plaintiffs' injuries.[28]

---

[23]*Id.* at 1319 n.11.

[24]*Id.* at 1319 n.10.

[25]*Id. But see* Lanni v. State of New Jersey, 177 F.R.D. 295, 302 (D.N.J. 1998) (opponent of the proposed expert testimony must demonstrate a prima facie case of unreliability before an evidentiary hearing is required).

[26]*Daubert,* 43 F.3d. at 1319.

[27]The law professor who argued the *Daubert* case on behalf of the plaintiffs in the Supreme Court and in the Ninth Circuit on remand argues that psychiatric and psychological evidence should not be subject to *Daubert* because psychiatric diagnosis is not "testable." *See* M. Gottesman, *Admissibility of Expert Testimony After Daubert: The "Prestige" Factor*, 43 EMORY L.J. 867 (Summer 1994). As is demonstrated below, however, courts *have* applied *Daubert* to psychiatric and psychological evidence, as well as to other types of medical evidence. *See also* Tyus v. Urban Search Management, 102 F.3d 256, 263 (7th Cir. 1996) (*Daubert* framework for assessing expert testimony "is applicable to social science experts, just as it applies to experts in the hard sciences").

[28]43 F.3d at 1319.

After concluding that "[p]ersonal opinion, not science, is testifying here," the Ninth Circuit rejected this expert's testimony under *Daubert*. The opinion of a psychiatric or psychological expert—given without considering the possible role of alternative stressors—that a particular workplace event caused a plaintiff to suffer severe psychological injury may similarly be vulnerable to a *Daubert* challenge.

As discussed in more detail below, the Ninth Circuit in *Daubert* went on to reject testimony from other experts that Benedictin is "capable of causing" birth defects. The court observed that "what plaintiffs must prove is not that Benedictin causes some birth defects, but that it caused *their* birth defects."[29] An analogy also might be drawn between this principle and proffered expert testimony in many employment cases to the effect that merely being fired is "capable of causing" depression or that sexual harassment "is capable of causing" posttraumatic stress disorder.

In *Kumho Tire Co. v. Carmichael*,[30] the Supreme Court extended *Daubert* to all expert testimony, not just that involving "pure science." At issue in *Kumho Tire* was the admissibility of testimony of an expert in tire failure analysis. The Court held that *Daubert* and the "gatekeeping" role it assigns to district courts applies to "technical" and "other specialized" knowledge, as well as scientific knowledge. Thus, the fact that psychiatry and clinical psychology are not pure experimental sciences does not provide a justification for failure to apply a rigorous *Daubert* analysis.[31]

Daubert and *Kumho Tire* therefore should have a profound impact on the admissibility of expert testimony offered to prove that workplace incidents caused significant psychological injury, in a number of respects. First, they may prevent testimony from "experts" who lack sufficient training and experience in clinical diagnosis of mental illness. Second, they may bar testimony from experts who, while possessing the requisite training and experience, fail to employ standard diagnostic principles derived through application of the scientific method, such that their testimony is little more than unsupported conjecture. Third, they may prevent experts from basing their opinions on the body of academic "research" that purports to suggest a link between employment discrimination (particularly sexual harassment) and significant psychological injury, as such "research" is not scientific in nature.

The Expert's Training and Experience

Should a mental health professional attempt to base on his or her clinical skills and experience an opinion that employment-related conduct such as

[29]*Id.* at 1322.

[30]526 U.S. 137 (1999).

[31]*But see* Wilson v. Phillips, 73 Cal. App. 4th 250, 254, 86 Cal.Rptr.2d 204, 207 (1999) (holding that *Kelly-Frye* rule in California applies only to cases involving "novel devices or processes," not to expert medical or psychological testimony).

discrimination or harassment caused significant psychological injury, such an opinion may be inadmissible under *Daubert* if the expert lacks the proper clinical training or lacks the requisite clinical experience with such cases.

Courts have applied *Daubert* specifically to the qualifications of a proffered psychological expert. In *Isley v. Capuchin Province,*[32] the court set forth two prerequisites that a psychological expert must meet before being found qualified to testify. First, the expert must demonstrate that he or she has education and training in the discipline at issue "sufficient to give him/her expertise or special knowledge such that any opinions that the expert has will be of assistance to the jury in its fact-finding responsibilities."[33] Second, the expert must show that he or she has personal experience in treating patients with the condition at issue.[34] For example, a licensed clinical psychologist who has never treated patients with personality disorders would have the requisite training and education but would lack the requisite clinical experience to qualify to give an opinion as to whether a plaintiff in an employment lawsuit does or does not suffer from a personality disorder.

Education and Training

Case law construing *Daubert* appears to require that psychological experts possess sufficient education and training such that their opinions will carry a measure of scientific reliability. With respect to psychiatrists and clinical psychologists, this should not ordinarily be a problem, provided that the expert testifies about a subject within the scope of his or her expertise. Psychiatrists and clinical psychologists receive rigorous training in the use of scientific principles in diagnosing mental illness. Although the nature of the training varies somewhat between the two professions, its substance is essentially the same. The psychiatrist or clinical psychologist is trained in the process of differential diagnosis, by which mental illness is diagnosed by posing and ruling out a number of alternative hypotheses based on the symptoms presented before arriving at a final diagnosis. For example, when diagnosing posttraumatic stress disorder (PTSD), it is the normal standard of practice in forensic evaluations to first rule out Acute Stress Disorder, adjustment disorders, anxiety disorders, personality disorders, and malingering before settling on a diagnosis of PTSD.[35]

Other mental health professionals who may seek to give expert testimony in employment lawsuits, such as marriage and family counselors, social workers, and educational psychologists, typically lack this training in scientifically based diagnosis, however. These professionals may have a nominal clinical orientation

---

[32]877 F. Supp. 1055 (E.D. Mich. 1995).

[33]*Id.* at 1063.

[34]*Id.*

[35]J. McDonald & P. Lees-Haley, *Avoiding "Junk Science" in Sexual Harassment Litigation*, 21 Employee Rel. L.J. 51, 59 (1995).

but lack the rigorous training in scientific principles of diagnosis that competent psychiatrists and clinical psychologists possess. The focus of many of these professionals' practices is on counseling and assisting clients with situational difficulties, such as marital discord, which ordinarily do not involve the diagnosis of mental disorders. Moreover, the licensure statutes governing these classes of professionals may limit the scope of their practice in a way that would prevent them from testifying in court as a forensic expert.[36]

A number of courts have refused to allow these mental health professionals to give expert testimony. For example, in *Jackson v. Bayou Industries,*[37] the court in a race discrimination case refused to allow testimony from a "licensed professional counselor" that the plaintiffs suffered PTSD as a result of race discrimination, although it allowed her to testify about her interviews with the plaintiffs, any behavioral characteristics she observed during those interviews, and the course of counseling she pursued with the plaintiffs. In refusing to allow the counselor to testify that discrimination caused the plaintiffs to suffer PTSD, the court observed that the counselor

> is not a psychiatrist, she is not a licensed psychologist, nor has she ever practiced in the field of psychology. She testified that she has a masters degree in psychology and is in the process of getting a doctorate degree in social work. The witness stated that she has only had one formal course at the non-college level in Diagnostic Statistical Manuals in addition to one 3 hour afternoon seminar on Diagnostic Statistical Manuals. Finally, she stated that she does not specialize in psychiatric testing and did not administer psychiatric tests to the plaintiffs.[38]

Similarly, the district court in the Paula Jones lawsuit against President Clinton rejected the plaintiff's proffer of a declaration from what the court described as a "purported expert with a Ph.D. in education and counseling" who, after a 3.5 hour meeting with the plaintiff and her husband, concluded that Jones' alleged encounter with then-Governor Clinton caused her to suffer severe emotional distress and "consequent sexual aversion." The court refused to give credit to this declaration.[39]

Some courts have taken a contrary view, however. For example, in *Sanfelice v. Dominick's Finer Foods,*[40] the court permitted expert testimony from a

---

[36]For example, in California, marriage and family counselors are authorized to treat marital and family problems but not to diagnose mental illness. *See* CAL. BUS. & PROF. CODE §4980.02.

[37]1995 WL 143538 (E.D. La. 1995).

[38]*Id.* at *1. *See also* Karlin v. Foust, 975 F. Supp. 1177 (W.D. Wis. 1997) (rejecting, pursuant to *Daubert*, proffered testimony by Ph.D. in "family social science" that abortion causes PTSD), *aff'd in part, rev'd in part*, 188 F.3d 446 (7th Cir. 1999); State v. Willis, 256 Kan. 837, 888 P.2d 839 (1995) (reversing trial court's admission of testimony from social worker diagnosing rape victim with PTSD; social worker lacked qualifications to make medical diagnosis of PTSD).

[39]Jones v. Clinton, 990 F.Supp. 657, 678, 76 FEP Cases 589 (E.D. Ark. 1998).

[40]1995 WL 608602 (N.D. Ill. 1995).

psychotherapist in spite of the fact that he did not have a degree in psychology.[41] The court emphasized, however, that the expert was "trained extensively in the area of psychotherapy" and had been performing therapy and counseling continuously since 1956.[42]

In addition, there is an ever-growing class of "experts" in employment cases, such as social psychologists, organizational psychologists, sociologists, and so-called "victimologists" and "discriminatologists," who may not possess any clinical orientation at all, but who come from a more general social science or human resources background. Some may attempt to offer diagnoses of psychological disorders, while others may seek to offer opinions on such issues as whether a particular workplace was a "hostile working environment" or that the plaintiff's failure to complain contemporaneously is consistent with the profile of a "typical victim" of harassment (and thus should not undercut her credibility).[43] Although some courts have admitted this kind of testimony,[44] an increasing number are refusing to do so.[45]

For example, in *Lipsett v. University of Puerto Rico,*[46] the court disallowed testimony from a social worker and a social psychologist who sought to testify that unlawful sexual harassment existed in the defendant's workplace. The court held both that the proffered experts could not qualify as experts and that their testimony would not assist the jury. With respect to an expert's qualifications, the *Lipsett* court ruled that an expert must be a member of a traditional profession that maintains ethical standards and requires extensive education and mastery of a specialized field of knowledge. Absent these qualifications, a proffered expert's testimony "would not possess the professional safeguards ensuring objectivity."[47]

---

[41]It is not clear from the court's opinion in just which field, if any, the therapist was degreed.

[42]*See also* Lanni v. State of New Jersey, 177 F.R.D. 295, 302–03 (D.N.J. 1998) (rejecting plaintiff's challenge of defendant's expert's qualifications to diagnose learning disabilities, court remarked that the defendant's psychiatrist "need not be the best qualified expert" so long as he is qualified).

[43]*See* Karibian v. Columbia Univ., 930 F. Supp. 134, 71 FEP Cases 325 (S.D.N.Y. 1996).

[44]For example, in *Flavel v. Svedala Industries Inc.,* 1994 WL 761447 (E.D. Wis. 1994), the court permitted an industrial psychologist to testify regarding "stereotypes in the employment context and management conduct and practices which reflect age consciousness and age stereotypes" to establish the motive for the actions taken by the defendant.

[45]*See, e.g.,* United States v. Rouse, 111 F.3d 561, 571 (8th Cir. 1997) (assessing the reliability or credibility of a victim's accusations is the exclusive function of the jury; psychological expert's opinions about witness credibility are properly excluded), *cert. denied,* 118 S. Ct. 261 (1997); *Karibian,* 930 F. Supp. at 140 (excluding testimony of social worker that plaintiff's failure to complain of sexual harassment was attributable to "reluctance of people to complain about sexual harassment;" noting that this is "such an oversimplification of the issue that it would be of no real help to the jury and could be misleading").

[46]740 F. Supp. 921, 54 FEP Cases 257 (D.P.R. 1990).

[47]*Id.* at 924, 54 FEP Cases at 259.

The *Lipsett* court additionally maintained that testimony of a social worker or social psychologist to the effect that sexual harassment existed in a workplace "would not bring to the jury anything more than the lawyers can offer in argument." *Lipsett* is an important step toward eliminating so-called expert testimony that involves more advocacy than true expertise and that addresses matters more appropriately within the province of the jury to decide.[48]

Thus, neither the status of "professional" nor the title "doctor" necessarily makes an expert witness. The expert must have advanced training and experience in a recognized field of knowledge that is beyond the common sense and life experience of the average juror. Moreover, although a proffered psychological expert's various credentials may sound impressive, what matters from an evidentiary standpoint is whether that expert's training included adequate, scientifically based training in clinical diagnostics. For experts who are not licensed clinical psychologists or Board-certified psychiatrists,[49] this threshold will be difficult to meet.

Lack of Clinical Experience

Even if a proffered expert has had the requisite basic clinical training in diagnosing mental disorders, that expert's testimony may not be admissible unless it can be shown that the expert additionally has sufficient personal experience in the diagnosis of patients with the type of condition at issue in the lawsuit.[50] As one authority has observed, with respect to experts on the issue of Posttraumatic Stress Disorder: "Qualification as an expert witness is not generic but rather issue specific. Licensure as a physician who practices psychiatry, or even a board certification in psychiatry, should not, in and of itself, result in qualification as an expert on PTSD."[51]

Courts have used *Daubert* as a basis for excluding testimony by medical experts grounded solely in the expert's clinical experience where the expert lacks extensive experience in diagnosing the condition at issue. For example,

---

[48]Similarly, in *United States v. Whitted*, 11 F.3d 782 (8th Cir. 1993), a sexual abuse case, the court permitted a physician to testify about the alleged victim's bedwetting, nightmares, and inability to sleep at night, but it refused to allow the physician to testify that the alleged victim had suffered "repeated child sexual abuse." *Id.* at 786. The court explained that because the physician's diagnosis rested solely on his acceptance of the victim's account, his testimony amounted to nothing more than an invitation to the jury to believe his assessment of the victim's truthfulness. *Id.*

[49]Upon the completion of a psychiatric residency, a physician is eligible to sit for the certification examination in psychiatry administered by the American Board of Psychiatry and Neurology. Although in most jurisdictions a physician need not be Board-certified to practice psychiatry, only Board certification in psychiatry will guarantee that the physician has received the proper clinical training in psychiatry.

[50]Isley v. Capuchin Province, 877 F. Supp. 1055, 1063–64 (E.D. Mich. 1995).

[51]D. Shuman, *Persistent Reexperiences in Psychiatry and Law: Current and Future Trends in Posttraumatic Stress Disorder Litigation*, in POSTTRAUMATIC STRESS DISORDER IN LITIGATION 6–7 (R. Simon, ed. 1995).

in *O'Conner v. Commonwealth Edison Co.*,[52] the Seventh Circuit affirmed the trial court's exclusion of the testimony of the plaintiff's medical expert, who sought to testify that he could simply look at a cataract and determine whether it was caused by radiation exposure. The court began by rejecting the plaintiff's argument that the testimony of a treating physician is not governed by *Daubert.*[53] The court went on to note that the expert was basing his opinion on his prior experience with radiation-induced cataracts, but then observed: "However, Dr. Scheribel has treated only five patients with radiation-induced cataracts in his 20 years of practice. We do not believe that this limited exposure to radiation-induced cataracts qualifies as a basis for a scientifically sound opinion."[54] The Seventh Circuit took a similar position in rejecting testimony of a physician who sought to testify that, based upon his experience, ibuprofen can cause a type of kidney failure known as anti-GBM RPGN.[55] The court noted that the testimony failed to satisfy the *Daubert* standards because the physician "has encountered only about five cases of anti-GBM RPGN in his career."[56]

Similarly, in *Antoine-Tubbs v. Local 513, Transport Workers Union*,[57] the court cited *Daubert* in refusing to admit testimony of a doctor of osteopathy that the plaintiff's being yelled at by her boss caused her to develop preeclampsia and lose her baby. The court noted that the doctor had been in practice for only two years, had been involved in only one case of preeclampsia while in her residency program, and not encountered any such cases in her own practice. The doctor also admitted that she was aware of no literature or studies indicating that work stress could cause preeclampsia. The court described the doctor's opinion as just "subjective belief and unsupported speculation."[58]

Thus, in the mental health context, an expert who seeks to testify that workplace incidents caused a plaintiff to become depressed may have to demonstrate sufficient personal experience in diagnosing not only patients complaining of depression but also patients who claim to have been the victims of similar workplace conduct. Although most mental health professionals will have sufficient experience in diagnosing and treating depressed patients, for example, relatively few will have diagnosed and treated a sufficient number of sexual harassment victims suffering from depression to reach this threshold. Moreover, even clinicians who have previously treated a few harassment victims likely would not have treated a sufficient number of victims of the type of conduct alleged in the instant case to permit meaningful clinical comparisons and generalizations to be drawn.

The following example illustrates this problem. Suppose a plaintiff seeks to have her treating psychologist testify that, in his opinion, her depressed

---

[52]13 F.3d 1090 (7th Cir.), *cert. denied*, 512 U.S. 1222 (1994).

[53]*Id.* at 1105 n.14.

[54]*Id.* at 1107 n.19.

[55]Porter v. Whitehall Labs. Inc., 9 F.3d 607 (7th Cir. 1993).

[56]*Id.* at 614 n.6.

[57]50 F. Supp.2d 601 (N.D. Tex. 1998), *aff'd sub nom.* Tubbs v. TX Workers Union, 190 F.3d 537 (5th Cir. 1999) (table).

[58]*Id.* at 609.

condition is attributable solely to sexual harassment (in the form of repeated sexual joking and horseplay by co-workers) suffered at the defendant's workplace. Voir dire questioning of the psychologist indicates that although he is properly licensed and received the requisite general training in diagnostics, he has treated only two victims of sexual harassment previously—one patient who was raped by a co-worker and who did exhibit symptoms of a clinical depression, and one patient who was fired after ending a consensual affair with her boss and who felt angry and betrayed but did not suffer a diagnosable mental disorder. If such an expert seeks to base his opinion on his clinical skills and experience, he may well lack the requisite clinical experience with sexual harassment victims to support an opinion as to causation.

The Expert's Diagnostic Technique

To the extent that a psychological expert fails to follow standard clinical protocols and principles in reaching a diagnosis, that expert's opinion may be inadmissible under *Daubert*. Although the diagnosis of mental illness is not as precise a science as "hard" sciences such as chemistry and physics, a number of diagnostic protocols and principles have been developed through application of the scientific method. These have been validated through testing in field trials, and they are generally accepted by the psychiatric and psychological professions.

An expert's attempt to use *Daubert* to justify a departure from mainstream diagnostic protocols and principles on the ground that *Daubert* no longer absolutely requires that an expert's theories be generally accepted by the relevant scientific community would be misplaced, in that *Daubert* still requires that an expert's methodologies be based on the scientific method. In virtually every such case, the expert's chosen methodologies will not be based on the scientific method (and, in any event, will not have been subject to validity testing), so the *Daubert* standards will not be met.

In employment cases, experts most frequently fail to use standard clinical protocols and principles by failing to apply the diagnostic criteria set forth in the American Psychiatric Association's *Diagnostic and Statistical Manual of Mental Disorders* (the current edition of which is known as *DSM-IV*[59]), failing to apply principles of differential diagnosis, or failing to administer and interpret psychological testing properly.

Failure to Use the *DSM-IV*

DSM-IV is the only generally accepted diagnostic manual of the mental health professions in the United States. It contains objective diagnostic criteria for

---

[59] AMERICAN PSYCHIATRIC ASSOCIATION, DIAGNOSTIC AND STATISTICAL MANUAL OF MENTAL DISORDERS (4th ed. 1994) (hereinafter *DSM-IV*).

each of the recognized mental disorders, criteria that were formulated after lengthy study and debate among psychiatrists and psychologists and that have been subjected to extensive field testing.[60] Although no compendium of diagnostic criteria could be perfect, *DSM-IV* provides an essential measure of objectivity to the rather slippery subject matter of diagnosing mental illness.

Numerous plaintiffs' experts fail to follow *DSM-IV* in rendering a diagnosis, however. Instead, they employ subjective, idiosyncratic diagnostic criteria not found in any manual. Although at times this may be for the expedient purpose of maximizing the value of the plaintiff's claim, more often it is due to the fact that many plaintiffs' experts also serve as the plaintiffs' treating therapists, and strict adherence to standard diagnostic criteria is less important in the therapeutic context than in the forensic. Nonetheless, to the extent an expert's diagnosis of a plaintiff fails to conform with *DSM-IV* criteria, there is an issue as to whether that diagnosis will be admissible under *Daubert.*

One court has held that a psychologist's failure to utilize *DSM-IV* diagnostic criteria is not grounds to exclude her testimony under *Daubert*. In *Mancuso v. Consolidated Edison Co. of New York,*[61] the defendant sought to exclude the testimony of a psychologist diagnosing the plaintiffs' child as having a learning disorder. The defendant argued that the child could not have had a learning disorder as defined by *DSM-IV* criteria because none of her scores were two standard deviations below her overall intelligence score, as required by *DSM-IV* for such a diagnosis.[62] The court refused to exclude the testimony. It first noted that it could find no case law requiring that an expert use *DSM-IV* criteria to qualify to testify. It then observed that it appeared that the psychologist's diagnosis could nonetheless fit within the *DSM-IV* category of "Learning Disorder Not Otherwise Specified,"[63] that the diagnosis was based upon the administration of several well-recognized intelligence tests, and that it conformed with the diagnostic criteria in another authoritative text on learning disabilities.[64] The court maintained that the defendant's attack on the psychologist's failure to adhere to *DSM-IV* diagnostic criteria was an issue as to the weight, but not the admissibility, of the evidence.

Mancuso appears to be inconsistent with the Ninth Circuit's mandate on remand in *Daubert* that an expert "assiduously follow" scientific protocol.[65] Several courts in the wake of *Daubert*, moreover, have noted that even though clinical practitioners such as psychiatrists and psychologists need not be held to the same rigorous scientific standards as are researchers in the "hard" sciences, *Daubert* nonetheless requires that they utilize the methodologies and protocols commonly utilized in their field. For example, in *Moore v. Ashland Chemical Inc.,*[66] the court addressed the applicability of *Daubert* to a clinical physician's

---

[60]*See id.* at xviii–xix for a discussion of these field tests.

[61]967 F. Supp. 1437 (S.D.N.Y. 1997).

[62]*See DSM-IV, supra* note 59, at 46–47.

[63]*Id.* at 53.

[64]967 F. Supp. at 1454–57.

[65]*See* 43 F.3d 1311, 1319 n.10 (9th Cir.), *cert. denied*, 516 U.S. 869 (1995).

[66]126 F.3d 679 (5th Cir. 1997), *cert. denied*, 119 S. Ct. 1454 (1999).

expert opinion on the cause of the plaintiff's respiratory disease. It maintained that although the *Daubert* standards for determining the evidentiary reliability of scientific evidence are not appropriately applied to clinical medicine (as opposed to research or laboratory medicine), Federal Rule of Evidence 702, as interpreted by *Daubert*, still requires that the district court examine the soundness of the evidence involved prior to admitting it. As the *Moore* court explained:

> [U]nder Rule 702, an opinion based on other technical or specialized knowledge must be grounded in the principles, methods and procedures of the particular field of knowledge involved. Every discipline employs a body of methods, rules and postulates, i.e., methodology, both in its ordinary functions and in developing and adopting new concepts, techniques and analogues. . . . Thus, the proffered opinion of any expert in a field of knowledge, in order to be evidentiarily reliable, must either be based soundly on the current knowledge, principles and methodology of the expert's discipline or be soundly inferred or derived therefrom.[67]

Thus, as the current edition of the *DSM* is the only commonly accepted diagnostic manual of the mental health professions, an expert's failure to adhere to the *DSM*'s diagnostic criteria would make that expert's methodology highly vulnerable to a *Daubert* challenge.

One common situation in which a plaintiff's expert may fail to adhere to standard diagnostic protocols occurs where the expert evaluated the plaintiff prior to the commencement of litigation, with an eye toward prescribing treatment rather than toward giving testimony in court. For example, in *Gier v. Educational Service Unit No. 16,*[68] the court excluded expert testimony from various mental health professionals seeking to demonstrate that the plaintiffs had been sexually and emotionally abused. The court explained:

> Plaintiffs have failed to demonstrate by a preponderance of the evidence that their experts' methodologies for evaluating the plaintiffs in this particular case are reliable for the investigative purposes plaintiffs now seek to use them. The witnesses all testified that their purposes in evaluating plaintiffs were for the provision of therapy, not investigation. The methods used here may well have been sufficiently reliable for purposes of choosing a course of psychotherapy for these disturbed children, a course which must, to some extent, rely upon perception as well as reality, and upon the subjective reports of parents and others. However, the methodologies have not been shown to be reliable enough to provide a sound basis for investigative conclusions and confident legal decision-making.[69]

---

[67]*Id.* at 686–87. *Accord* Watkins v. Telsmith Inc., 121 F.3d 984, 991 (5th Cir. 1997) (trial court must ensure that expert's opinion comports with applicable professional standards outside the courtroom); Tyus v. Urban Search Management, 102 F.3d 256, 263 (7th Cir. 1996) (social science testimony must adhere to same standards of intellectual rigor that apply in expert's professional field).

[68]845 F. Supp. 1342 (D. Neb. 1994), *aff'd*, 66 F.3d 940 (8th Cir. 1995).

[69]845 F. Supp. at 1353. *Accord* Isley v. Capuchin Province, 877 F. Supp. 1055, 1059 (E.D. Mich. 1995).

The *Gier* court quoted *Daubert* for the point that "scientific validity for one purpose is not necessarily scientific validity for other, unrelated purposes."[70] Diagnostic practice in the therapeutic setting tends to be less precise than in the forensic setting. In the therapeutic context, determining the cause and even the precise identity of a mental disorder is often less important than prescribing an effective treatment. If a patient consults a psychiatrist, complaining of being depressed, the psychiatrist can prescribe a course of medication or counseling therapy without necessarily determining whether the patient's condition would fall within the specific *DSM-IV* category of Major Depression, Dysthymic Disorder, Adjustment Disorder with Depressed Mood, or Depressive Disorder Not Otherwise Specified. The fact that the clinician may have applied idiosyncratic diagnostic criteria is not as important as whether the clinician has prescribed the right treatment.

In court, by contrast, the cause of a particular mental disorder is usually a central issue in the litigation. It also may be important to determine whether the patient suffers from Dysthymic Disorder (a chronic depressed state that often precedes the workplace events at issue in litigation[71]), or Adjustment Disorder with Depressed Mood (a short-term condition that is triggered by an identifiable stressor and resolves within six months[72]). In the litigation context, therefore, where a claim for substantial money damages is usually at stake, *Daubert* would appear to require faithful adherence to the rigorous diagnostic standards set forth in *DSM-IV*, at least in the absence of some other indicia carrying a similarly high degree of scientific reliability.

One common example of the application of idiosyncratic diagnostic criteria in employment cases is found in the diagnosis of PTSD in a plaintiff in a sexual harassment case where the alleged harassment did not involve a sexual assault. *DSM-IV* sets forth precise diagnostic criteria for PTSD.[73] One key criterion is that the person must have been subject to "an extreme traumatic stressor" of such a dramatic and profound nature that it involved "actual or threatened death or serious injury, or other threat to one's physical integrity."[74] *DSM-IV* provides the following examples of qualifying stressors: rape, robbery, mugging, kidnaping, being taken hostage, torture, incarceration as a prisoner of war, and natural or man-made disasters. Without such a stressor, a PTSD diagnosis will not be valid under *DSM-IV*. Stressors of a less serious nature—no matter how annoying, unpleasant, or persistent—simply do not qualify. For example, *DSM-IV* expressly provides that "being fired" is not a stressor sufficiently serious to justify a PTSD diagnosis.[75] Moreover, although *DSM-IV* loosens the diagnostic criteria for PTSD a bit over the previous edition of the manual, it does *not* recognize a "cumulative trauma" stressor for PTSD.[76]

---

[70]845 F. Supp. at 1353 (quoting *Daubert*, 509 U.S. at 591).

[71]*DSM-IV, supra* note 59, at 345–49.

[72]*Id.* at 623–27.

[73]*Id.* at 424–29.

[74]*Id.* at 424.

[75]*Id.* at 427.

[76]*See* R. Simon, *Toward the Development of Guidelines in the Forensic Psychiatric Examination of Posttraumatic Stress Disorder Claimants,* in POSTTRAUMATIC STRESS

Nonetheless, many plaintiffs' experts will insist that their patients suffered PTSD as a result of sexual harassment. They may attempt to justify this position by noting that rape is a qualifying stressor for PTSD, and by then asserting that because sexual harassment is "like rape," sexual harassment must similarly constitute a qualifying stressor for PTSD. This position is wrong on a number of counts. First, sexual harassment is *not* "like rape." Such an imprecise comparison is based in ideology, not science. Second, nothing in *DSM-IV* suggests that such incidents as a boss's sexual proposition, a co-worker's unwanted kiss or hug or pat on the buttocks, overhearing dirty jokes, viewing "pinup" posters, or even being called foul and insulting names are sufficient to cause PTSD. A plaintiff's expert who nonetheless diagnoses PTSD in cases involving non-assaultive sexual harassment[77] therefore cannot be relying on the *DSM-IV* diagnostic criteria. There are no other generally accepted diagnostic criteria for PTSD, however, so such an expert must be relying on his or her own idiosyncratic diagnostic criteria that, ordinarily lacking any grounding in the scientific method and incapable of being tested, may be inadmissible under *Daubert*.

Other diagnoses that frequently appear in discrimination and harassment cases—such as major depression and panic disorder—similarly carry strict diagnostic criteria that are set forth in *DSM-IV*. To the extent that a plaintiff seeks to introduce evidence of a diagnosis of one of these conditions in court where the *DSM-IV* diagnostic criteria have not been met, such a diagnosis may be vulnerable to a *Daubert* challenge.

Failure to Conduct Differential Diagnosis

It is a fundamental precept of forensic psychiatry and psychology that any mental evaluation must include an exploration of significant prior and concurrent events in the plaintiff's life, to determine whether there may be an alternative cause—besides the alleged acts or omissions of the defendant—for the mental condition at issue in the litigation. Specifically, the examining clinician must probe the plaintiff's prior psychological history for evidence of preexisting mental disorders (for example, bipolar disorder or chronic depression), personality disorders,[78] or significant prior traumas such as sexual assault[79] or childhood sexual abuse.[80] The clinician also must explore whether concurrent stressors

DISORDER IN LITIGATION 31, 51–52 (R. Simon ed., 1995) ("Stressor research has not clarified whether a minor stress, if experienced long enough, can produce sufficient traumatic stress to cause PTSD").

[77]Of course, where the alleged sexual harassment involved actual rape, a diagnosis of PTSD could be appropriate if the *DSM-IV* criteria are otherwise met.

[78]For a detailed discussion of personality disorders, see M. STONE, ABNORMALITIES OF PERSONALITY (1993) and T. MILLION, DISORDERS OF PERSONALITY (1981).

[79]S. Feldman-Schorrig & J. McDonald, *The Role of Forensic Psychiatry in the Defense of Sexual Harassment Cases*, 20 J. PSYCHIATRY & L. 5, 13 (1992).

[80]*See* J. McDonald & S. Feldman-Schorrig, *The Relevance of Childhood Sexual Abuse in Sexual Harassment Cases*, 20 EMPLOYEE REL. L.J. 221 (1994).

exist in the plaintiff's personal life that may have affected that person's psychological condition, such as marital problems or substance abuse.

The clinician must not only ask questions of the plaintiff about these matters during the clinical interview but also must, in addition, review all available records pertaining to the plaintiff. This records review should include medical and psychological records, employment records, criminal records, divorce records, and school records. Such a records review is essential because the plaintiff's own account of his or her history may at best be subject to memory lapses, and at worst be intentionally misrepresented.

Only after a comprehensive review of the plaintiff's prior psychological history and potential concurrent stressors can a clinician render an objective opinion as to the causation of the plaintiff's current condition. The clinician must rule out preexisting mental or personality disorders, prior traumas, and concurrent stressors as potential causes of the plaintiff's current condition to render any scientifically valid opinion that sexual harassment caused the plaintiff's current psychopathology.

Numerous courts have excluded expert testimony under *Daubert* because the clinician failed to conduct such a process of differential diagnosis.

A leading case on this subject is *In re Paoli Railroad Yard PCB Litigation,*[81] in which the Third Circuit affirmed exclusion of expert testimony of two physicians who failed to employ differential diagnosis. The court remarked that "at the core of differential diagnosis is a requirement that experts at least consider alternative causes—this almost has to be true of any technique that tries to find a cause of something."[82] The court went on to state:

> Defendants' experts explained that a reliable differential diagnosis generally requires a physical examination of the patient, a review of medical records, taking a history and conducting of laboratory tests, and always requires careful consideration of alternative causes. We agree with the defendants that performance of physical examinations, taking of medical histories, and employment of laboratory tests all provide significant evidence of a reliable differential diagnosis, and that their absence makes it much less likely that a differential diagnosis is reliable.[83]

The *Paoli* court noted that a clinician does not have to employ *all* of these techniques for a differential diagnosis to be reliable, however. The court held that where one of the plaintiff's experts had either examined the plaintiff or reviewed the plaintiff's medical records and considered alternative causation, her testimony would be admissible.

The *Paoli* court was emphatic, however, that a medical expert may not rely simply upon a plaintiff's own self-report of symptoms and causation. It affirmed the exclusion of the testimony of one physician who had simply given the plaintiffs a written questionnaire and based his diagnosis on the answers

---

[81] 35 F.3d 717 (3d Cir. 1994), *cert. denied sub nom.* General Elec. Co. v. Ingram, 513 U.S. 1190 (1995).

[82] *Id.* at 759.

[83] *Id.* at 758.

given by the plaintiffs. It described such questionnaires as "an unreliable source of information."[84] Other courts similarly have condemned plaintiffs' experts' failure to employ differential diagnosis to take into account the potential impact of alternative psychosocial stressors on a plaintiff's mental condition.[85]

Nonetheless, many plaintiffs' experts—particularly those who were initially engaged to provide therapy—fail to take a comprehensive patient history or to review records. They may diagnose the plaintiff as suffering from one or more mental disorders based upon the plaintiff's self-report of symptoms and then simply endorse the plaintiff's view that workplace events were the sole cause of the emotional difficulties, without conducting any independent inquiry into alternative causation. There is nothing at all scientific about such an approach, however. In *Huey v. United Parcel Service Inc.*[86] a "forensic vocational expert" with a Ph.D. in human resource development was prevented by the district court from testifying that the employer retaliated against the plaintiff for his prior claim of discrimination. On appeal, the Seventh Circuit condemned the unscientific approach employed by the expert: "[The expert] did not do anything except talk to [the plaintiff], read documents [the plaintiff's] counsel sent, and write a letter. . . . Asked if he did more than accept [the plaintiff's] view that UPS retaliated, [the expert] replied, 'I think he's the one that [sic] best knows what happened in the situation.' This will not do as the work of an expert."[87]

Misuse of Psychological Testing

An increasing number of mental health experts on both sides in wrongful discharge, employment discrimination, and sexual harassment cases use a variety of psychological testing instruments in the course of evaluating a plaintiff's mental condition. Psychological tests are commonly *mis*used in employment

---

[84] *Id.* at 762–63.

[85] *See, e.g.,* Mancuso v. Consolidated Edison Co., 967 F. Supp. 1437, 1451 (S.D.N.Y. 1997) (failure of plaintiffs' expert to employ differential diagnosis "is particularly disturbing in light of the common nature of many of the plaintiffs' complaints"); Alberts v. Wickes Lumber Co., 69 FEP Cases 304, 306 (N.D. Ill. 1995) (condemning plaintiff's expert's acceptance of plaintiff's version of events as true and failing to consider other possible causes of plaintiff's condition). *See also* Borawick v. Shay, 68 F.3d 597, 609 (2d Cir.) (in part because there was no record of the procedures that the plaintiff's expert used, the expert's testimony was excluded because the court had no means, independent of the expert's testimony, to determine whether or not appropriate methodology was applied), *cert. denied*, 517 U.S. 1229 (1996); Sanfelice v. Dominick's Finer Foods Inc., 1995 WL 608602 (N.D. Ill. 1995) (court considered *Daubert* challenge to expert's alleged failure to follow accepted methodology for diagnosis of PTSD, but found that expert followed methodology).

[86] 165 F.3d 1084 (7th Cir. 1999).

[87] *Id.* at 1086.

litigation, however. The expert on the stand may opine that psychological testing "proves" that the plaintiff suffered severe emotional injury at the hands of the defendant employer. Such testimony often may sound impressive to a jury and can be difficult to rebut. A thorough grasp of *Daubert* and an understanding of the methods and limits of psychological testing, however, can assist counsel in preventing the trier of fact from being misled by testimony that is in fact scientifically worthless.

Psychological testing may be misapplied in a number of ways. Some of the more common examples are explored further here.

Lack of Expert's Qualifications in Testing

For a psychological test to be valid, the examiner must be qualified to administer and interpret the test. Psychologists typically are the most highly qualified experts with respect to psychological testing. Every psychologist has a unique pattern of professional training, however, so competency cannot be presumed. For example, many psychologists whose primary interest is in psychotherapy or research do not maintain their proficiency in psychological testing (in some cases, they never developed expertise in the first place). Most psychiatrists, social workers, marriage and family counselors, and pastoral counselors have little or no expertise in psychological testing. As courts have held that an expert's qualifications may properly be the subject of a *Daubert* challenge,[88] a clinician who lacks training and expertise in psychological testing might thus be prevented from testifying about psychological test results.[89]

It is not uncommon, moreover, for psychiatrists and other clinicians who are not experts in test interpretation to administer the Minnesota Multiphasic Personality Inventory-2 (MMPI-2) and have it interpreted by a commercial scoring service that provides them with an interpretive report. These experts are vulnerable to cross-examination due to a lack of understanding of test methodology, unfamiliarity with the contents of the test, misunderstanding of the meaning of the interpretive report, inability to answer questions about the significance of specific scores, and the like.

Some clinicians will attempt to circumvent such cross-examination by claiming that these tests are analogous to a laboratory test. They will assert that they know how to interpret the results of the tests even if they are not familiar with the manner in which the tests are scored and interpreted. An enterprising opponent might obtain the plaintiff's raw test data from such a clinician, submit it to several different scoring services, and point out that the interpretations vary depending on which scoring service is used. Experts who

---

[88] *See, e.g.*, Isley v. Capuchin Province, 877 F. Supp. 1055, 1063 (E.D. Mich. 1995).

[89] In *Gier v. Educational Service Unit No. 16*, 845 F. Supp. 1342, 1351 (D. Neb. 1994), *aff'd*, 66 F.3d 940 (8th Cir. 1995), the court excluded testimony about the results of psychological testing in part because the examiners lacked adequate training in the tests administered.

rely on external scoring and interpretation services often are at a loss when confronted with such results and are unable to explain contradictory interpretations.

Lack of Scientific Basis in the Test

Although some tests such as the MMPI are grounded in the scientific method and have been validated extensively, many other psychological testing instruments used in employment litigation are of dubious scientific validity. Examples of tests that have little or no scientific basis in the forensic context are the so-called "projective" tests—Human Figure Drawings, the Thematic Apperception Test, Sentence Completion Tests, and the Rorschach Ink Blot Test. Examiners using these instruments have plaintiffs draw pictures of houses or people or trees, or make up sentences and stories, or describe what they see in a series of ambiguous ink blots, and then claim that they can reliably and validly measure emotional distress by interpreting this material. These tests are so subjective in nature, however, that they permit the examiner to base virtually any opinion upon results of the test.

Other instruments are merely inventories of symptoms that purport to measure the quality of a plaintiff's life but which by their nature are so subjective and prone to manipulation that they are scientifically worthless. Many of these instruments carry impressive-sounding titles such as "Emotional Distress Rating Scale" or "Loss of Enjoyment of Life Quantitative Scale," but these questionnaires often are written by the clinicians who administer them and have not been validated. Many of these questionnaires in fact are merely checklists that ask leading questions suggesting the existence of symptoms that the plaintiff might not otherwise list. Unfortunately, many courts fail to appreciate the complete lack of scientific basis inherent in these instruments. They may conclude that if the examiner felt the instrument to have been helpful in reaching a diagnosis, the test result should be admitted. This sort of an approach is not only inconsistent with *Daubert*, but it is highly dangerous in that a jury may believe that what in reality is just a description of the plaintiff's self-reported symptoms carries the mantle of scientific proof derived from a methodologically sound test.

One recent case in which such a self-report inventory was rejected as inconsistent with *Daubert* is *McGuire v. City of Santa Fe.*[90] In that case, a psychologist designed and administered a "Lost Pleasure of Life Scale" to a plaintiff in an employment lawsuit and, in conjunction with an economist, determined that the defendants' harassment and termination of the plaintiff caused between $1,430,000 and $2,300,000 worth of "lost enjoyment of life." The court noted that *Daubert* requires that any methodology that lies at the root of expert testimony must have an acceptable error rate, and then observed of the test instrument at issue:

---

[90]954 F. Supp. 230 (D.N.M. 1996).

> Dr. Murphy's report states the "Lost Pleasure of Life Scale," which she used to calculate the relevant percentages to be attributed to Plaintiff's hedonic losses, "has been found to be moderately reliable and that moderate reliability and validity means that results are greater than chance." This is hardly a quantifiable error rate and it hardly seems useful to provide the fact finder with "expert" testimony on figures that are only touted as slightly more reliable than those which might be drawn out of a hat.[91]

A *Daubert* challenge therefore may be raised with regard to an opponent's attempted use of instruments that do not constitute scientifically valid tests. Should the court reject such a challenge and allow the results of such instruments to be admitted, the examiner should be vigorously cross-examined so that the instruments might be demystified for the jury. For example, the actual ink blots used in the Rorschach, or the pictures of houses or trees drawn by the plaintiff, might be shown to the jury at the same time the expert is questioned closely about how he or she was able to reach diagnostic conclusions from such materials. The speculative nature of such testimony soon should become apparent. Similarly, symptom checklists completed by the plaintiff should be shown to the jury, to demonstrate that they largely consist of leading questions and to make it obvious how any plaintiff seeking to obtain emotional distress damages in a lawsuit might answer them.

Improper Test Administration

For the results of a psychological test to be valid, the test must be administered correctly. Correct administration of a psychological test requires careful control over how, where, and when the test is taken.

A psychological test should be administered in a clinical setting under the examiner's supervision; it should never be sent home with the subject for completion. The subject may become distracted while taking the test, may receive assistance with the test from family or friends, or may even be coached by the subject's own therapist or attorney. A plaintiff whose own expert or treating therapist has conducted psychological testing should be questioned closely in discovery concerning the conditions under which the test was administered. If the test was not properly administered in a clinical setting, a *Daubert* challenge to the admissibility of the test result should be considered.

Correct instructions also are essential if test results are to be valid. For example, in administering the MMPI-2, the correct procedure is to instruct the subject to answer in terms of his or her current condition at the time of testing, not his or her condition during or immediately after the events that led to the litigation.

Finally, some examiners give only portions of a test instead of the entire test. Although there are certain circumstances in which this may be appropriate, some experts engage in highly questionable practices, such as testing only for

---

[91]*Id.* at 233.

their predetermined conclusions, and omitting the parts of the test that address malingering or preexisting conditions. An example would be the expert who administers only the PTSD scale of the MMPI-2, omitting the validity scales and questions dealing with chronic personality problems. These practices produce results that are highly vulnerable to attack.

Improper Test Scoring

Psychological test scoring is done either by hand or via computer. Either method of scoring is prone to error, however. Counsel therefore should obtain the raw test data and have it re-scored by a reliable scoring method. Should such a re-scoring reveal errors in the original scoring, the opposing expert's conclusions based upon those erroneous scores obviously would be suspect.

Improper Test Interpretation

Interpretation is the process of determining what test scores mean. Psychological test scores are sometimes misinterpreted in employment cases.

For example, some experts—particularly those lacking sufficient training in interpretation of the MMPI-2—may attempt to interpret each clinical scale by itself, or may interpret only selected scales, such as the depression scale. This kind of select interpretation is unscientific and improper.[92] For a valid interpretation of the MMPI-2 to occur, its clinical scales must be interpreted together.

It is important to note that many psychological tests do not clarify whether the subject's condition is the result of workplace events, or instead is preexisting. Psychological testing cannot prove causation. An MMPI-2 result indicating that the plaintiff is depressed, for example, does not constitute proof that being fired or harassed caused the depression. It is just as reasonable to assume that the plaintiff suffers from a chronic and preexisting depression. Attempts by litigants to use psychological test results as proof that a workplace incident caused the plaintiff to suffer a mental disorder are scientifically invalid.

Psychopathology revealed on psychological tests, moreover, is not equivalent to vocational impairment. The fact that a plaintiff may have a number of psychological problems does not necessarily mean that the plaintiff is disabled from working. There are many individuals with serious psychological problems who work full time, often at a high level of performance. Psychopathology may affect the subjective happiness and personal relationships of a person without preventing that person from working. Although there are a number of tests that measure vocational abilities, it is scientifically suspect for an expert to testify that, based upon test results indicating the presence of psychopathology, the plaintiff is unable to work.

---

[92]*See* P. Lees-Haley & J. McDonald, *The Use (and Misuse) of Psychological Testing in Employment Litigation*, 23 EMPLOYEE RELATIONS L.J. 37, 49 (1997).

Some tests, such as the MMPI-2, contain their own validity scales to ensure that a particular administration of the test is valid. There are numerous influences that may cause tests to produce invalid results. Lack of cooperation, drug or alcohol intoxication, medical illnesses, psychological disorders interfering with test performance, malingering, illiteracy, cultural characteristics, improper test administration, and inappropriate testing conditions may each possibly lead to an invalid test administration. Some experts will either disregard validity scale results on the MMPI-2 indicating an invalid profile or characterize an invalid profile as a "cry for help" and attempt to use a malingered profile as evidence of injury. There is no empirical research in the scientific literature supporting the "cry for help" hypothesis; it is merely the product of clinical folklore.[93]

Other Issues

Coaching

Coaching of plaintiffs by their attorneys in preparing for the mental examination or psychological testing is an increasing problem.[94] For example, one recent survey found that 63 percent of attorneys surveyed felt that they should provide clients with information about psychological test validity measures (47 percent of attorneys surveyed believed that they should "always or usually" provide such information to their clients before the testing, and another 16 percent said that they should "sometimes" do so). Of the 63 percent of attorneys who believed they should provide such information, 42 percent said that they should provide as much as possible and another 42 percent said that they believed they should provide a "moderate" amount of information.[95]

The validity of a psychologist's expert opinions based upon psychological test results obviously may be compromised by attorney coaching. The outcome of coaching may be that the expert's results mislead rather than inform the trier of fact.

Coaching with respect to psychological testing may be prevented to an extent by refusing to divulge to the opposition in advance the identity of the tests to be administered during the Rule 35 mental examination. In *Ragge v.*

---

[93]*See* R. Greene, *Assessment of Malingering and Defensiveness by Objective Personality Inventories,* in CLINICAL ASSESSMENT OF MALINGERING AND DECEPTION 149–50 (R. Rogers ed., 1988).

[94]*See, e.g.*, R. Baer et al., *Effects of Information About Validity Scales on Underreporting of Symptoms on the MMPI-2: An Analogue Investigation*, 2 ASSESSMENT 189 (1995); M. Youngjohn, *Confirmed Attorney Coaching Prior to Neuropsychological Evaluation*, 2 ASSESSMENT 279 (1995).

[95]J. Wetter & B. Corrigan, *Providing Information to Clients About Psychological Tests: A Survey of Attorneys' and Law Students' Attitudes*, 26 PROF. PSYCHOLOGY: RES. & PRAC. 474 (1995).

MCA/Universal Studios,[96] for example, the court refused to order the defense examiner to disclose in advance the specific psychological tests to be administered. Certainly, requests by plaintiffs' counsel for copies of tests to be administered during the Rule 35 examination must be vigorously resisted; the defense examiner may cite in support the ethical requirement of psychologists to maintain the integrity and security of psychological tests.[97]

Although questioning of a plaintiff concerning whether his or her attorney provided coaching concerning the symptoms necessary to support a particular diagnosis is likely to draw an objection based upon the attorney–client privilege, one authority points out that another way to get at this issue is to ask the plaintiff's expert and/or treating therapist on cross-examination: "Doctor, did you attempt to determine whether Plaintiff's attorney explained to him what the symptoms of PTSD are?"[98] As this authority notes: "This does not ask for privileged information, it only concerns the adequacy of the methodology of the examination."[99]

Failure to Take and Maintain Notes

Recently, a trend has emerged among plaintiff's experts of not taking extensive notes of the history of patients who are involved in employment litigation, so as to prevent discovery by defense counsel of potential alternative stressors.[100] This practice is not only a blatant breach of professional ethics for the clinician, but it also amounts to a fraud on the court.

There is an ethical code that applies to psychologists engaged in forensic practice. It is known as the Specialty Guidelines for Forensic Psychologists, and it was promulgated by Division 41 of the American Psychological Association and the American Board of Forensic Psychology. Section VI.B of the Specialty Guidelines provides:

> Forensic psychologists have an obligation to document and be prepared to make available, subject to court order or the rules of evidence, all data that form the basis for their evidence or services. The standard to be applied to such documentation or recording *anticipates* that the detail and quality of such documentation will be subject to reasonable judicial scrutiny; this standard is higher than the normative standard for general clinical practice. When forensic psychologists conduct an examination or engage in treatment of a party to a legal proceeding, with foreknowledge that their professional services will be used in an adjudicative forum,

---

[96] 165 F.R.D. 605 (C.D. Cal. 1995).

[97] American Psychological Association, Ethical Principles of Psychologists and Code of Conduct §2.10 (1992).

[98] J. Ziskin, Coping with Psychiatric and Psychological Testimony 107 (5th ed. Supp. 1997).

[99] *Id.*

[100] *See Importance of Dealings With Psychologists in Harassment Cases Is Stressed by Panel*, 3 Employment Discrimination Rep. (BNA) 52–53 (July 13, 1994).

they incur a special responsibility to provide the best documentation possible under the circumstances.[101]

Psychologists and other mental health professionals who fail or refuse to take adequate history and treatment notes may therefore be in violation of ethical requirements governing their profession, and their entire testimony may be vulnerable to challenge under *Daubert* as a result. Even putting aside ethical considerations, for a clinician to consciously refrain from inquiring about and recording potential alternative stressors violates fundamental principles of clinical practice and is decidedly unscientific.

Academic Studies Purporting to Prove That Sexual Harassment Causes Mental Disorders

Mental health professionals who testify that a plaintiff suffered significant psychological injury as the result of sexual harassment in the workplace sometimes base their opinions on academic studies supposedly demonstrating that sexual harassment "causes" various types of mental disorders. This can be problematic from both a legal[102] and a scientific standpoint.

Although there are a number of academic studies that purport to find a link between sexual harassment and psychological injury, they lack the scientific grounding necessary to satisfy the test for admissibility under the Supreme Court's decision in *Daubert*. Quite simply, there is no reliable scientific evidence proving that sexual harassment causes mental disorders. One of the leading researchers in this field recently admitted as much when she conceded: "It is admittedly the case that scientifically defensible linkages between harassment behaviors . . . and [their] outcomes have been more hypothesized than demonstrated."[103] Others have pointed out that most studies to date have "used samples of convenience or special populations, utilized terms that were not operationally defined, and contained nonstandardized measures of psychological or physical distress. In other words, few well-controlled investigations in this area have been conducted."[104]

---

[101]Committee on Ethical Guidelines for Forensic Psychologists, *Specialty Guidelines for Forensic Psychologists*, reprinted in Main Volume at 168–75.

[102]*See* United States v. Rouse, 111 F.3d 561, 571 (8th Cir.) (district court was well within its discretion in ruling that psychological expert should not embellish his own research and opinions by telling the jury about the research and writings of other psychologists because these works have not produced a consistent body of scientific knowledge and therefore admission of other theories and writings would result in a battle of experts that could confuse or even mislead the jury), *cert. denied*, 118 S. Ct. 261 (1997).

[103]L. Fitzgerald et al., *Antecedents and Consequences of Sexual Harassment in Organizations: A Test of an Integrated Model*, 81 J. App. Psychology 1, 11 (1997).

[104]B. Dansky & D. Kilpatrick, *Effects of Sexual Harassment*, in Sexual Harassment: Theory, Research and Treatment 152, 154 (W. O'Donohue ed., 1997).

As another article acknowledges:

> Carefully controlled studies of effects of harassment have not been done. Information about impacts comes primarily from self-reported effects included in prevalence studies, convenience samples, specialized populations such as victims who have filed complaints or visited a counseling center, and anecdotal accounts of harassment. This review of outcomes yields a list of possible effects but does not allow conclusions about their prevalence or the conditions under which any particular effect will occur.[105]

There is a series of significant hurdles that thus far have prevented researchers from demonstrating a relationship between sexual harassment and psychological symptomatology. These include definitional problems, selection bias, accurately describing and measuring the pathology, variability of effect, and alternative causation. All are discussed below.

Definitional Problems

There is no generally accepted definition of sexual harassment in the scientific community. The nature and extent of the traumatic event must be reasonably well understood, however, if experts wish to assert that they know how it is related to psychological symptoms. To answer basic questions about the prevalence, incidence, or effects of sexual harassment, it is necessary to define it reliably. Unreliable definitions thwart efforts to conduct quality scientific research, and they may lead to abuse and exploitation in legal contexts.

For example, one recent definition by a leading authority in this area concededly is so broad as to assume that "all sexist or sexual behaviors constitute harassment when they occur within the framework of a formal power differential, since the woman is not considered able either to consent or to resist freely."[106] Among other things, such an overbroad definition ignores the fact that truly consensual romantic relationships sometimes do develop between a supervisor and a subordinate, and it rather oddly declares that all workplace conduct of a sexual nature is necessarily sexual harassment, whether or not it is actually perceived as such by the recipient.[107] Such an extreme definition of sexual harassment is neither consistent with the law[108] nor scientifically useful.

---

[105]B. Gutek & M. Koss, *Changed Women and Changed Organizations: Consequences and Coping With Sexual Harassment*, 42 J. Vocational Behav. 28, 31 (1993).

[106]L. Fitzgerald & A. Ormerod, *Breaking Silence: The Sexual Harassment of Women in Academia and the Workplace*, in Psychology of Women 553, 556 (F. Denmark & M. Paludi eds., 1993).

[107]*See also* N. Betz & L. Fitzgerald, The Career Psychology of Women 245 (1987) ("Other studies seem to imply that if a behavior is not perceived to be harassment, then it is not. Such interpretations are clearly incorrect").

[108]Although the law defining what constitutes sexual harassment is not entirely clear, what is clear is that not all workplace conduct or conversations of a sexual nature are unlawful harassment. To be unlawful, workplace sexual harassment must be so severe or pervasive as to create a hostile or offensive working environment for a

Overbroad definitions are scientifically problematic because the scope of the definition necessarily will affect the outcome of the research. From a purely epidemiological standpoint, if a broad definition is used (as is mostly the case in research conducted to date), the research will likely result in a finding that harassment is less pervasive than might be supposed. Taken a step further, where the purpose of a study is to determine the effects of sexual harassment, an overbroad definition of sexual harassment will likely result in a finding (assuming a totally objective study) of fewer adverse effects. This is because victims of such relatively harmless conduct as "suggestive looks" and nonoffensive flirtation by co-workers are unlikely to have suffered resulting psychopathology.

Thus, until the scientific community can agree on a common definition of sexual harassment (which may be difficult, given the legal community's lack of success so far in this regard), meaningful research on the psychological effects of sexual harassment will be impossible. As one authority in the field of sexual harassment research admits:

> Since definitions are the source of operationalizations, each new study has tended to develop its own methodology, yielding a literature that is littered with conflicting estimates of incidence rates, behaviors and other forms of noncomparable data. Among the problems that this has created has been the diminished credibility of these studies within the legal system. . . .[109]

This glaring defect in the state of sexual harassment research causes such research to fall far short of the *Daubert* standard requiring that evidence of this nature be scientifically valid.

Selection Bias

Any valid study must select its subjects as randomly as possible. Yet most research on sexual harassment depends heavily on samples of self-identified victims.[110] For example, one oft-cited study used as its sample women who had sought assistance or counseling relating to sexual harassment from the "Working Women's Institute."[111] Not surprisingly, 90 percent of the respondents in that study complained of psychopathology.[112] Numerous studies concerning the effects of sexual harassment similarly chose as their subjects persons who had already identified themselves as victims of harassment. These subjects obviously had a heightened interest in the topic, and the possibility that their responses might have been skewed by a desire to achieve certain external legal

---

reasonable person of the same gender as the plaintiff. *See* Harris v. Forklift Sys. Inc., 114 S. Ct. 367, 370–71 (1993); Ellison v. Brady, 924 F.2d 872 (9th Cir. 1991).

[109]Fitzgerald & Ormerod, *supra* note 106, at 554.

[110]*Id.* at 574.

[111]P. Crull, *Stress Effects of Sexual Harassment on the Job: Implications for Counseling*, 52 AM. J. ORTHOPSYCHIATRY 539, 540 (1982).

[112]*Id.*

or therapeutic objectives, such as pursuing a lawsuit for damages or qualifying for counseling or treatment under a health insurance plan, cannot be ignored.

Telephone and mail surveys may appear more random in nature, in that targets may be selected blindly. The appearance of randomness is only superficial, however, because those subjects who choose to participate in the survey may do so on account of their own biases and experiences. Not everyone who is invited agrees to participate in research, and it is doubtful that volunteers who accept are entirely unbiased. For example, several studies have established that pro-feminist attitudes increase the likelihood that sexual harassment will be perceived.[113] Where participation in a survey is voluntary, those who have never felt harassed, and those who may have felt harassed but who dealt with it effectively and experienced no resulting psychopathology, may not be inclined to participate. Likewise, individuals who are skeptical of the importance of the issues surveyed are less likely to respond.

A truly scientific study of the psychological effects of sexual harassment would be one in which the people studied are selected *prospectively* at random and observed over a period of time, and in which those who are harassed during that time are compared with those who are not. The psychological functioning of persons who experienced harassment would then be compared with the psychological functioning of persons who did not experience harassment. Although relatively straightforward in principle, such a study would require a complex experimental model that may well be too costly and time-consuming to carry out. The difficulty and costs associated with constructing a scientifically valid experiment cannot justify reliance on scientifically invalid evidence, however.

Describing and Measuring Psychopathology

A further defect in the present research is that it does not describe and measure with sufficient precision the psychopathology that is said to result from sexual harassment. There is almost no literature comparing the assessment procedures among various investigators to establish that they possess a shared reliable methodology for measuring the extent of emotional distress caused by sexual harassment. Moreover, to date, no studies based on in-person interviews have been published;[114] all have relied on written or oral surveys. The obvious problem is that a survey respondent's subjective report of symptomatology may not necessarily meet the criteria for a diagnosable mental disorder that must ordinarily be applied by an experienced clinician in the course of a face-to-face clinical interview. A respondent's survey response indicating that she felt "depressed" following an episode of sexual harassment is not the same as a clinician's diagnosis of major depression, yet research surveys conducted to

---

[113]Fitzgerald & Ormerod, *supra* note 106, at 561.

[114]L. Fitzgerald & S. Shullman, *Sexual Harassment: A Research Analysis and Agenda for the 1990's*, 42 J. VOCATIONAL BEHAV. 5, 11 (1993).

date tend to equate the two. To draw the conclusion from such a study that sexual harassment causes depression is scientifically invalid.

Some studies use terms so general as to be meaningless; for example, "general tension" and "nervousness."[115] Although tension and nervousness—or anger, irritability, or similar reactions usually listed on surveys in sexual harassment research—may be associated with mental disorders, they are not themselves mental disorders or necessarily even *symptoms* of mental disorders. These sorts of surveys merely support the unremarkable proposition that victims of sexual harassment may experience some unpleasant reactions. They do not, however, support a conclusion that sexual harassment causes mental disorders. As such, they cannot validly be relied on by an expert witness to support an opinion that sexual harassment caused the plaintiff to suffer distress or impairment.

Variability of Effect

Although various stressors (such as overhearing a dirty joke, a boss's sexual proposition, or a sexual assault) may be rank-ordered in the aggregate by their relative severity,[116] it is not scientifically valid to assume such data to confirm that a specific individual suffered a specific psychological injury as a result of a particular stressor.

This is because various events that might be termed sexual harassment affect different individuals in vastly different ways, depending on a host of factors including the individual's background, ideology,[117] and coping mechanisms. An incident that one individual might shrug off without a second thought might cause another individual to suffer a serious psychological injury. Thus, even if there *were* a scientifically valid study (which there is not) proving that in the aggregate, sexual harassment more often than not causes depression, it would be of limited utility in proving that one particular plaintiff suffered a clinical depression following an incident of sexual harassment.

Alternative Causation

Alternative explanations are rarely explored in any depth in research exploring the psychological effects of sexual harassment. Researchers often just assume

---

[115] Crull, *supra* note 111, at 541.

[116] P. Lees-Haley et al., *Sexual Harassment and Emotional Distress: A Ranking of Social-Sexual Behavior*, 15 AM. J. FORENSIC PSYCHIATRY 5 (1994).

[117] As one set of researchers recently observed:

> [C]onsiderable data exist suggesting that attitude and belief sets may influence victim appraisal in important ways. For example, [one study] found that victims' feminist ideology was a predictor of the perceived offensiveness of harassing behaviors, with women who identified more strongly as feminist generally finding harassment to be more offensive.

L. Fitzgerald et al., *But Was It Really Sexual Harassment?,* in SEXUAL HARASSMENT: THEORY, RESEARCH AND TREATMENT 5, 19 (W. O'Donohue ed., 1997).

that because a respondent claims both to have been harassed and to have suffered psychopathology, sexual harassment caused the psychopathology. For example, one study noted that 37 percent of women suffering from PTSD and 31 percent of women suffering from depression reported that they had been told "sex stories" by a supervisor (compared with 17 percent who did not suffer from PTSD or depression but had been told "sex stories"), and then concluded that

> [w]omen suffering from PTSD and depression were more likely to have been sexually harassed than women who have never experienced PTSD or depression, suggesting that sexual harassment may contribute to depression and PTSD.[118]

This sort of reasoning is incorrect. It is equally plausible that the PTSD and depression existed prior to the sexual harassment, and it is even possible that preexisting PTSD caused a hypersensitivity to sexual cues that led the subject to believe that she was being sexually harassed where a "reasonable woman" of normal sensitivities would not have felt harassed.

In most instances, psychological problems have more than one cause. For example, a test subject who indicates that she suffers from depression and that she was sexually harassed may well have suffered from depression prior to the incident of harassment. Most cases of chronic severe depression are the result of complex causative factors, not the result of a single incident or even a few episodes of boorish behavior by a boss or co-worker. Yet no study conducted to date concerning the psychological effects of sexual harassment has accounted for the possibility that the symptomatology reported by the subjects in the study might have been caused by other stressors.

This problem cannot be solved, moreover, by asking survey respondents simply if they suffered from depression (or any other mental disorder) prior to the incident of harassment. Lay survey respondents would not be qualified to make such a diagnosis, even if they had complete recall and were wholly objective. Such a determination may validly be made only in a clinical setting by an experienced examiner.

Thus, because current research confuses correlation with causation and relies on self-reporting, it is not a scientifically valid means of determining whether sexual harassment causes specific mental disorders. Attempts by mental health experts to rely upon such research may be attacked as inconsistent with *Daubert*.

---

[118]B. Gutek & M. Koss, *Changed Women and Changed Organizations: Consequences and Coping With Sexual Harassment*, 42 J. VOCATIONAL BEHAV. 28, 34, (1993).

CHAPTER 12

PREPARING THE CASE FOR THE EXPERT

Counsel's thorough preparation of the case for the expert is essential to a successful resolution. Even the best experts cannot be expected simply to show up with little preparation and give testimony that will win the case. Advance planning and the collection—usually via subpoena—of a considerable amount of background information on the plaintiff are both essential. Close communication with the expert and thorough preparation of the expert's testimony also are very important.

Obtaining the Maximum Benefit from the Expert

Although the expert must maintain professional objectivity to be credible and effective, counsel should not overlook the fact that the expert is an important member of the litigation team.

Formulating the Theory of the Case

The expert can be helpful in developing the theory of the case, not only with respect to emotional damage issues but often with respect to liability issues as well. In fact, it is essential that counsel and the expert communicate early in the case to determine whether the anticipated role for the expert will be consistent with the overall theory of the case. For example, it would be inconsistent for the defense's fact witnesses to claim unequivocally in a sexual harassment case that the acts alleged by the plaintiff never occurred, while the defense's psychiatric expert simultaneously opines that the plaintiff has a personality disorder that causes her to be hypersensitive to sexual cues and to misperceive the actions and motivations of others. A better approach might be to determine whether there was in fact a kernel of truth to the plaintiff's allegations (i.e., that some relatively innocuous comments were in fact made, but that the plaintiff may have misperceived those comments or taken them out of context as a result of her personality disorder). Obviously, such a theory of the case needs to be fully developed before fact witnesses testify under oath at a deposition.

Orientation to the Litigation Process

In addition, if the expert is not experienced in forensic work, counsel should advise the expert in advance concerning the nature of the litigation process, including the unpredictability of court schedules and the nature of cross-examination. The expert should commit in advance to take the time necessary to review all relevant documents prior to the mental examination of the plaintiff, to spend sufficient time conducting the examination, and to devote the time necessary to preparation of deposition and trial testimony. If a potential expert's schedule will not accommodate these time commitments, counsel should consider whether another expert might be more suitable.

The Expert's Background

Counsel also should inquire in advance of designating the expert whether the prospective expert has any blemishes in his or her background that might be exploited by the opposition on cross-examination. Examples include malpractice lawsuits, revocation of licenses or professional discipline, loss of hospital privileges, unpaid student loans, and similar matters. Such matters need not necessarily disqualify an expert, but counsel should be aware of them in advance and be prepared to explain them if they become an issue in the litigation.

Experts from Outside the Jurisdiction

If the expert is coming in from out of town, counsel should ensure that arrangements are made to secure an adequate facility for the conduct of the mental examination of the plaintiff. Another mental health professional's office borrowed for the occasion, an executive suite facility, or a hotel conference room are the best options. Examinations should not be conducted in an attorney's office, as the atmosphere may be too adversarial. Hotel sleeping rooms similarly should be avoided—particularly where the plaintiff and the examiner are of the opposite gender—for obvious reasons.

If the expert will be testifying in a jurisdiction in which he or she is not licensed, counsel must determine whether permission from or notification of the forum jurisdiction's licensing board is required. This is because the conduct of a forensic mental examination and the giving of expert testimony are considered the practice of medicine or psychology in most jurisdictions. Although it is not ordinarily difficult for an out-of-state expert to obtain permission to come into a jurisdiction for the limited purpose of performing a forensic evaluation, the failure to abide by local requirements in this regard could lead to disqualification of the expert.

Financial Arrangements

Finally, counsel and the expert should develop a realistic budget for the cost of the expert's services, particularly if limited funds are available for expert fees. Failure to communicate in this regard can lead to an expert's bill that counsel's client may view as excessive, placing counsel in the difficult position of going into a trial with both an unhappy client and an unhappy expert. Any billing problems must be resolved in advance of trial, moreover. If a party owes its expert a substantial amount of money at the time of trial and this fact is exploited by the opposition, the expert's credibility can suffer in the eyes of the factfinder as it may appear that the expert's ability to collect outstanding fees may be contingent upon the outcome of the trial.

Obtaining Discovery of the Information That the Expert Will Need

As experts do not have subpoena power, it is the obligation of counsel to obtain and provide to the expert all of the documents that the expert will need to conduct a thorough evaluation, such as records, pleadings, deposition transcripts, and the like. These should be provided to the expert *prior* to the mental examination of the plaintiff, if possible, so that the expert can construct a context in which to place the data obtained during the examination. On the other hand, counsel must be careful not to inundate the expert with unnecessary documents, as such will likely just confuse the issues and unnecessarily increase the cost of the expert's services.

Legal Documents to Provide to the Expert

Counsel should provide the expert with the following documents from counsel's own files or as they become available:

- complaint or last amended version
- transcripts of the deposition of the plaintiff
- transcripts of the depositions of key defense witnesses, such as the decision maker in a termination case or the alleged harasser in a harassment case
- any other discovery responses (for example, interrogatory responses, statement of damages) relating to alleged emotional injuries
- transcripts of the depositions of opposing medical and psychological treatment providers and experts

The entire transcript of a particular deposition should be provided. If counsel provides only excerpts of the transcript, the expert could be vulnerable on cross-examination; for example: "Doctor, did you review all the material you considered important, or just that selected information that opposing counsel allowed you to see?"

Records to Obtain and Provide to the Expert

Counsel additionally should obtain and provide the following records to the expert.

Exhibit 12-1S Sample Language for Subpoena for Psychiatric or Psychological Treatment Records

Any and all medical, psychiatric, and psychological records relating to the diagnosis and/or treatment of [NAME OF PLAINTIFF], SSN: __________, DOB: __________. This request includes, but is not limited to, any and all intake documents, patient questionnaires, patient history notes, patient diaries, clinical notes, MMPI/MMPI-2 and all other psychological testing materials (including answer sheets and scoring analyses), laboratory test results, therapy notes, treatment records, medications administered and/or prescriptions written, insurance records, billing records, medical-legal reports, correspondence with attorneys for the patient, records relating to referrals to this patient to other health care providers, reports and records of other health care providers relied upon by you in diagnosing and treating this patient, and any other records or reports pertaining to the treatment and/or evaluation of this patient.

Psychotherapy and Other Treatment Records

Records of all of the plaintiff's treating physician(s) and psychotherapist(s) should be obtained, including patient questionnaires, treatment notes, billing records, and psychological testing materials and answer sheets (see Exhibit 12-1S).

Patient questionnaires should be obtained, because these often contain a detailed account in the plaintiff's own handwriting of family history and even prior sexual abuse; prior major illnesses, hospitalizations, and mental health treatment; and a description of current symptoms.

Treatment notes may reveal a variety of useful information.[1] They often reflect discussions between patient and therapist concerning prior or concurrent alternative stressors, such as childhood sexual abuse or marital discord. They may additionally reflect treatment for medical conditions that produce psychological symptoms; for example, thyroid imbalances. They also may reveal that the patient is taking medications that may produce relevant side effects.

Billing records should be obtained for two purposes. First, they will ordinarily indicate whether the expert is owed any significant amount of money at the time of trial that may indicate a financial bias. Second, billing records should be matched with treatment notes, to ensure that all such notes were produced. If there are billing entries but no therapy notes for particular therapy sessions, further inquiry of the treatment provider should be made.

Psychological testing materials and answer sheets should be obtained so that the tests may be re-scored. Data-entry or hand-scoring errors are not

---

[1]*See* Magee v. Paul Revere Life Ins. Co., 178 F.R.D. 33 (E.D.N.Y. 1998) (where plaintiff's therapist refused to produce treatment notes covering therapy conducted during certain period, therapist was precluded from testifying at trial concerning any aspect of therapy conducted during that period).

uncommon, and sometimes an expert or treatment provider will take only selected portions of a test's results into account in rendering a diagnosis instead of the entire test profile. A re-scoring of the test data and an interpretation of the entire test profile may reveal significant errors in the opposing expert's test interpretation. If the opposing expert or treatment provider refuses on ethical grounds to produce testing materials to counsel, arrangements should be made for the production of such materials directly to counsel's expert.

Exhibit 12-2S Sample Language for Subpoena for Medical Records

Any and all medical, billing, and insurance records related to your admission, diagnosis, evaluation, and/or treatment of [NAME OF PLAINTIFF], SSN: _____________, DOB: _____________. This request includes, but is not limited to, any and all intake documents, patient questionnaires, patient history notes, clinical notes, results, surgical records, radiology reports, laboratory test results, therapy notes, treatment records, medications administered and/or prescriptions written, insurance records, billing records, medical-legal reports, correspondence with attorneys for the patient, records relating to referrals to this patient to other health care providers, reports and records of other health care providers relied upon by you in diagnosing and treating this patient, and any other records or reports pertaining to the treatment and/or evaluation of this patient.

Prior Medical Records

Records should be subpoenaed from the plaintiff's family or general practice physician, other physicians who treated the plaintiff in the past, any providers of prior mental health treatment, and any hospitals in which the plaintiff was treated. These records are essential for determining whether the physical and mental symptoms attributed by the plaintiff to the workplace are not in fact the result of other causes (see Exhibit 12-2S).

For example, many plaintiffs claim that workplace events caused them to suffer depression and/or anxiety. Yet depression and anxiety are often chronic conditions that existed prior to and apart from any specific workplace events. The best evidence of a preexisting depression or anxiety consists of prior medical records reflecting treatment for those conditions. In many cases, such treatment is provided by a primary care physician (family practitioner or internist) or gynecologist. Records from those providers may contain references to patient complaints of depression or anxiety, to referrals to mental health professionals, or to prescriptions for antidepressant or antianxiety medications (see Exhibits 12-3S and 12-4S).

Another type of preexisting depressive condition is bipolar disorder (formerly known as manic-depressive disorder), which is characterized by periods of depression punctuated by episodes of mania. It is commonly treated with lithium carbonate, Eskalith, Tegretol, or Depakote.

Exhibit 12-3S Common Antidepressant Medications

Brand Name	*Generic Name*
Prozac	fluoxetine
Paxil	paroxetine
Zoloft	sertraline
Serzone	nefazodone
Wellbutrin	buproprion
Desyrel	trazodone
Elavil	amitriptyline
Effexor	venlafaxine
Tofranil	imipramine
Pamelor	nortriptyline
Sinequan	doxepin
Luvox	fluvoxamine
Anafranil	clomipramine

Exhibit 12-4S Common Antianxiety Medications

Brand Name	*Generic Name*
Buspar	buspirone
Xanax	alprazolam
Ativan	lorazepam
Librium	chlordiazepoxide
Valium	diazepam
Klonopin	clonazepam
Serax	oxazepam
Tranxene	clorazepate

These (and other) medications often may cause side effects that a plaintiff may misattribute to the workplace. For example, a common side effect of popular antidepressant medications such as Prozac, Paxil, and Zoloft is diminished libido. Often, plaintiffs in employment cases claim that being fired or harassed caused them to lose interest in sex. In such situations, it should be determined whether diminished libido may in fact be attributable to side effects of antidepressant or other medications.

Plaintiffs in employment cases often complain of insomnia as a result of job difficulties or termination. An examination of the plaintiff's medical records should be conducted to determine whether such insomnia preexisted the workplace events at issue. Medications commonly prescribed for insomnia include Halcion, Ambien, Dalmane, ProSom, and Restoril.

Finally, the plaintiff may have a medical disorder that produces psychological symptoms.[2] One such disorder that sometimes appears in employment cases is hyperthyroidism, which also is known as Graves' Disease. Hyperthyroidism, which occurs predominantly in women, results from an overactive thyroid gland and is characterized by symptoms such as tension, agitation, irritability, insomnia, anxiety, and emotional lability. The opposite condition, hypothyroidism, is characterized by symptoms such as fatigue, weakness, depression, and impaired memory and concentration. These conditions are diagnosed via a series of blood tests known as a thyroid panel. Results of these thyroid panels may be found in the records of a plaintiff's primary care physician, gynecologist, internist, or endocrinologist. There are three main tests in the thyroid panel—T3, T4, and TSH (thyroid stimulating hormone). The thyroid panel report is easy to interpret, as most reports indicate the normal range for each test and indicate when a score is out of range. An abnormally high T3 or T4 score, or an abnormally low TSH score, may indicate hyperthyroidism. An abnormally low T3 or T4 score, or an abnormally high TSH score, may indicate hypothyroidism. Any thyroid panel results in a plaintiff's medical records thus should be examined closely, in consultation with a qualified medical practitioner, to determine whether the plaintiff's reported psychiatric symptoms may actually be attributable to a thyroid condition.

Another common condition in women is mitral valve prolapse, which is a heart valve abnormality that causes the heart to race and the person to experience anxiety and even panic attacks. As one authority recently noted, "every patient who presents with panic or generalized anxiety disorder should be asked about prior cardiac history."[3] Thus, where a plaintiff complains that the workplace caused her to suffer anxiety or "panic attacks," her medical records should be examined for evidence of mitral valve prolapse.

Records of prior hospitalizations also should be examined, to determine whether the plaintiff suffered a prior trauma or serious illness that may have produced lingering emotional symptoms. Hospitalizations resulting from prior sexual assaults or domestic violence ordinarily would be extremely relevant in a sexual harassment lawsuit. Certainly, records of any prior psychiatric hospitalizations should be scrutinized carefully for evidence of suicidal behavior, psychotic episodes, chronic depressive conditions, and substance abuse.

Personnel Records

The plaintiff's personnel files from current and prior employers should be obtained and provided to the expert (see Exhibit 12-5S). Personnel files frequently contain valuable information concerning the plaintiff's behavior in other workplaces that might provide clues to the existence of a personality disorder or other psychopathology. Performance evaluations from prior employers, for example, might contain admissions by the plaintiff concerning certain personality traits relevant to the instant litigation, such as difficulty getting

---

[2]*See* E. KLONOFF & H. LANDRINE, PREVENTING MISDIAGNOSIS OF WOMEN (1997).
[3]*Id.* at 81.

along with co-workers and supervisors. Multiple complaints of harassment or unfair treatment in prior jobs may indicate hypersensitivity or a "victimlike" mentality. Varying employment histories given on different employment applications may evidence a deceptive or evasive quality. Multiple job terminations for misconduct might reveal an antisocial personality, whereas an unstable pattern of moving from job to job in a variety of industries may suggest an identity disturbance characteristic of a borderline personality.

Exhibit 12-5S Sample Language for Subpoena for Personnel Records

All documents contained in the personnel file of [NAME OF PLAINTIFF], SSN: ____________, DOB: ____________, including, but not limited to, all documents reflecting terms of employment, employment applications, resumes, documents reflecting compensation and earnings, benefits, job duties, discipline, reasons for leaving, internal complaints or grievances, and any claims or lawsuits filed against your organization by this individual.

Exhibit 12-6S Sample Language for Subpoena for School Records

Any and all academic records pertaining to [NAME OF PLAINTIFF], SSN: ____________, DOB: ____________, including, but not limited to, academic transcripts, disciplinary records, counseling records, and attendance records.

Educational Records

The plaintiff's high school and college records should be obtained (see Exhibit 12-6S). Dropouts, disciplinary problems, and teenage substance abuse may be evidence of a personality disorder. For example, the American Psychiatric Association notes that "[i]ndividuals with Borderline Personality Disorder may have a pattern of undermining themselves at the moment a goal is about to be realized (e.g., dropping out of school just before graduation)."[4] Similarly, diagnosis of Antisocial Personality Disorder requires evidence of a conduct disorder (such as aggression to people or animals, destruction of property, deceitfulness or theft, or serious rule violations) prior to age 15.[5] Although subpoenas for such records sometimes will draw an objection that a plaintiff's

---

[4]American Psychiatric Association, Diagnostic and Statistical Manual of Mental Disorders 652 (4th ed. 1994).

[5]*Id.* at 650.

educational records are too remote in time to be relevant to the issues in an employment lawsuit later in adult life, it is precisely because they are so remote that they are so relevant. Personality disorders, by definition, begin in adolescence or early adulthood.[6] Although educational records are not by any means the only vehicle for diagnosing personality disorders, they can provide a key form of confirmation that a plaintiff's dysfunctional behavior and psychiatric symptomatology are the result of a personality disorder that long preexisted the plaintiff's entry into the defendant employer's workplace.

Records of Divorce and Child Custody Proceedings

Court files in divorce cases may contain relevant information on the plaintiff's background, such as financial problems, prior mental health treatment, and even criminal activity. Affidavits given in support of motions for protective orders may contain information about the other spouse's violent tendencies, emotional instability, or substance abuse problems. Of course, the source of such information must be taken into account. Accusations launched in the midst of a bitter divorce may not be the most reliable source of information on a plaintiff, but they might at least provide valuable leads for further investigation.

Information relating to a plaintiff's ex-spouse's violent or abusive behavior also might reveal that the plaintiff is displacing the undesirable traits of the ex-spouse onto an accused harasser in the workplace.

Records of contested child custody proceedings, although sealed in some jurisdictions, may contain considerable detail of a plaintiff's prior emotional and substance abuse problems. They also may contain reports of formal psychiatric or psychological evaluations performed to determine the plaintiff's fitness as a parent. These reports also may contain valuable information about a plaintiff's mental health treatment history.

Prior Criminal and Civil Litigation Files

Civil and criminal index searches ordinarily should be run on a plaintiff. A criminal history not only may be relevant to possible impeachment of the plaintiff's trial testimony, it may suggest the existence of a personality disorder, particularly where theft, violence, or substance abuse is involved.

A plaintiff's prior civil lawsuits may reveal a pattern of similar behavior with other employers. A plaintiff who claims to have experienced the same kind of harassment or discrimination at the hands of several unrelated employers may suffer from more than just unfortunate coincidence. In addition, transcripts of the plaintiff's depositions in other recent lawsuits should be subpoenaed from the court reporting service or one of the lawyers involved. Such transcripts may reveal not only a similar fact pattern to that in the instant litigation, they may also contain sworn testimony that the plaintiff suffered severe and debilitating emotional distress as a result of the acts of another defendant, thus constituting fairly potent evidence of alternative causation.

---

[6] *Id.* at 629.

Workers' Compensation Files

A number of employment lawsuits are preceded by, or proceed concurrently with, a workers' compensation proceeding involving some of the same issues of emotional injury. The file relating to the workers' compensation proceeding may include psychiatric reports on the plaintiff, including psychological test results. Also, the plaintiff may have given testimony at a hearing or deposition in the workers' compensation case that may be inconsistent with the theory of the plaintiff's case in the subsequent lawsuit. If the plaintiff has initiated a workers' compensation proceeding, all files relating to that proceeding therefore should be obtained.

CASE EXAMPLE

The plaintiff in a sexual harassment lawsuit claimed to have suffered severe emotional injuries causing her to be unable to work for two years, to be hospitalized in a psychiatric institution, and even to have attempted suicide. Yet a review of the records of her most recent psychiatric hospitalization revealed that the plaintiff told intake personnel that "family problems" were the cause of her most recent suicide attempt. The court file relating to her prior divorce and child custody case contained an affidavit of her ex-husband that described an earlier suicide attempt and psychiatric hospitalization, as well as her participation in a drug rehabilitation program. Records of her gynecologist revealed that she suffered two miscarriages during the last 18 months. Her high school records indicated that she dropped out during her freshman year after failing every class but one. Personnel files from her prior employers revealed that she had been fired from several jobs, that she misrepresented her academic and work history on several employment applications, and that she had filed a sexual harassment charge against a prior employer. Court records revealed prior convictions for prostitution and passing bad checks. All of these factors would suggest, at the very least, that the plaintiff's current emotional condition is not wholly the result of what happened to her at her last job.

Information to Obtain During Plaintiff's Deposition

Defense counsel can greatly assist the expert by obtaining some basic background information on the plaintiff during the plaintiff's deposition. This not only provides the expert with a "base" of information on the plaintiff prior to conducting the Rule 35 mental examination, it elicits the information at a stage in the litigation where the plaintiff is not as likely to have been coached. The following questions might be asked, depending upon the nature of the plaintiff's claims.

Symptoms Suffered

1. **What specific symptoms of emotional distress have you suffered?**
2. [For each symptom:] **When did you begin experiencing the symptom?**
3. [For each symptom:] **When did you stop experiencing the symptom?**

4. [For each symptom:] **How often did you experience the symptom?**
5. [For each symptom:] **Is there anyone who can verify that you experienced the symptom?**
6. [For each symptom:] **Did you ever experience that symptom prior to** [the workplace incident that led to the lawsuit]?
7. [For each symptom:] **Did this symptom prevent you from working? How? For how long? Did it affect your life in any other way? How? For how long?**

Medical Treatment Received

1. [For each symptom:] **Did you receive any treatment for it? From whom?**
2. [For each doctor:] **What was the doctor's full name and office address? What kind of doctor?** [e.g., psychiatrist, psychologist, counselor, internist, chiropractor].
3. [For each doctor:] **When did you first see this doctor? Are you still seeing him/her? When was your last visit? How many times did you see him/her?**
4. [For each doctor:] **Who referred you to this doctor?**
5. [For each doctor:] **Who is paying this doctor?** [e.g., private health insurance, workers' compensation, lien against lawsuit proceeds].
6. [For each psychiatrist/psychologist/marriage/family counselor (MFCC):] **Did you fill out a questionnaire during your first visit? Did you answer the questions honestly?**
7. [For each psychiatrist/psychologist/MFCC:] **Did you take any psychological tests? Did you take a test of about 500 true-false questions?** [MMPI] **Did you take it home with you to fill out or did you do it in the doctor's office? Did the doctor show you a series of ink blots and ask you what you saw?** [Rorschach]
8. [For each psychiatrist/psychologist/MFCC:] **Did the doctor interview you during your first visit? For how long? What kinds of questions did he/she ask? Was anyone else present? Did the doctor take notes?**
9. [For each psychiatrist/psychologist/MFCC:] **Did the doctor arrive at a diagnosis? What was it? Did the doctor prescribe a treatment plan? What was it?**
10. [If treatment involved counseling:] **How many counseling sessions did you attend? Who conducted them? Were they group or individual? Did the doctor take notes during the session? Did the doctor ask you to keep a diary or take notes of any kind?**
11. [If treatment involved counseling:] **Did you talk about** [the workplace incident] **with the doctor during counseling? What did the two of you discuss about it? What other issues did you talk about in counseling?**
12. [If treatment involved counseling:] **Are you still going to counseling? When was your last visit? Did the counseling help? Has the doctor told you how long you will need to continue counseling?**
13. [For each psychiatrist:] **Did the doctor prescribe any medicines? Which ones?**
14. [For each medication:] **When did you start taking it? Are you still taking it? When did you last take it? Did it help? Did it produce any side effects? Describe.**

15. [For each medical doctor:] **Did you fill out a questionnaire during your first visit? Did you answer the questions honestly?**
16. [For each medical doctor:] **Did the doctor run any tests? Which ones? Do you know what the results were?**
17. [For each medical doctor:] **Did the doctor prescribe any medicines? Which ones?**
18. [For each medication:] **When did you start taking it? Are you still taking it? When did you last take it? Did you stop taking it on your own, or at your doctor's direction? Did it help? Did it produce any side effects? Describe.**
19. [For each medical doctor:] **How many times did you see the doctor for this condition? Did you get better? Are you still seeing the doctor for this condition?**

Medical History

1. **Have you ever been hospitalized? When? What for?**
2. **Were you ever treated at a psychiatric institution? When? What for? Inpatient? Outpatient?**
3. **Have you ever received treatment or counseling from a psychiatrist? From a psychologist? From any other mental health professional? Identify each doctor, including office address.**
4. [For each period of treatment:] **Why did you seek treatment? What was the diagnosis? What treatment did you receive? How long did you receive treatment? Were you given medication? What kinds? Did you take them? For how long? Any side effects?**
5. **Have you ever suffered from:**
   —depression?
   —anxiety?
   —panic attacks?
   —manic-depressive disorder?
   —nervous condition?
   —heart disease (including, for women, mitral valve prolapse)?
   —cancer?
   —high blood pressure?
   —thyroid problems?
   —sexual difficulties?
   —alcoholism? (ever go to Alcoholics Anonymous?)
   —drug addiction?
   —eating disorders (anorexia or bulimia)?
   —head injury?
6. **Has anyone in your family suffered from:**
   —depression?
   —manic-depressive disorder?
   —alcoholism?
   —drug addiction?
   —Has anyone attempted suicide? Did they succeed?
7. **Identify all doctors seen, for whatever reason, during your period of employment. Include type of doctor, office address, and what prompted the visit.**

8. **Identify (including office address) all doctors who served as your personal physician (general practitioner/family doctor) for the 10 years prior to the start of your employment.**

Relevant Social History

1. **Have you ever been divorced? [If so, get:**
   —name of spouse
   —date of divorce
   —court in which divorce decree was entered
   —who got custody of children. (Was it contested?)]
2. **Have you ever applied for a restraining order against anyone? [Get details.]**
3. **Are your parents living? Where?** [If deceased:] **When did they die?** [If deceased after plaintiff began working for defendant:] **How did the death affect you?**
4. **Have you ever had a spouse die? A child?**
5. [For women, in a sex harassment case:] **Have you ever been raped or sexually assaulted?**
6. [For women, in a sex harassment case:] **Were you ever molested by your father or a male relative? Were you a victim of incest? [Get details.]**
7. [If incest or molestation:] **Did you ever receive counseling or treatment? [Get details.]**
8. **Have you ever been fired from a job? [Get details.]**
9. **Did you ever feel harassed or discriminated against in previous jobs? Did you file a complaint, either internally or with an outside agency? Did you file a lawsuit?**
10. [If married:] **Have you ever been separated? Have you ever received marriage counseling?**
11. **Have you ever sued anyone? Have you ever been sued by anyone?**
12. **Have you ever been convicted of or pled guilty to a crime?**
13. **Have you ever filed for bankruptcy?**

Privilege and Privacy Issues in Discovery

Attempts by counsel to obtain medical or psychotherapy records or other information needed by the expert to conduct a comprehensive evaluation of the plaintiff may be met with objections that the information sought is irrelevant, privileged, or subject to a constitutional or common law right to privacy. The law in this area has been rapidly developing, although not without inconsistencies.[7]

---

[7]For a sample brief to enforce a subpoena for a plaintiff's psychotherapy records, see Appendix C.

Scope and Waiver of Privileges [Renamed Topic]

With greater frequency, subpoenas or requests for a plaintiff's medical and psychotherapy records are countered with the claim that the records are covered by the physician–patient or psychotherapist–patient privilege. In *Jaffee v. Redmond,*[8] the U.S. Supreme Court recognized a federal common law psychotherapist–patient privilege. Noting that all 50 states and the District of Columbia recognize such a privilege,[9] the Court held that such a privilege will extend in federal cases to communications between a psychiatrist, psychologist, or licensed social worker and a patient in the course of psychotherapy. The Court noted, however, that "[l]ike other testimonial privileges, the patient may of course waive the protection."[10] This has produced considerable litigation over whether and to what extent a plaintiff waives the psychotherapist-patient privilege by asserting a claim for psychological injuries in an employment lawsuit.

Cases Viewing Waiver Broadly [New Topic]

One group of cases holds that a plaintiff waives the physician–patient or psychotherapist–patient privilege in litigation by asserting a claim for physical or mental injuries. For example, in *Sarko v. Penn-Del Directory Co.,*[11] the plaintiff sued, alleging that her discharge violated Title VII, the Age Discrimination in Employment Act (ADEA), and the Americans With Disabilities Act (ADA). She claimed an ADA violation in that she alleged she was suffering from clinical depression at the time of her termination. The defendant sought records of each of the plaintiff's medical providers identified in interrogatory responses, including those of her psychiatrist. The court rejected the plaintiff's claim of privilege, holding that a plaintiff waives the psychotherapist–patient privilege recognized in *Jaffee* by placing her mental condition in issue in a case. The *Sarko* court thus ordered the production of all of the plaintiff's medical and psychiatric records, emphasizing that to allow a plaintiff to hide behind a claim of privilege when the condition is placed directly at issue in a case would be contrary to the most basic sense of fairness and justice.[12]

---

[8]116 S. Ct. 1923 (1996).

[9]*Id.* at 1929 n.11.

[10]*Id.* at 1931 n.14.

[11]170 F.R.D. 127, 7 AD Cases 195 (E.D. Pa. 1997).

[12]*Accord* EEOC v. St. Michael Hosp. of Franciscan Sisters, Milwaukee Inc., 74 FEP Cases 993, 994 (E.D. Wis. 1997) (ordering disclosure of marriage counseling records where plaintiff claimed that workplace discrimination disrupted her marriage; "it is axiomatic that a plaintiff cannot brandish a sword and deny the defense a shield"); EEOC v. Kidder, Peabody & Co., 62 FEP Cases 899 (S.D.N.Y. 1993) (ordering production of records of plaintiff's medical doctors where plaintiff claimed that the workplace caused her to suffer various medical conditions); Ferrell v. Glen-Gery Brick, 678 F. Supp. 111, 112, 46 FEP Cases 502, 503–04 (E.D. Pa. 1987) (holding that right to privacy in medical records is waived by plaintiff's placing her mental state in issue, and noting that "an individual who wishes to receive the benefits of the judicial system should not be allowed to impose an additional burden on the system by withholding

Courts that take a broad view of the waiver of the psychotherapist-patient privilege typically hold that once a plaintiff has put her mental condition in issue by alleging that the defendant caused her to suffer emotional distress, the defendant may explore the plaintiff's psychological history to determine whether alternative causes of the plaintiff's psychological condition may exist. In *Cleveland v. International Paper Co.,*[13] for example, the plaintiff sought to prevent discovery of her medical history by arguing that she suffered only "ordinary" stresses and psychological injury as a result of discrimination and harassment, and by pointing out that she did not seek treatment for any of the matters raised in her lawsuit. The court rejected this rationale, holding that where a plaintiff seeks to recover damages for mental anguish and emotional distress, the defendant is entitled to conduct discovery into the plaintiff's medical history to show that the claimed emotional distress "was caused at least in part by events and circumstances that were not job related."[14]

The plaintiffs in *Lanning v. Southeastern Pennsylvania Transportation Authority*[15] similarly sought to bar the defendant from gaining access to their psychiatric and gynecological records by arguing that they were not seeking damages for any specific psychiatric injury, they did not plan to offer expert witness testimony on their emotional damage claim, they did not seek to recover the costs of mental health treatment, and they were not pursuing a separate claim for intentional infliction of emotional distress. The court nonetheless held that the plaintiffs had waived the psychotherapist–patient privilege, and that in spite of the plaintiffs' attempts "to limit damages regarding emotional distress, the claim for emotional distress remains a part of plaintiffs' action."[16] Further, reasoned the court, the defendant's right to discovery does not depend upon the manner in which the plaintiffs choose to present their claim. As long as they seek to recover damages for emotional distress, "[d]efense counsel has a right to inquire into plaintiffs' pasts for the purpose of showing that their emotional distress was caused at least in part by events and circumstances that were not job related."[17]

Likewise, in *Miranda v. Mount Sinai School of Medicine,*[18] the court rejected the plaintiff's argument that the defendant should be able to discover only those medical records that related to the issue of whether and to what extent the defendant's discrimination caused the plaintiff to suffer emotional harm. The court refused to impose such a narrow limitation. It maintained that

---

necessary information central to her claim" (quoting Note, *Developments in the Law—Privileged Communications,* HARV. L. REV. 1450, 1554 (1985)).

[13]74 FEP Cases 1661 (N.D.N.Y. 1997).

[14]*Id.* at 1664 (quoting Bridges v. Eastman Kodak Co., 850 F. Supp. 216, 223 (S.D.N.Y. 1994)).

[15]1997 WL 597905 (E.D. Pa. 1997).

[16]*Id.* at *2.

[17]*Id.* (citing Lowe v. Philadelphia Newspapers Inc., 101 F.R.D. 296, 298, 44 FEP Cases 1224, 1226 (E.D. Pa. 1983)).

[18]68 FEP Cases 546 (S.D.N.Y. 1995).

the defendant is entitled to explore other possible stressors that are not job related that could have caused the plaintiff's emotional distress.[19]

In *Gatewood v. Stone Container Corp.*,[20] the plaintiff in a race discrimination action attacked the defendant's subpoena for his medical and psychiatric records as overbroad, irrelevant, and an invasion of privacy and stressed that he did not receive any treatment for the emotional distress allegedly resulting from discrimination. Noting that the defendant was seeking $100,000 in damages for mental and emotional anguish, the court narrowed the scope of the subpoena somewhat but permitted the discovery. It remarked:

> Generally, a defendant is entitled to discover whether there have been other stressors relating to plaintiff's mental and physical health during the relevant time period which may have contributed to the claimed emotional distress. This is not diminished by the fact [that] plaintiff has not sought medical or mental health care for the emotional distress resulting from the claimed discrimination.[21]

In *Fritsch v. City of Chula Vista*,[22] the district court overruled a magistrate judge's ruling that a plaintiff did not waive the psychotherapist-patient privilege by asserting a claim for emotional distress. The court opined that, if presented with the question, the Supreme Court would adopt a broad view of the waiver. It noted that the Supreme Court had submitted a proposed Rule of Evidence, Rule 504(d)(3), stating that the psychotherapist-patient privilege would not apply to communications regarding a patient's emotional condition if that patient relies upon that condition as an element of a claim in litigation. The court also observed that California has a similar psychotherapist-patient privilege,[23] accompanied by a statutory patient-litigant exception,[24] and that the California Supreme Court had ruled that a patient seeking damages for severe emotional distress waives the privilege.[25] Noting that the plaintiff sought $1 million in damages for emotional distress, the court maintained:

> Fritsch can testify to her emotions near the incident, and defendant is free to cross examine her about the depth of her emotional damage and other factors in her life at the time. But to insure a fair trial, particularly on the elemant of causation, the court concludes that defendants should have access to evidence that Fritsch's emotional state was caused by something else.[26]

---

[19]*Id.* at 547. *But see* Pasternak v. Texaco Inc., 1997 WL 621267 (S.D.N.Y. 1997) (denying motion to compel plaintiff's preinjury medical records, on the ground that speculation that plaintiff may have suffered some unknown physical condition that might have in turn caused a psychological injury is insufficient to justify intrusive discovery).

[20]170 F.R.D. 455, 78 FEP Cases 1251 (S.D. Iowa 1996).

[21]*Id.* at 460, 78 FEP Cases at 1253.

[22]1999 WL 799213 (S.D. Cal. 1999).

[23]CAL. EVID. CODE §1010.

[24]CAL. EVID. CODE §1016.

[25]*In re* Lifschutz, 2 Cal. 3d 415, 85 Cal. Rptr. 829 (1970).

[26]1999 WL 799213 at *8.

Courts have allowed discovery into a variety of potential alternative stressors. In *Alden v. Time Warner Inc.,*[27] noting that by seeking $2 million in damages for emotional distress allegedly caused by age discrimination, the plaintiff "clearly placed his emotional health at issue," the court compelled disclosure of the plaintiff's marriage counseling records. It explained: "Marital difficulties significant enough to prompt counseling are likely to have been an independent cause of emotional distress."[28] The court also ordered production of the plaintiff's substance abuse treatment records, noting that "drug and alcohol abuse surely contribute to emotional distress."[29] The court did not permit discovery of the plaintiff's family doctor's records, however, pointing out that the plaintiff was not claiming to have suffered any physical injury as a result of discrimination and that the defendant did not identify any physical condition that might have been an independent cause of the plaintiff's emotional distress. Conversely, in *Workman v. Carolina Freight Carriers Corp.,*[30] the court permitted discovery of medical records indicating that the plaintiff had been diagnosed with a sexually transmitted disease, because "the revelation that a person had a sexually transmitted disease would cause considerable emotional distress."[31]

Courts that view the waiver broadly also reject attempts by plaintiffs to limit a defendant's access to evidence of potential alternative stressors via manipulative litigation tactics. For example, in *Vann v. Lone Star Steakhouse,*[32] the court ordered disclosure of the plaintiff's psychotherapist's records where the plaintiff was seeking damages for emotional distress allegedly resulting from sexual harassment. In *Vann*, the plaintiff designated her treating psychiatrist as a testifying expert, but then sought to prevent the disclosure of the psychiatrist's records on the ground that they were exempt from discovery under a state law providing that personal notes of a therapist are exempt from discovery. The court held that state law exemptions from discovery do not apply in nondiversity cases, and that there is no similar exemption under federal law.

Similarly, in *Doolittle v. Ruffo,*[33] the plaintiff initially claimed that all of her psychological problems were the fault of the defendants. When it was discovered that the plaintiff had suffered some significant childhood traumas, she attempted to limit discovery into those matters by changing her claim to exclude damage from childhood incidents and arguing that the defendants should be barred from discovery into those matters. The court rejected that ploy and maintained that the defendants were entitled to explore other potential stressors.

---

[27]1995 WL 679238 (S.D.N.Y. 1995).

[28]*Id.* at *2. *But see* Tylo v. Superior Court, 55 Cal. App. 4th 1379, 64 Cal. Rptr. 2d 731 (1997) (limiting deposition questioning of plaintiff concerning prior marital difficulties pursuant to California's constitutional right to privacy).

[29]*Id.* at *3.

[30]65 FEP Cases 1209 (M.D. Ala. 1994).

[31]*Id.* at 1210.

[32]967 F. Supp. 346, 75 FEP Cases 1131 (C.D. Ill. 1997).

[33]1997 WL 151799 (N.D.N.Y. 1997).

In *Sidor v. Reno*,[34] the court rejected the plaintiff's challenge to the defendant's subpoena for her treating psychologist's records. The plaintiff argued that, because she did not plan to call her psychologist to testify at trial (but planned to designate a different clinician as her expert), there was no waiver of the psychotherapist–patient privilege. The court observed: "[P]laintiff may not in fairness select from the psychiatric testimony available and preclude defendant from learning the content of other records."[35] Similarly, the court in *EEOC v. Danka Industries Inc.*[36] rejected the plaintiffs' attempt to bar discovery of the records of their prior psychotherapists. It observed: "[F]airness requires a waiver of privilege. Plaintiffs cannot rely on advice given by certain psychotherapists to support their claims while at the same time expect to keep confidential advice given by other psychotherapists that may weaken their claims."[37]

One court has held that a defendant may conduct discovery of a plaintiff's psychiatric history even where the plaintiff is not seeking damages for emotional distress. In *Covell v. CNG Transmission Corp.*,[38] the plaintiff in a sexual harassment case withdrew her claims for emotional distress. Yet the court still ordered her to submit her psychiatric records to the court for in camera inspection to determine if they might be relevant to the issue of liability. Specifically, the *Covell* court, citing a previous case in which a witness's mental illness affected his "interpretation of reality,"[39] noted that "[r]eports concerning plaintiff's mental condition might be relevant to her subjective perceptions [of an abusive working environment], and would rebut her contention that the allegedly hostile work environment altered the conditions of her employment."[40]

Cases Viewing Waiver Narrowly [New Topic]

Other courts have taken a much more restrictive view of waiver, however. In *Vanderbilt v. Town of Chilmark*,[41] the defendant in a discrimination and retaliation case argued that by seeking damages for emotional distress, the plaintiff put her emotional state at issue and, therefore, waived any privilege in her psychotherapy records that might exist. The court disagreed, holding that subsequent to the Supreme Court's *Jaffee*[42] decision, a plaintiff does not waive the privilege simply by putting his or her emotional state at issue. Instead, according to the *Vanderbilt* court, a plaintiff must use the privileged communication as

---

[34] 8 AD Cases 18 (S.D.N.Y. 1998).

[35] *Id.* at 20. *See also* Kirchner v. Mitsui & Co., 184 F.R.D. 124 (M.D. Tenn. 1998) (district court reversed magistrate judge's ruling that the plaintiff was only required to produce those of her medical, psychological, and social worker records as would be relied upon by her expert at trial).

[36] 990 F. Supp. 1138, 75 FEP Cases 685 (E.D. Mo. 1997).

[37] *Id.* at 1142, 75 FEP Cases at 688.

[38] 863 F. Supp. 202, 70 FEP Cases 914 (M.D. Pa. 1994).

[39] United States v. Diamond (*In re* Doe), 964 F.2d 1325 (2d Cir. 1992).

[40] 863 F. Supp. at 206, 70 FEP Cases at 916.

[41] 174 F.R.D. 225, 74 FEP Cases 685 (D. Mass. 1997).

[42] 116 S. Ct. 1923 (1996).

evidence herself before she waives the privilege: "Were she to introduce evidence regarding the substance of her conversations with her psychotherapist in order to further her claim of emotional damage, this court would agree that she could not shield the communication from others. She has, however, done no such thing."[43] The *Vanderbilt* court concluded that the privilege would be waived if the plaintiff called her psychotherapist as a witness, or if she testified herself about the substance of her discussions with her therapist. The court also emphasized that the mere fact that the plaintiff had therapy, and the dates of such therapy (including therapy that preexisted the injury at issue) are not privileged.

In *Vasconcellos v. Cybex International Inc.,*[44] the court quashed as overbroad a subpoena for all of the plaintiff's psychiatrist's records. Although noting that the plaintiff was pursuing a separate claim for intentional infliction of emotional distress as well as damages for emotional distress flowing from her other employment claims, the court held that the plaintiff "has a right to have discovery limited to information that is directly relevant to the lawsuit."[45] The court did not define just what it considered to be "directly relevant," although it quoted the following passage from an earlier case:

> [A]lthough the defendants will be permitted to inquire into plaintiff's personal histories, it must be emphasized that defendants may not engage in a fishing expedition by inquiring into matters totally irrelevant to the issue of emotional distress. In other words, the scope of the inquiry must be limited to whether, and to what extent, the alleged harassment caused plaintiffs to suffer emotional harm.[46]

The *Vasconcellos* court also suggested that the defendant could issue a new, narrower subpoena, and that the plaintiff was free to withdraw her claims for emotional injury if she wanted to avoid discovery into that area.[47]

In *Bottomly v. Leucadia National,*[48] a sexual harassment case, the court similarly narrowed the scope of the defendant's discovery of the plaintiff's psychotherapy records, noting that although a plaintiff "waives privacy claims as to those matters which are related to causation and damages as to her claim, plaintiff does not waive privacy interests on matters unrelated to the case or not calculated to lead to admissible evidence."[49] The court's application of this principle was somewhat muddled, however. It held that discovery must be allowed as to (1) all material the plaintiff's experts could reasonably rely on to address the relevant issues in the case, and (2) information needed by the defendants' experts to form a basis for any counter-opinion. The *Bottomly* court then gave conflicting directives, however. First, it said that

---

[43]174 F.R.D. at 230, 74 FEP Cases at 688.

[44]962 F. Supp. 701, 4 WH Cases 2d 1446 (D. Md. 1997).

[45]*Id.* at 708, 4 WH Cases at 1452.

[46]*Id.* at 709, 4 WH Cases at 1452 (citing Bridges v. Eastman Kodak Co., 850 F. Supp. 216, 223 (S.D.N.Y. 1994)).

[47]*Id.*, 4 WH Cases 2d at 1452.

[48]163 F.R.D. 617 (D. Utah 1995).

[49]*Id.* at 619.

> matter that is not related to causation and extent of damage, but which merely goes to the plaintiff's character is outside of proper bounds of discovery. Matters that are remote to what an expert may legitimately use for foundation for an expert opinion but which may be helpful in a clinical treatment mode or for a psychoanalytic personality analysis are too broad and intrusive and not needed for an expert opinion on the issues. A clinical whole person approach is not especially functional in the legal context of the case and is unjustifiably intrusive. A full personality inventory is not necessary for an expert witness to address the relevant issues of damages and causation.[50]

The court then said, however, that the defense expert's opinion must be "founded on what an expert in the discipline would reasonably rely on given the issues in the case," and that the defendants may have access to material that is related and relevant to what is appropriate for an expert to give or base an opinion on.[51] The problem with this formulation is that psychiatric and psychological experts in sexual harassment cases must consider whether the plaintiff has one or more personality disorders that may be relevant not only to causation of damages, but to the very genesis of the workplace dispute at issue.[52] The *Bottomly* court seemed to at least partially recognize the importance of this inquiry by noting that it had permitted extensive questioning of the plaintiff concerning her prior sexual harassment claims against other employers. It acknowledged that "if a modus operandi of sexual harassment claims can be shown, such evidence may be admissible on whether the harassment alleged in this case really occurred."[53] In light of this concession to the relevance of the plaintiff's personality structure to the issues in a sexual harassment case,[54] the *Bottomly* court's prior comments on the inappropriateness of such discovery seem particularly difficult to reconcile.

---

[50]*Id.* at 620.

[51]*Id.* at 621.

[52]*See* Chapter 4, "Personality Disorders and Traits," of the Supplement and of the Main Volume. *See also* J. McDonald & P. Lees-Haley, *Personality Disorders in the Workplace: How They May Contribute to Claims of Employment Law Violations*, 22 EMPLOYEE REL. L.J. 57 (1996). The court in *Covell v. CNG Transmission Corp.*, 863 F. Supp. 202, 70 FEP Cases 914 (M.D. Pa. 1994), recognized this point in holding that psychiatric records would be discoverable if they bear on the plaintiff's subjective perceptions in the workplace, even where the plaintiff had withdrawn her claim for emotional distress damages. *Id.* at 206, 70 FEP Cases at 916.

[53]163 F.R.D. at 622 n.3.

[54]A history of sexual harassment claims brought against a variety of employers may be evidence of hypersensitivity to sexual cues or a repetition compulsion, each of which may be related to a personality disorder, and each of which is relevant to whether actionable sexual harassment occurred. *See* discussion in Chapter 10 of this Supplement in text accompanying notes 104–18. *See also* S. Feldman-Schorrig & J. McDonald, *The Role of Forensic Psychiatry in the Defense of Sexual Harassment Cases*, 20 J. PSYCHIATRY & L. 5 (1992); J. McDonald & S. Feldman-Schorrig, *The Relevance of Childhood Sexual Abuse in Sexual Harassment Cases*, 20 EMPLOYEE REL. L.J. 221 (1994).

Cases Taking a Balanced View [New Topic]

Some courts have attempted to avoid the extremes presented by the opposing lines of cases construing the waiver of the psychotherapist-patient privilege and have instead taken a more balanced and pragmatic approach.

In *Fox v. Gates Corp.,*[55] the plaintiff alleged that she was not hired in violation of the Americans With Disabilities Act on account of her two disabled sons and that she suffered emotional distress as a result. The defendant sought to discover her psychotherapy records going back five years prior to and subsequent to the incident at issue. The court adopted an "applicable time period test," holding that the defendant was entitled to the plaintiff's therapy records preceding the incident because those records may reveal that the cause of the plaintiff's emotional distress was some other stressor in her life. As the plaintiff admitted that her emotional distress ceased prior to her obtaining additional therapy after the incident, the court held that the defendants were not entitled to disclosure of the postincident therapy records. The court cautioned, however, that if the plaintiff subsequently claimed that her emotional distress was continuing, the defendant would be entitled to discovery of the postincident therapy records.

In *Santelli v. Electro-Motive,*[56] the plaintiff testified at deposition that she was seeing a psychotherapist for emotional distress allegedly suffered as a result of sex discrimination. Upon the defendant's seeking disclosure of her psychotherapy, alcohol and drug treatment and HIV testing records, the plaintiff changed course and represented that she would seek damages only for humiliation and embarrassment, not for emotional distress. The court ruled that the plaintiff's narrowing of her claim made her psychotherapy records irrelevant, but the court also precluded the plaintiff at trial from introducing evidence of any symptoms (such as sleeplessness, nervousness, or depression), or of any medical or psychological diagnosis. Rather, the court maintained, the plaintiff would only be allowed to testify that she felt humiliated, embarrassed, angry, or upset. The court went on to say: "This may be a meager victory for [the plaintiff]. Bare testimony of humiliation or disgust may prevent her from fully recovering for her alleged emotional distress. She may be better off disclosing her psychological records, which would allow her to make a broader damage claim."[57]

Discovery of Other Records [Renamed Topic]

Courts typically have permitted discovery of other types of records pertaining to plaintiffs in employment cases. In *EEOC v. Danka Industries,*[58] the court rejected the plaintiffs' motion to quash the defendant's subpoenas for records of a former employer of one plaintiff, the high school and college records of

---

[55] 179 F.R.D. 303 (D. Colo. 1998).
[56] 188 F.R.D. 306 (N.D. Ill. 1999).
[57] *Id.* at 309.
[58] 990 F. Supp. 1138, 75 FEP Cases 685 (E.D. Mo. 1997).

three other plaintiffs, and even the medical examiner's records relating to the death of the boyfriend of one of the plaintiffs. The court maintained that because the plaintiffs had no claim of privilege in any of the subpoenaed documents, they had no standing to request that the subpoenas be quashed.

In *J.J.C. v. Fridell,*[59] the court ordered production of the plaintiff's file relating to his charge filed with the Equal Employment Opportunity Commission (EEOC), which the defendant sought to determine whether the plaintiff had made any inconsistent statements to that agency. The court ruled that because the EEOC had created special disclosure rules permitting disclosure of its files to parties in litigation, the plaintiff was required to produce documents relating to her EEOC filing.

In two cases, courts have compelled plaintiffs in sexual harassment cases to turn over their diaries. In *Topol v. Trustees of the University of Pennsylvania,*[60] the court ordered the plaintiff to produce her diary of events during the time period she alleged she was being sexually harassed. The court rejected the plaintiff's invocation of the psychotherapist–patient privilege, holding that the plaintiff waived that privilege by putting her emotional state in issue. The court similarly rejected the plaintiff's claim of privilege with respect to a journal he kept at the suggestion of his psychiatrist in *Pfeifer v. State Farm Insurance Co.,*[61] albeit on the ground that the journal was not a "confidential communication" between patient and therapist.

Depositions

Plaintiffs, their therapists, and others[62] ordinarily may be deposed concerning the nature and causation of the plaintiff's emotional distress.[63] Controversies sometimes arise, however, over whether and to what extent a defendant may question a plaintiff or the plaintiff's therapist about the plaintiff's psychological history.

In *Bridges v. Eastman Kodak Co.,*[64] the court rejected the plaintiffs' motion for a protective order restricting the defendant's questioning of the plaintiffs and their therapists about the plaintiffs' psychological histories. It explained:

> Although having to answer questions about their personal histories is to some extent an intrusion into their privacy, and may in fact inhibit some plaintiffs from

---

[59]165 F.R.D. 513 (D. Minn. 1995).

[60]74 FEP Cases 899 (E.D. Pa. 1995).

[61]1997 WL 276085 (E.D. La. 1997).

[62]*See* Alden v. Time Warner Inc., 1995 WL 679238 (S.D.N.Y. 1995) (holding that plaintiff's wife may be deposed regarding manifestations of plaintiff's emotional distress).

[63]*But see* Allen v. Cook County Sheriff's Dep't, 1999 WL 168466 (N.D. Ill. 1999) (defendant may not depose plaintiff's psychotherapists unless she designates them as expert witnesses).

[64]850 F. Supp. 216, 64 FEP Cases 1100 (S.D.N.Y. 1994).

> proceeding with their claims, such an inquiry is warranted since plaintiffs are seeking compensation for their mental anguish. Moreover, since plaintiffs seek to prove that they have suffered emotional distress as a result of the sexual harassment through their testimony and the testimony of their therapists, defense counsel has a right to inquire into plaintiffs' pasts for the purpose of showing that their emotional distress was caused at least in part by events and circumstances that were not job related. Indeed, as far as the testimony of their therapists is concerned, defendants must be allowed to inquire into all relevant information upon which the therapists' opinions [are] based, not necessarily only information directly related to their employment.[65]

The only limitation on deposition questioning imposed by the *Bridges* court was that defendants could not engage in a "fishing expedition" by inquiring into matters "totally irrelevant" to the issue of emotional distress.[66]

In *Pfeifer v. State Farm,*[67] the court granted the defendant's motion to compel the plaintiff to answer questions regarding his illegal drug use while an employee of the defendant. The court noted that the answers to such questions could be relevant to the cause of the plaintiff's claimed mental illness, and it rejected the plaintiff's invocation of a Fifth Amendment privilege against self-incrimination.

Interrogatories

In *Hilt v. SFC Inc.,*[68] the court ruled insufficient a plaintiff's answer to an interrogatory asking her to list all physicians, psychologists, and counselors who had treated or consulted with plaintiff. The plaintiff listed the requested information for only a five-year period, and referred the defendant to her medical records for further information. The court ordered the plaintiff to submit a complete response to the interrogatory, noting that it was relevant to the extent and causation of her damages. The court also maintained that an interrogatory "is not necessarily overly broad or unduly burdensome simply because it is unlimited in time and scope."[69]

---

[65] 850 F. Supp. at 216, 64 FEP Cases at 1104–05.

[66] *Id.* at 223, 64 FEP Cases at 1105. As an example, the *Bridges* court stated that "it would be inappropriate for defendants to question plaintiffs about their past sexual histories in order to show that sexually promiscuous people are less likely to be offended, and thus less damaged, than those who are not as sexually active." *Id.* at n.5, 64 FEP Cases at 1105 n.5.

[67] 1997 WL 276085 (E.D. La. 1997).

[68] 170 F.R.D. 182 (D. Kan. 1997).

[69] *Id.* at 186.

APPENDIX A

RULE 412, FEDERAL RULES OF EVIDENCE*

(as amended in 1994)

Rule 412. Sex Offense Cases; Relevance of Alleged Victim's Past Sexual Behavior or Alleged Sexual Predisposition

(a) Evidence generally inadmissible.—The following evidence is not admissible in any civil or criminal proceeding involving alleged sexual misconduct except as provided in subdivisions (b) and (c):

(1) Evidence offered to prove that any alleged victim engaged in other sexual behavior.

(2) Evidence offered to prove any alleged victim's sexual predisposition.

(b) Exceptions.—

(1) In a criminal case, the following evidence is admissible, if otherwise admissible under these rules:

(A) evidence of specific instances of sexual behavior by the alleged victim offered to prove that a person other than the accused was the source of semen, injury or other physical evidence;

(B) evidence of specific instances of sexual behavior by the alleged victim with respect to the person accused of the sexual misconduct offered by the accused to prove consent or by the prosecution; and

(C) evidence the exclusion of which would violate the constitutional rights of the defendant.

(2) In a civil case, evidence offered to prove the sexual behavior or sexual predisposition of any alleged victim is admissible if it is otherwise admissible under these rules and its probative value substantially outweighs the danger of harm to any victim and of unfair prejudice to any party. Evidence of an alleged victim's reputation is admissible only if it has been placed in controversy by the alleged victim.

(c) Procedure to determine admissibility.—

(1) A party intending to offer evidence under subdivision (b) must—

(A) file a written motion at least 14 days before trial specifically describing the evidence and stating the purpose for which it is offered unless the court, for good cause requires a different time for filing or permits filing during trial; and

(B) serve the motion on all parties and notify the alleged victim or, when appropriate, the alleged victim's guardian or representative.

Editor's Note: For a discussion of this rule, see the preface to this Supplement.

(2) Before admitting evidence under this rule the court must conduct a hearing in camera and afford the victim and parties a right to attend and be heard. The motion, related papers, and the record of the hearing must be sealed and remain under seal unless the court orders otherwise.

(As amended Pub.L. 100–690, Title VII, § 7046(a), Nov. 18, 1988, 102 Stat. 4400; Apr. 29, 1994, eff. Dec. 1, 1994; Pub.L. 103–322, Title IV, § 40141(b), Sept. 13, 1994, 108 Stat. 1919.)

ADVISORY COMMITTEE NOTES

1994 Amendments

Rule 412 has been revised to diminish some of the confusion engendered by the original rule and to expand the protection afforded alleged victims of sexual misconduct. Rule 412 applies to both civil and criminal proceedings. The rule aims to safeguard the alleged victim against the invasion of privacy, potential embarrassment and sexual stereotyping that is associated with public disclosure of intimate sexual details and the infusion of sexual innuendo into the factfinding process. By affording victims protection in most instances, the rule also encourages victims of sexual misconduct to institute and to participate in legal proceedings against alleged offenders.

Rule 412 seeks to achieve these objectives by barring evidence relating to the alleged victim's sexual behavior or alleged sexual predisposition, whether offered as substantive evidence of [*sic*] for impeachment, except in designated circumstances in which the probative value of the evidence significantly outweighs possible harm to the victim.

The revised rule applies in all cases involving sexual misconduct without regard to whether the alleged victim or person accused is a party to the litigation. Rule 412 extends to "pattern" witnesses in both criminal and civil cases whose testimony about other instances of sexual misconduct by the person accused is otherwise admissible. When the case does not involve alleged sexual misconduct, evidence relating to a third-party witness' alleged sexual activities is not within the ambit of Rule 412. The witness will, however, be protected by other rules such as Rules 404 and 608, as well as Rule 403.

The terminology "alleged victim" is used because there will frequently be a factual dispute as to whether sexual misconduct occurred. It does not connote any requirement that the misconduct be alleged in the pleadings. Rule 412 does not, however, apply unless the person against whom the evidence is offered can reasonably be characterized as a "victim of alleged sexual misconduct." When this is not the case, as for instance in a defamation action involving statements concerning sexual misconduct in which the evidence is offered to show that the alleged defamatory statements were true or did not damage the plaintiff's reputation, neither Rule 404 nor this rule will operate to bar the evidence; Rule 401 and 403 will continue to control. Rule 412 will, however, apply in a Title VII action in which the plaintiff has alleged sexual harassment.

The reference to a person "accused" is also used in a non-technical sense. There is no requirement that there be a criminal charge pending against the person or even that the misconduct would constitute a criminal offense. Evidence offered to prove allegedly false prior claims by the victim is not barred by Rule 412. However, the evidence is subject to the requirements of Rule 404.

Subdivision (a). As amended, Rule 412 bars evidence offered to prove the victim's sexual behavior and alleged sexual predisposition. Evidence, which might otherwise be admissible under Rules 402, 404(b), 405, 607, 608, 609 of [*sic*] some other evidence rule, must be excluded if Rule 412 so requires. The word "other" is used to suggest some flexibility in admitting evidence "intrinsic" to the alleged sexual misconduct. *Cf.* Committee Note to 1991 amendment to Rule 404(b).

Past sexual behavior connotes all activities that involve actual physical conduct, i.e. sexual intercourse or sexual contact. *See, e.g., United States v. Galloway,* 937 F.2d 542 (10th Cir. 1991), *cert. denied,* 113 S.Ct. 418 (1992) (use of contraceptives inadmissible since use implies sexual activity); *United States v. One Feather,* 702 F.2d 736 (8th Cir. 1983) (birth of an illegitimate child inadmissible); *State v. Carmichael,* 727 P.2d 918, 925 (Kan. 1986) (evidence of venereal disease inadmissible). In addition, the word "behavior" should be construed to include activities of the mind, such as fantasies of [*sic*] dreams. *See* 23 C. Wright and K. Graham, Jr., *Federal Practice and Procedure,* § 5384 at p. 548 (1980) ("While there may be some doubt under statutes that require 'conduct,' it would seem that the language of Rule 412 is broad enough to encompass the behavior of the mind.").

The rule has been amended to also exclude all other evidence relating to an alleged victim of sexual misconduct that is offered to prove a sexual predisposition. This amendment is designed to exclude evidence that does not directly refer to sexual activities or thoughts but that the proponent believes may have a sexual connotation for the factfinder. Admission of such evidence would contravene Rule 412's objectives of shielding the alleged victim from potential embarrassment and safeguarding the victim against stereotypical thinking. Consequently, unless the (b)(2) exception is satisfied, evidence such as that relating to the alleged victim's mode of dress, speech, or life-style will not be admissible.

The introductory phrase in subdivision (a) was deleted because it lacked clarity and contained no explicit reference to the other provisions of the law that were intended to be overridden. The conditional clause, "except as provided in subdivisions (b) and (c)" is intended to make clear that evidence of the types described in subdivision (a) is admissible only under the strictures of those sections.

The reason for extending the rule to all criminal cases is obvious. The strong social policy of protecting a victim's privacy and encouraging victims to come forward to report criminal acts is not confined to cases that involve a charge of sexual assault. The need to protect the victim is equally great when a defendant is charged with kidnapping, and evidence is offered, either to prove motive or as background, that the defendant sexually assaulted the victim.

The reason for extending Rule 412 to civil cases is equally obvious. The need to protect alleged victims against invasions of privacy, potential embarrassment, and unwarranted sexual stereotyping, and the wish to encourage victims to come forward when they have been sexually molested do not disappear because the context has shifted from a criminal prosecution to a claim for damages or injunctive relief. There is a strong social policy in not only punishing those who engage in sexual misconduct, but in also providing relief to the victim. Thus, Rule 412 applies in any civil case in which a person claims to be the victim of sexual misconduct, such as actions for sexual battery or sexual harassment.

Subdivision (b). Subdivision (b) spells out the specific circumstances in which some evidence may be admissible that would otherwise be barred by the general rule expressed in subdivision (a). As amended, Rule 412 will be virtually unchanged in criminal cases, but will provide protection to any person alleged to be a victim of sexual misconduct regardless of the charge actually brought against an accused. A new exception has been added for civil cases.

In a criminal case, evidence may be admitted under subdivision (b)(1) pursuant to three possible exceptions, provided the evidence also satisfies other requirements for admissibility specified in the Federal Rules of Evidence, including Rule 403. Subdivisions (b)(1)(A) and (b)(1)(B) require proof in the form of specific instances of sexual behavior in recognition of the limited probative value and dubious reliability of evidence of reputation or evidence in the form of an opinion.

Under subdivision (b)(1)(A), evidence of specific instances of sexual behavior with persons other than the person whose sexual misconduct is alleged may be admissible if it is offered to prove that another person was the source of semen, injury or other physical evidence. Where the prosecution has directly or indirectly asserted that the physical evidence originated with the accused, the defendant must be afforded an opportunity to prove that another person was responsible. See *United States v. Begay,* 937 F.2d 515, 523 n.10 (10th Cir. 1991). Evidence offered for the specific purpose identified in this subdivision may still be excluded if it does not satisfy Rules 401 or 403. *See, e.g., United States v. Azure,* 845 F.2d 1503, 1505–06 (8th Cir. 1988) (10 year old victim's injuries indicated recent use of force; court excluded evidence of consensual sexual activities with witness who testified at in camera hearing that he had never hurt victim and failed to establish recent activities).

Under the exception in subdivision (b)(1)(B), evidence of specific instances of sexual behavior with respect to the person whose sexual misconduct is alleged is admissible if offered to prove consent, or offered by the prosecution. Admissible pursuant to this exception might be evidence of prior instances of sexual activities between the alleged victim and the accused, as well as statements in which the alleged victim expresses an intent to engage in sexual intercourse with the accused, or voiced sexual fantasies involving that specific accused. In a prosecution for child sexual abuse, for example, evidence of uncharged sexual activity between the accused and the alleged victim offered by the prosecution may be admissible pursuant to Rule 404(b) to show a pattern of behavior. Evidence relating to the victim's alleged sexual predisposition is not admissible pursuant to this exception.

Under subdivision (b)(1)(C), evidence of specific instances of conduct may not be excluded if the result would be to deny a criminal defendant the protections afforded by the Constitution. For example, statements in which the victim has expressed an intent to have sex with the first person encountered on a particular occasion might not be excluded without violating the due process right of a rape defendant seeking to prove consent. Recognition of this basic principle was expressed on subdivision (b)(1) of the original rule. The United States Supreme Court has recognized that in various circumstances a defendant may have a right to introduce evidence otherwise precluded by an evidence rule under the Confrontation Clause. *See, e.g., Olden v. Kentucky,* 488 U.S. 227 (1988) (defendant in rape cases had right to inquire into alleged victim's cohabitation with another man to show bias).

Subdivision (b)(2) governs the admissibility of otherwise proscribed evidence in civil cases. It employs a balancing test rather than the specific exceptions stated in subdivision (b)(1) in recognition of the difficulty of foreseeing future developments in the law. Greater flexibility is needed to accommodate evolving causes of action such as claims for sexual harassment.

The balancing test requires the proponent of the evidence, whether plaintiff or defendant, to convince the court that the probative value of the proffered evidence "substantially outweighs the danger of harm to any victim and of unfair prejudice of any party." This test for admitting evidence offered to prove sexual behavior or sexual propensity in civil cases differs in three respects from the general rule governing admissibility set forth in Rule 403. First, it Reverses [*sic*] that [*sic*] usual procedure spelled out in Rule 403 by shifting the burden to the proponent to demonstrate admissibility rather than making the opponent justify exclusion of the evidence. Second, the standard expressed in subdivision (b)(2) is more stringent than in the original rule; it raises the threshold for admission by requiring that the probative value of the evidence *substantially* outweigh the specified dangers. Finally, the Rule 412 test puts "harm to the victim" on the scale in addition to prejudice to the parties.

Evidence of reputation may be received in a civil case only if the alleged victim has put his or her reputation into controversy. The victim may do so without making a specific allegation in a pleading. *Cf.* Fed.R.Civ.P. 35(a).

Subdivision (c). Amended subdivision (c) is more concise and understandable than the subdivision it replaces. The requirement of a motion before trial is continued in the amended rule, as is the provision that a late motion may be permitted for good cause shown. In deciding whether to permit late filing, the court may take into account the conditions previously included in the rule: namely whether the evidence is newly discovered and could not have been obtained earlier through the existence of due diligence, and whether the issue to which such evidence relates has newly arisen in the case. The rule recognizes that in some instances the circumstances that justify an application to introduce evidence otherwise barred by Rule 412 will not become apparent until trial.

The amended rule provides that before admitting evidence that falls within that prohibition of Rule 412(a), the court must hold a hearing in camera at which the alleged victim and any party must be afforded the right to be present and an opportunity to be heard. All papers connected with the motion must be kept and remain under seal during the course of trial and appellate proceedings unless otherwise ordered. This is to assure that the privacy of the alleged victim is preserved in all cases in which the court rules that proffered evidence is not admissible, and in which the hearing refers to matters that are not received, or are received in another form.

The procedures set forth in subdivision (c) do not apply to discovery of a victim's past sexual conduct or predisposition in civil cases, which will be continued to be governed by Fed. R. Civ. P. 26. In order not to undermine the rationale of Rule 412, however, courts should enter appropriate orders pursuant to Fed. R. Civ. P. 26 (c) to protect the victim against unwarranted inquiries and to ensure confidentiality. Courts should presumptively issue protective orders barring discovery unless the party seeking discovery makes a showing that the evidence sought to be discovered would be relevant under the facts and theories of the particular case, and cannot be obtained except through discovery. In an action for sexual harassment, for instance, while some evidence of the alleged victim's sexual behavior and/or predisposition in the workplace may perhaps be relevant, non-work place conduct will usually be irrelevant. *Cf. Burns v. McGregor Electronic Industries, Inc.,* 989 F.2d 959, 962–63 (8th Cir. 1993) (posing for a nude magazine outside work hours is irrelevant to issue of unwelcomeness of sexual advances at work). Confidentiality orders should be presumptively granted as well.

One substantive change made in subdivision (c) is the elimination of the following sentence: "Notwithstanding subdivision (b) of Rule 104, if the relevancy of the evidence which the accused seeks to offer in trial depends upon the fulfillment of a condition of fact, the court, at the hearing in chambers or at a subsequent hearing in chambers scheduled for such purpose, shall accept evidence on the issue of whether such condition of fact is fulfilled and shall determine such issue." On its face, this language would appear to authorize a trial judge to exclude evidence of past sexual conduct between alleged victim and an accused or a defendant in a civil case based upon the judge's belief that such past acts did not occur. Such an authorization raises questions of invasion of the right to a jury trial under the Sixth and Seventh Amendments. *See* 1 S. Saltzburg & M. Martin, *Federal Rules of Evidence Manual,* 396–97 (5th ed. 1990).

The Advisory Committee concluded that the amended rule provided adequate protection for all persons claiming to be the victims of sexual misconduct, and that it was inadvisable to continue to include a provision in the rule that has been confusing and that raises substantial constitutional issues.

[Advisory Committee Note adopted by Congressional Conference Report accompanying Pub.L. 103–322. See H.R. Conf. Rep. No. 103–711, 103rd Cong., 2nd Sess., 383 (1994).]

HISTORICAL NOTES

Subd. (b). Pub.L. 100–690, § 7046(a)(2), substituted "an offense under chapter 109A of title 18, United States Code" for "rape or of assault with intent to commit rape".

Subd. (b)(2)(B). Pub.L. 100–690, § 7046(a)(5), substituted "such offense" for "rape or assault".

Subd. (c)(1). Pub.L. 100–690, § 7046(a)(4), substituted "an offense under chapter 109A of title 18, United States Code" for "rape or assault with intent to commit rape".

Subd. (d). Pub.L. 100–690, § 7046(a)(4), substituted "an offense under chapter 109A of title 18, United States Code" for "rape or assault with intent to commit rape".

Legislative History

For legislative history and purpose of Pub.L. 100–690, see 1988 U.S. Code Cong. and Adm. News, p. 5937.

1994 Amendments

Pub.L. 103–322, § 40141(b), completely revised rule, substituting provisions relating to admissibility of evidence regarding relevance of alleged victim's past sexual behavior or alleged sexual predisposition in sex offense cases, for provisions relating to admissibility of evidence regarding relevance of victim's past sexual behavior in sex offense cases.

1988 Amendment

Heading. Pub.L. 100–690, § 7046(a)(1), substituted "Sex Offense" for "Rape".

Subd. (a). Pub.L. 100–690, § 7046(a)(2), (3), substituted "an offense under chapter 109A of title 18, United States Code" and "offense" for "rape or of assault with intent to commit rape" and "rape or assault", respectively.

(as enacted in 1978)

Rule 412. Rape Cases; Relevance of Victim's Past Behavior

(a) Notwithstanding any other provision of law, in a criminal case in which a person is accused of rape or of assault with intent to commit rape, reputation or opinion evidence of the past sexual behavior of an alleged victim of such rape or assault is not admissible.

(b) Notwithstanding any other provision of law, in a criminal case in which a person is accused of rape or of assault with intent to commit rape, evidence of a victim's past sexual behavior other than reputation or opinion evidence is also not admissible, unless such evidence other than reputation or opinion evidence is—

(1) admitted in accordance with subdivisions (c)(1) and (c)(2) and is constitutionally required to be admitted; or

(2) admitted in accordance with subdivision (c) and is evidence of—

(A) past sexual behavior with persons other than the accused, offered by the accused upon the issue of whether the accused was or was not, with respect to the alleged victim, the source of semen or injury; or

(B) past sexual behavior with the accused and is offered by the accused upon the issue of whether the alleged victim consented to the sexual behavior with respect to which rape or assault is alleged.

(c)(1) If the person accused of committing rape or assault with intent to commit rape intends to offer under subdivision (b) evidence of specific instances of the alleged victim's past sexual behavior, the accused shall make a written motion to offer such evidence not later than fifteen days before the date on which the trial in which such evidence is to be offered is scheduled to begin, except that the court may allow the motion to be made at a later date, including during trial, if the court determines either that the evidence is newly discovered and could not have been obtained earlier through the exercise of due diligence or that the issue to which such evidence relates has newly arisen in the case. Any motion made under this paragraph shall be served on all other parties and on the alleged victim.

(2) The motion described in paragraph (1) shall be accompanied by a written offer of proof. If the court determines that the offer of proof contains evidence described in subdivision (b), the court shall order a hearing in chambers to determine if such evidence is admissible. At such hearing the parties may call witnesses, including the alleged victim, and offer relevant evidence. Notwithstanding subdivision (b) of rule 104, if the relevancy of the evidence which the accused seeks to offer in the trial depends upon the fulfillment of a condition of fact, the court, at the hearing in chambers or at a subsequent hearing in chambers scheduled for such purpose, shall accept evidence on the issue of whether such condition of fact is fulfilled and shall determine such issue.

(3) If the court determines on the basis of the hearing described in paragraph (2) that the evidence which the accused seeks to offer is relevant and that the probative value of such evidence outweighs the danger of unfair prejudice, such evidence shall be admissible in the trial to the extent an order made by the court specifies evidence which may be offered and areas with respect to which the alleged victim may be examined or cross-examined.

(d) For purposes of this rule, the term "past sexual behavior" means sexual behavior other than the sexual behavior with respect to which rape or assault with intent to commit rape is alleged.

(Added Pub.L. 95–540, § 2(a), Oct. 28, 1978, 92 Stat. 2046.)

APPENDIX B

SAMPLE CROSS-EXAMINATION OF PLAINTIFF'S EXPERT

The following is a simulated cross-examination of a plaintiff's psychological expert in a sexual harassment lawsuit.

QUALIFICATIONS

ATTORNEY: Doctor, you really are not a psychologist, are you?

EXPERT: I most certainly am.

ATTORNEY: Are you licensed to practice psychology in this state?

EXPERT: I'm licensed as a marriage and family counselor. And, as I said, I have a Ph.D. in psychology.

ATTORNEY: But you are not licensed to *practice* psychology, are you?

EXPERT: I am fully licensed for the kind of therapy I perform.

ATTORNEY: Doctor, are you a licensed psychologist?

EXPERT: No.

ATTORNEY: Is it not true, doctor, that the licensure statute for marriage and family counselors in this state provides that such counselors may provide counseling to assist persons with marital, family, and other relational difficulties?

EXPERT: Yes, I think so.

ATTORNEY: That statute does not authorize marriage and family counselors to diagnose mental illness, does it?

EXPERT: I'm not familiar with the specific language of the law.

ATTORNEY: Your Honor, I ask the Court to take judicial notice of the licensure statute for marriage and family counselors, and that I may approach the witness.

THE COURT: Judicial notice is taken. You may approach.

ATTORNEY: Doctor, would you please look at the statute that authorizes you to practice, and tell me where it authorizes you to diagnose mental illness.

EXPERT: Well, I guess it really doesn't.

ATTORNEY: Doctor, have you ever taken the examination for licensure as a psychologist?

EXPERT: No. I've been so busy with my practice that I have not had time.

ATTORNEY: Doctor, did you perform a clinical internship after you received your Ph.D.?

EXPERT: No.

ATTORNEY: Such an internship is a prerequisite to licensure as a psychologist in this state, is it not?

EXPERT: I'm really not sure.

ATTORNEY: You're really not sure because you're really not a psychologist, are you?

OPPONENT: Objection. Argumentative; asked and answered.

THE COURT: Sustained. Move on.

ATTORNEY: Doctor, are you a Diplomate of the American Board of Professional Psychology?

EXPERT: No.

ATTORNEY: Are you a member of the American Psychological Association?

EXPERT: No. I am a member of the American Association of Marriage and Family Therapists.

FAILURE TO CONSIDER ALTERNATIVE STRESSORS

ATTORNEY: Doctor, you testified that all of the plaintiff's emotional distress is the result of sexual harassment at my client's place of busincss, corrcct?

EXPERT: That and her being forced to quit her job as a result of the sexual harassment.

ATTORNEY: Did you consider any other stressors in her life that might have caused her to suffer emotional distress?

EXPERT: Well, she was so obviously upset about what happened to her at work, I really didn't have to consider anything else.

ATTORNEY: So your answer, doctor, is that you did not consider any other potential stressors, correct?

EXPERT: That's correct.

ATTORNEY: So you don't know whether any other stressors played a role in causing the plaintiff's present emotional condition, do you?

EXPERT: Well, I believe my patient when she tells me that the sexual harassment and loss of her job has had a devastating effect on her emotionally.

ATTORNEY: By the way, doctor, who referred the plaintiff to you?

EXPERT: Her attorney.

ATTORNEY: So she was already contemplating litigation when she came to see you?

EXPERT: I don't know. We did not discuss that initially.

ATTORNEY: Well, has her attorney referred other clients to you?

EXPERT: Yes.

ATTORNEY: How many?

EXPERT: I would estimate seven or eight.

ATTORNEY: Did all of those people file lawsuits?

EXPERT: I don't know for sure. Some of them did.

ATTORNEY: Did you testify for any of them?

EXPERT: Three, I think.

ATTORNEY: So the plaintiff was the eighth or ninth person referred to you by her attorney, right?

EXPERT: That's right.

ATTORNEY: Yet you feel you are able to be completely objective, right?

EXPERT: Yes.

ATTORNEY: But you did not consider any alternative causes of the plaintiff's emotional distress, did you?

OPPONENT: Objection. Asked and answered.

THE COURT: Sustained.

ATTORNEY: Well, did you know, for example, that the plaintiff was under a psychiatrist's care for anxiety and depression before she ever went to work for my client?

EXPERT: I do now.

ATTORNEY: But you did not know that until I informed you of that fact when I took your deposition, did you?

EXPERT: No, I did not.

ATTORNEY: And you did not know that when you wrote your report in this case giving your opinions, did you?

EXPERT: No.

ATTORNEY: Did you know that the plaintiff was involved in a physically abusive relationship during the time she was employed by my client?

EXPERT: She mentioned that.

ATTORNEY: Are you aware that her ex-husband had a severe drinking problem?

EXPERT: That's what she told me.

ATTORNEY: Are you aware that after a drinking binge, her ex-husband once beat her so severely that she spent three days in the hospital?

EXPERT: Yes.

ATTORNEY: And that she received that beating about a month before she left my client's employment?

EXPERT: Approximately.

ATTORNEY: And that while she was in the hospital, her ex-husband took her child and left the state?

EXPERT: I'm aware of that.

ATTORNEY: And that he had cleaned out their bank account, leaving her with no money?

EXPERT: She mentioned that.

ATTORNEY: And that she was evicted from the apartment she had shared with her ex-husband?

EXPERT: She mentioned that, too.

ATTORNEY: Did she also mention that a week before she complained of sexual harassment and walked off the job, she asked her supervisor, whom she is now accusing of harassment, for a loan?

EXPERT: She did tell me that.

ATTORNEY: Did she tell you that she told her supervisor that her life was a mess and she needed money badly?

EXPERT: She told me she had asked him for a loan so she could hire an attorney to help get her child back.

ATTORNEY: So the plaintiff told you that her ex-husband beat her, stole her child, and left her homeless with no money, is that right?

EXPERT: I'm not sure she put it quite that way, but . . .

ATTORNEY: But she told you about all of those things, did she not?

EXPERT: Yes.

ATTORNEY: Yet, you still feel that all of her emotional distress is the result of sexual harassment?

EXPERT: Well, I would have to say that it was the major cause.

ATTORNEY: Major cause? Meaning that you now concede that there may have been other causes as well?

EXPERT: Perhaps, but when she was in an especially vulnerable position, she looked to her employer for protection and all she got was harassment and abuse.

ATTORNEY: I'm sorry, doctor, I don't think you answered my question. Are you saying there were other causes of the plaintiff's emotional distress?

EXPERT: Yes, but sexual harassment was the major cause.

ATTORNEY: So are you changing your opinion, doctor? Are you now saying that sexual harassment was a major cause instead of the sole cause?

EXPERT: I would say major cause.

ATTORNEY: But at the time you wrote your report, doctor, you did not consider any other causes, did you?

EXPERT: No.

FAILURE TO CONSIDER PERSONALITY DISORDER

ATTORNEY: Doctor, did you find the plaintiff to be suffering from a personality disorder?

EXPERT: No.

ATTORNEY: Did you at least consider the possibility of a personality disorder?

EXPERT: I always consider the possibility of a personality disorder.

ATTORNEY: You consider yourself fully qualified to diagnose personality disorders?

EXPERT: Absolutely.

ATTORNEY: Well, how did you rule out a personality disorder in this case?

EXPERT: Based on my clinical experience, I just do not feel that the plaintiff has a personality disorder.

ATTORNEY: Before reaching that conclusion, did you examine any of the plaintiff's prior medical records?

EXPERT: No, I did not have those records.

ATTORNEY: So you did not know that five years ago, the plaintiff was admitted to a psychiatric hospital after trying to kill herself?

EXPERT: Well, I found out about that in the course of this lawsuit.

ATTORNEY: So the plaintiff did not tell you about that?

EXPERT: I did not ask her.

ATTORNEY: Doctor, did the plaintiff tell you that she had been admitted to a psychiatric institution five years ago after she tried to kill herself?

EXPERT: No.

ATTORNEY: Are prior suicide attempts not an indication that a personality disorder may be present?

EXPERT: They could be.

ATTORNEY: During your therapy sessions with the plaintiff, you and she discussed her cocaine addiction, did you not?

EXPERT: Well, yes. But as I said previously, oftentimes victims of sexual harassment will attempt to self-medicate their pain through drugs or alcohol.

ATTORNEY: But, doctor, your own notes indicate that the plaintiff's drug problems pre-dated her employment with my client, do they not?

EXPERT: Yes.

ATTORNEY: And is not a history of substance abuse another indication that a personality disorder might be present?

EXPERT: It could be.

ATTORNEY: Your notes also indicate that the plaintiff was sexually molested by her stepfather when she was young, do they not?

EXPERT: Yes.

ATTORNEY: And is there not a substantial body of medical evidence indicating that childhood sexual abuse can cause a personality disorder to develop later in life?

EXPERT: Well, I don't know if I agree with that. . . .

ATTORNEY: Doctor, my question was whether there is a substantial body of medical evidence indicating that childhood sexual abuse causes personality disorders to develop, not whether you agree or disagree with that evidence.

OPPONENT: Objection. Argumentative. No question pending.

ATTORNEY: OK. Once more. Doctor, is there not a substantial body of medical evidence indicating that childhood sexual abuse can cause a personality disorder to develop?

EXPERT: Yes.

ATTORNEY: In particular, it can cause what's known as a Borderline Personality Disorder to develop, can it not?

EXPERT: That's what the literature says.

ATTORNEY: And one feature of a Borderline Personality Disorder is a chaotic course of interpersonal relationships, is it not?

EXPERT: It can be.

ATTORNEY: And yet, you attribute the collapse of the plaintiff's relationship with her boyfriend solely to the events at work?

EXPERT: Well, it was after she was forced to quit that they broke up.

ATTORNEY: Do you know how many other times in the past the plaintiff has broken off a relationship?

EXPERT: No. I never asked her that.

ATTORNEY: In fact, doctor, people with personality disorders often have difficulty getting along with others, do they not?

EXPERT: It's possible.

ATTORNEY: Well, doctor, a personality disorder would affect a person's ability to get along with co-workers, would it not?

EXPERT: It could.

ATTORNEY: Personality disorders often affect a person's perceptions of the words or actions of others, correct?

EXPERT: That's correct.

ATTORNEY: So a person with a personality disorder may misinterpret the words or actions of co-workers, correct?

EXPERT: It's possible.

ATTORNEY: Doctor, you also are aware, are you not, that the plaintiff has suffered from bulimia off and on for the past 17 years?

EXPERT: That's what her medical records indicate.

ATTORNEY: Medical records that you did not review until you prepared to testify in this case?

OPPONENT: Objection. Argumentative.

THE COURT: Counsel?

ATTORNEY: I'm simply trying to find out when the doctor informed himself of the plaintiff's medical history. It goes to the basis of his opinion.

THE COURT: Overruled.

ATTORNEY: Bulimia is another indication that a personality disorder may be present, is it not, doctor?

EXPERT: It can be.

ATTORNEY: Doctor, you are also aware, are you not, that the plaintiff dropped out of high school in the 11th grade?

OPPONENT: Objection. Irrelevant. This has nothing to do with sexual harassment.

ATTORNEY: Your Honor, this witness has testified that he does not think the plaintiff has a personality disorder, yet he has admitted that the existence of such a personality disorder might constitute an alternative explanation for some of the problems the plaintiff seeks to blame on her employer. I'm just trying to determine how careful the doctor was in ruling out the possibility of a personality disorder here.

THE COURT: Overruled. But counsel, you seem to be reaching a bit far, and we need to move on.

ATTORNEY: Doctor, you are aware, are you not, that the plaintiff dropped out of high school in the 11th grade?

EXPERT: Yes.

ATTORNEY: And that's another indication that a personality disorder may be present, is it not?

EXPERT: Not necessarily. I don't think that's a valid statement.

ATTORNEY: Doctor, you relied on the American Psychiatric Association's *Diagnostic and Statistical Manual* in your diagnosis of the plaintiff, did you not?

EXPERT: Yes, basically.

ATTORNEY: In fact, the DSM is the standard diagnostic manual relied upon by the mental health professions, is it not?

EXPERT: Yes.

ATTORNEY: Did you bring your manual to court with you today?

EXPERT: Actually, no . . .

ATTORNEY: Here, doctor, you can use mine. Your Honor, may I approach?

THE COURT: You may.

ATTORNEY: Doctor, please turn to page 652 of the DSM. What do you find there?

EXPERT: Well, it's a description of Borderline Personality Disorder.

ATTORNEY: Doctor, please read the first full paragraph.

EXPERT: "Individuals with Borderline Personality Disorder may have a pattern of undermining themselves at the moment a goal is about to be realized. For example, dropping out of school just before graduation . . ."

ATTORNEY: Is there more?

EXPERT: "Or destroying a good relationship just when it is clear that the relationship could last."

ATTORNEY: Thank you, doctor. Doctor, in light of all of your answers to my questions about personality disorders today, is it still your belief that the plaintiff does not have a personality disorder?

MISDIAGNOSIS OF PTSD

ATTORNEY: Now, doctor, you said you diagnosed the plaintiff as suffering from Posttraumatic Stress Disorder, correct?

EXPERT: Yes.

ATTORNEY: Did you diagnose her based on the criteria set forth in DSM-IV?

EXPERT: That and my clinical experience.

ATTORNEY: Well, did you rely on DSM-IV or not?

EXPERT: I did.

ATTORNEY: So you are aware, are you not, doctor, that valid diagnosis of PTSD requires the occurrence of an event or events that involved actual or threatened death or physical injury or a threat to the physical integrity of oneself or others?

EXPERT: I'm familiar with the definition.

ATTORNEY: So, doctor, what traumatic event in the workplace did the plaintiff experience that you believe triggered her PTSD?

EXPERT: As I testified earlier, the sexual harassment.

ATTORNEY: Well, what incident or incidents specifically do you feel triggered PTSD?

EXPERT: The assault, for one.

ATTORNEY: You are referring to her boss putting his arm around her?

EXPERT: And suggesting that he would pay her to be his girlfriend.

ATTORNEY: Aren't you referring to the supervisor's testimony that when the plaintiff asked him for a loan, he said, "Well, it's not like you're my girlfriend or anything"?

EXPERT: That's his version. My patient perceived him to be pressuring her for sex.

ATTORNEY: Any other traumas that you believed triggered PTSD?

EXPERT: Well, she had to endure a daily barrage of off-color jokes and innuendo, and she ultimately lost her job, which was quite a serious trauma for her.

ATTORNEY: But doctor, doesn't DSM-IV, at page 427, specifically state that getting fired is not a sufficient trigger for PTSD?

EXPERT: But the plaintiff was not fired. She was forced to quit on account of the sexual harassment.

ATTORNEY: So, doctor, are you saying that overhearing some off-color jokes and comments is a trauma involving actual or threatened death or physical injury or a threat to her physical integrity?

EXPERT: Well, sexual harassment is like rape, and rape is certainly a recognized PTSD stressor.

ATTORNEY: Doctor, are you saying that what the plaintiff claimed happened to her was the equivalent of rape?

EXPERT: In her mind she certainly felt it was. Keep in mind, this woman has been in therapy for a year and a half as the result of what happened to her at work.

ATTORNEY: Therapy that you conducted, right, doctor?

EXPERT: That's right.

ATTORNEY: And after a year and a half, she's *still* in therapy?

EXPERT: This was a very traumatic experience for her.

ATTORNEY: And during that year and a half of therapy, doctor, did you ever suggest to her that maybe she was overreacting?

EXPERT: Oh, no. To have done so would have been very harmful to her.

ATTORNEY: So you just took her word for it, doctor?

EXPERT: Well, of course, she had no reason to lie to me.

ATTORNEY: No reason to lie?! She's suing for money, she was sent to you by her attorncy, and you don't think she had any reason to lie?

OPPONENT: Objection. Argumentative.

THE COURT: Sustained. Move on.

ATTORNEY: Well, doctor, did you consider whether her being beaten, put in the hospital, and thrown out on the street by her ex-husband might have caused this so-called PTSD?

EXPERT: Yes, I considered it, but I think what finally made her snap was her supervisor sexually propositioning her when she turned to him for help.

ATTORNEY: Doctor, here, look at DSM-IV and tell me where it says that having your boss make a pass at you can cause PTSD.

EXPERT: Well, it does not say that per se, but one might interpret it that way.

ATTORNEY: When the PTSD diagnosis was developed, it was designed to apply to war veterans, wasn't it?

EXPERT: Yes.

ATTORNEY: And the DSM says other people who might be expected to suffer from PTSD are prisoners of war and torture victims, does it not?

EXPERT: Yes.

ATTORNEY: And you equate the plaintiff's boss making a pass at her, even if he did, as being the same as being a POW or a torture victim?

EXPERT: Well, it did make her very uncomfortable.

FINANCIAL BIAS

ATTORNEY: Doctor, how many therapy sessions did you say you had with the plaintiff?

EXPERT: Well, twice a week for six months, and then about once a week for the last year.

ATTORNEY: So about 100 sessions?

EXPERT: Give or take a few; I'd say that sounds about right.

ATTORNEY: Did you charge her for those sessions?

EXPERT: Of course.

ATTORNEY: How much per session?

EXPERT: My normal rate is $100.

ATTORNEY: Well, is that what you charged her?

EXPERT: Yes.

ATTORNEY: So 100 sessions at $100—that comes to $10,000, correct?

EXPERT: Yes.

ATTORNEY: Have you been paid any of that money?

EXPERT: Her insurance covered part of it.

ATTORNEY: What part of it?

EXPERT: Ten sessions.

ATTORNEY: Do you expect to get any more insurance money?

EXPERT: No. I understand that 10 sessions is all her policy covers.

ATTORNEY: So she still owes you for 90 sessions, correct?

EXPERT: Correct.

ATTORNEY: Has she paid you anything?

EXPERT: No, she couldn't afford to after she was forced to quit her job with your client.

ATTORNEY: So the plaintiff now owes you $9,000?

EXPERT: Approximately.

ATTORNEY: Has she made any arrangements to pay you?

EXPERT: Not yet, but I trust her.

ATTORNEY: Doctor, you are testifying as the plaintiff's expert as well as her treating therapist in this case, are you not?

EXPERT: Yes.

ATTORNEY: And in your role as expert, you are trying to be objective, are you not?

EXPERT: Of course.

ATTORNEY: Yet, if the plaintiff does not win this lawsuit and collect some money, you are not likely to get paid, are you?

OPPONENT: Objection. Argumentative.

ATTORNEY: I'll withdraw it. No further questions.

APPENDIX C

SAMPLE BRIEF TO ENFORCE SUBPOENA FOR PLAINTIFF'S PSYCHOTHERAPY RECORDS

James J. McDonald, Jr.
State Bar No. 150605
FISHER & PHILLIPS LLP
4675 MacArthur Court
Suite 550
Newport Beach, California 92660
(949) 851-2424

Attorneys for Defendants
ABC Corporation
and Richard Roe

UNITED STATES DISTRICT COURT
SOUTHERN DISTRICT OF CALIFORNIA

JANE DOE,	) DOCKET NO. 999999
	)
Plaintiff,	) BRIEF OF DEFENDANTS RE
	) ENFORCEMENT OF MEDICAL
	) RECORDS SUBPOENA TO
	) DR. SIGMUND FREUD
ABC CORPORATION,	)
et. al.	)
	)
Defendants.	)
______________________________	)

INTRODUCTION

Whether the plaintiff suffered childhood sexual abuse and other prior sexual trauma is one of the most important issues from the defense standpoint in a sexual harassment lawsuit. *See* J. McDonald & S. Feldman-Schorrig, *The Relevance of Childhood Sexual Abuse in Sexual Harassment Cases,* 20 EMPLOYEE REL. L.J. 221 (1994); S. Feldman-Schorrig, *Special Issues in Sexual Harassment Cases, in* MENTAL AND EMOTIONAL INJURIES IN EMPLOYMENT LITIGATION 332–90 (J. McDonald & F. Kulick eds., 1994). Yet, while placing her emotional condition squarely at issue in this sexual harassment lawsuit by accusing Defendants of causing her grievous psychological injury, Plaintiff now seeks to hide behind a veil of "privacy" in an attempt to prevent Defendants from defending themselves.

FACTUAL BACKGROUND

Plaintiff Jane Doe filed the instant lawsuit against her former employer, ABC Corporation, and several of its employees. While Plaintiff alleges 10 separate causes of action, all essentially involve her allegation that she was sexually harassed and wrongfully terminated from her employment.

Specifically, Plaintiff alleges in her Complaint that she was sexually harassed by a co-worker, Defendant Larry Low, with whom she admits she previously had a consensual romantic relationship. She alleges that as a result of such harassment, she "has suffered and continues to suffer physical injury, pain and suffering, humiliation, mental anguish and emotional distress. . . ." She further alleges that "as a proximate result of the conduct of the defendants," she began seeing Dr. Sigmund Freud, a psychiatrist.

Accordingly, on or about September 20, 1999, Defendants served Dr. Freud with a subpoena for his psychiatric or psychological records pertaining to Plaintiff. Dr. Freud, on the instruction of Plaintiff's counsel, has refused to produce the subpoenaed records. Plaintiff's counsel has taken the position that some of Dr. Freud's records, which apparently relate to childhood sexual abuse or other prior sexual trauma, should not be produced based on the psychotherapist-patient privilege and Rule 412 of the Federal Rules of Civil Procedure. Neither constitutes good grounds to deny this discovery, however.

SUMMARY OF DEFENDANTS' POSITION

By expressly pleading in her Complaint that she suffered mental and emotional injuries as a result of Defendants' actions and that she had to seek treatment from Dr. Freud as a further result, Plaintiff has plainly placed her psychological condition in issue. Plaintiff claims that Defendants caused her to suffer a serious psychological injury, and Defendants need to be able to defend themselves. The first step in this defense is to discover (1) whether and to what extent Plaintiff actually has suffered psychological injury, and (2) if so, what was its cause.

But Plaintiff now seeks to bar Defendants from discovering the potential *true* cause of her psychological troubles. She wants the Court to prevent Defendants and their psychiatric experts from learning what other prior traumas and/or preexisting conditions might plausibly have caused or contributed to her current emotional problems, if any. She seeks to hide the truth behind a veil of privilege and a Rule of Evidence that does not even apply to discovery. This is wrong.

What this dispute boils down to is whether Defendants may discover evidence of prior sexual *trauma* on the part of Plaintiff that may account for her current emotional condition. Defendants are not interested in Plaintiff's prior consensual sexual affairs and they certainly do not seek to defend this case by arguing that Plaintiff is an "unchaste" woman. Defendants do seek to learn whether Plaintiff experienced prior sexual *trauma*—in the form of childhood sexual abuse and/or prior sexual assaults—because such trauma has such lasting psychological effects and plays such a pivotal role in understanding both Plaintiff's current psychological condition and the genesis of the very sexual harassment claim itself.

ARGUMENT

To deny the instant discovery would be to deny Defendants due process of law. The discovery sought here is barred neither by the psychotherapist-patient privilege nor Rule 412, moreover.

I. TO DENY THE INSTANT DISCOVERY IS TO DENY DEFENDANTS' RIGHT TO DUE PROCESS OF LAW

Plaintiff has alleged, and will likely present extensive evidence at trial, that she has suffered numerous serious physical and mental illnesses, *which are all Defendants' fault.* Yet, she simultaneously seeks to prohibit Defendants from challenging her claims by discovering and introducing evidence of other significant traumas in Plaintiff's life that could just as well have been the cause of her problems. This is a fundamental denial of due process.

It is a basic principle of procedural due process that a defendant be given an adequate opportunity to defend against civil claims brought against it in court. As the Supreme Court declared in *Joint Anti-Fascist Refugee Committee v. McGrath,* 341 U.S. 123 (1951):

> [T]he right to be heard before being condemned to suffer grievous loss of any kind, even though it may not involve the stigma and hardships of a criminal conviction, is a principle basic to our society.

Id. at 168. The "fair hearing" element of due process requires a hearing that allows the defendant a "meaningful opportunity" to defend against the charges. *Armstrong v. Manzo,* 380 U.S. 545, 552 (1965).

The California Supreme Court recognized this important principle of due process in the context of emotional distress damages claims in *Vinson v. Superior Court,* 43 Cal. 3d 833, 239 Cal. Rptr. 292 (1987). The defendant in *Vinson* sought a court order requiring a sexual harassment plaintiff to submit to a mental examination in order to determine whether the plaintiff's alleged emotional damages were attributable to the conduct of the defendant or were instead the result of alternative stressors. The plaintiff refused to submit to the mental examination on the grounds that the examination would violate her right to privacy, which is the same argument Plaintiff advances here.

The California Supreme Court in *Vinson* flatly rejected the plaintiff's arguments. It maintained: "A party who chooses to allege that he has mental and emotional difficulties can hardly deny his mental state is in controversy." *Id.* at 839, 239 Cal. Rptr. 292. The court continued:

> In the case at bar, plaintiff haled defendants into court and accused them of causing her various mental and emotional ailments. Defendants deny her charges. As a result, the existence and extent of her mental injuries is indubitably in dispute. *In addition, by asserting a causal link between her mental distress and defendants' conduct, plaintiff implicitly claims it was not caused by a preexisting mental condition, thereby raising the question of alternative sources for the distress.*

Id. at 839–40, 239 Cal. Rptr. 292 (emphasis added). Finally, the *Vinson* court acknowledged the principle that is central to Defendants' argument here—"*plaintiff cannot be allowed to make her very serious allegations without affording defendants an opportunity to put their truth to the test.*" *Id.* at 842, 239 Cal. Rptr. 292 (emphasis added). It is this very basic right of due process that Defendants seek here.

Defendants will be deprived of this crucial due process right if they are not granted access to *all* of Dr. Freud's records. It is not enough to allow Defendants to see merely those portions of Dr. Freud's records relating to the events at issue in this lawsuit, as to do so would deprive Defendants of their due process right, recognized by the California Supreme Court in *Vinson,* to challenge Plaintiff's theory of causation by identifying alternative stressors that might be responsible for Plaintiff's condition. Plaintiff cannot be permitted to hide evidence detrimental to her case behind a wall of "privacy."

This important principle was reaffirmed in *Ziemann v. Burlington County Bridge Commission,* 155 F.R.D. 497 (D.N.J. 1994). In that sexual harassment case, the court granted the defendant access to the records of the plaintiff's psychotherapist and of a marriage counselor whom she had previously consulted. The court explained:

> Indeed, the issues of causation and damages will depend heavily for their resolution upon the determination of how [the plaintiff's] first marriage and earlier experiences have contributed to her current mental state. *Without discovery relating to these earlier experiences, defendants will be unable to adequately prepare their defense on these issues.*

Id. at 506 (emphasis added).

Similarly, in *Cleveland v. International Paper Co.,* 74 FEP Cases 1661 (N.D.N.Y. 1997), the plaintiff sought to prevent discovery of her medical history by arguing that she suffered only "ordinary" stresses and psychological injury as a result of discrimination and harassment, and by pointing out that she did not seek treatment for any of the matters raised in her lawsuit. The court rejected this rationale, holding that where a plaintiff seeks to recover damages for mental anguish and emotional distress, the defendant is entitled to conduct discovery into the plaintiff's medical history to show that the claimed emotional distress "was caused at least in part by events and circumstances that were not job related." *Id.* at 1664 (*quoting Bridges v. Eastman Kodak Co.,*

850 F. Supp. 216, 223 (S.D.N.Y. 1994)). *Accord EEOC v. St. Michael Hosp.,* 74 FEP Cases 993, 994 (E.D. Wis. 1997) (ordering disclosure of marriage counseling records where plaintiff claimed that workplace discrimination disrupted her marriage; "it is axiomatic that a plaintiff cannot brandish a sword and deny the defense a shield"); *EEOC v. Kidder, Peabody & Co.,* 62 FEP Cases 899 (S.D.N.Y. 1993) (ordering production of records of plaintiff's medical doctors where plaintiff claimed that the workplace caused her to suffer various medical conditions); *Ferrell v. Glen-Gery Brick,* 46 FEP Cases 502, 503–04 (1987) (holding that right to privacy in medical records is waived by plaintiff's placing her mental state in issue, and noting that "an individual who wishes to receive the benefits of the judicial system should not be allowed to impose an additional burden on the system by withholding necessary information central to her claim").

II. PLAINTIFF WAIVED HER PSYCHOTHERAPIST–PATIENT PRIVILEGE BY ASSERTING CLAIMS FOR EMOTIONAL DAMAGES

It is true that in *Jaffee v. Redmond,* 116 S. Ct. 1923 (1996), the U.S. Supreme Court recognized a federal common law psychotherapist–patient privilege. The Court noted, however, that "[l]ike other testimonial privileges, the patient may of course waive the protection." *Id.* at 1931 n.14.

Courts hold that a plaintiff waives the psychotherapist–patient privilege in litigation by asserting a claim for physical or mental injuries. For example, in *Sarko v. Penn-Del Directory Co.,*170 F.R.D. 127, 7 AD Cases 195 (E.D. Pa. 1997), the plaintiff sued, alleging that her discharge violated Title VII, the Age Discrimination in Employment Act, and the Americans With Disabilities Act (ADA). She claimed an ADA violation in that she alleged she was suffering from clinical depression at the time of her termination. The defendant sought records of each of the plaintiff's medical providers identified in interrogatory responses, including those of her psychiatrist. The court rejected the plaintiff's claim of privilege, holding that a plaintiff waives the psychotherapist–patient privilege recognized in *Jaffee* by placing her mental condition in issue in a case. The *Sarko* court ordered the production of all of the plaintiff's medical and psychiatric records, emphasizing that to allow a plaintiff to hide behind a claim of privilege when the condition is placed directly at issue in a case would be contrary to the most basic sense of fairness and justice.

The plaintiffs in *Lanning v. Southeastern Pennsylvania Transportation Authority,* 1997 WL 597905 (E.D. Pa. 1997), similarly sought to bar the defendant from gaining access to their psychiatric and gynecological records by arguing that they were not seeking damages for any specific psychiatric injury, they did not plan to offer expert witness testimony on their emotional damage claim, they did not seek to recover the costs of mental health treatment, and they were not pursuing a separate claim for intentional infliction of emotional distress. The court nonetheless held that the plaintiffs had waived the psychotherapist–patient privilege, and that in spite of the plaintiffs' attempts "to limit damages regarding emotional distress, the claim for emotional distress remains a part of plaintiffs' action."*Id.* at *2. Further, reasoned the court, the defendant's right to discovery does not depend upon the manner in which the plaintiffs choose to present their claim. As long as they seek to recover damages for emotional distress, "[d]efense counsel has a right to inquire into plaintiffs' pasts for the purpose of showing that their emotional distress was caused at least in part by events and circumstances that were not job related."*Id.* (*citing Lowe v. Philadelphia Newspapers Inc.*, 101 F.R.D. 296, 298 (E.D. Pa. 1983)).

Likewise, in *Miranda v. Mount Sinai School of Medicine,* 68 FEP Cases 546 (S.D.N.Y. 1995), the court rejected the plaintiff's argument that the defendant should be able to discover only those medical records that related to the issue of whether and to what extent the defendant's discrimination caused the plaintiff to suffer emotional harm. The court refused to impose such a narrow limitation. It maintained that the defendant is entitled to explore other possible stressors that are not job related that could have caused the plaintiff's emotional distress.

In *Fritsch v. City of Chula Vista,* 1999 WL 799213 (S.D. Cal. 1999), the district court overruled a magistrate judge's ruling that a plaintiff did not waive the psychotherapist–patient privilege by asserting a claim for emotional distress. The court opined that, if presented with the question, the Supreme Court would adopt a broad view of the waiver. It noted that the Supreme Court had submitted a proposed Rule of Evidence, Rule 504(d)(3), stating that the psychotherapist–patient privilege would not apply to communications regarding a patient's emotional condition if that patient relies upon that condition as an element of a claim in litigation. Noting that the plaintiff sought $1 million in damages for emotional distress, the court maintained:

> Fritsch can testify to her emotions near the incident, and defendant is free to cross examine her about the depth of her emotional damage and other factors in her life at the time. But to insure a fair trial, particularly on the element of causation, the court concludes that defendants should have access to evidence that Fritsch's emotional state was caused by something else.

1999 WL 799213 at *8.

In *Sidor v. Reno*, 8 AD Cases 18 (S.D.N.Y. 1998), the court rejected the plaintiff's challenge to the defendant's subpoena for her treating psychologist's records. The plaintiff argued that since she did not plan to call her psychologist to testify at trial (but planned to designate a different clinician as her expert) there was no waiver of the psychotherapist–patient privilege. The court observed: "[P]laintiff may not in fairness select from the psychiatric testimony available and preclude defendant from learning the content of other records." Finally, the court in *EEOC v. Danka Industries Inc.,* 990 F. Supp. 1138, 75 FEP Cases 685 (E.D. Mo. 1997), rejected the plaintiffs' attempt to bar discovery of the records of their prior psychotherapists. It observed:

> [F]airness requires a waiver of privilege. Plaintiffs cannot rely on advice given by certain psychotherapists to support their claims while at the same time expect to keep confidential advice given by other psychotherapists that may weaken their claims.

III. FRE 412 DOES NOT BAR DISCOVERY OF PLAINTIFF'S PSYCHIATRIC RECORDS

Plaintiff alternatively argues that since a portion of Dr. Freud's records relate to Plaintiff's childhood sexual abuse, their production is barred by FRE 412. This argument is incorrect.

Several courts have held that Rule 412 does not apply at all in discovery. For example, in *Ramirez v. Nabil's Inc.*, 1995 WL 609415 (D. Kan. 1995), the court similarly declined to apply Rule 412 to discovery, noting that the rule is "a rule of admissibility." In that sexual harassment case, the defendant sought production of medical records pertaining to psychiatric treatment received by two of the plaintiffs when they were adolescents. While those plaintiffs did not expressly indicate that the treatment involved sexual matters, they raised Rule 412 in an attempt to bar the discovery. The court applied Federal Rule of Civil Procedure 26 instead and ordered the records produced. It stated that the discovery sought appeared "reasonably calculated to lead to the discovery of admissible evidence regarding the claims of emotional distress" by the plaintiffs. *See also Holt v. Welch Allyn Inc.*, 3 WH Cases 2d 1622 (N.D.N.Y. 1997) (refusing to apply Rule 412 in discovery).

In fact, the Advisory Committee Notes to the 1994 Amendments to Rule 412 provide that the procedures set forth in subdivision (c) of that Rule "do not apply to discovery of a victim's past sexual conduct or predisposition in civil cases, which will continue to be governed by Fed. R. Civ. P. 26," which requires only "relevance" as a prerequisite to discovery. The Notes go on to suggest that courts should issue appropriate orders under Rule 26(c) to "protect the victim against unwarranted inquiries and to ensure confidentiality." The Notes to Rule 412 thus suggest a different standard for discovery of information covered by Rule 412 than for its admissibility. In the Advisory Committee's view, a protective order should issue "unless the party seeking discovery makes a showing that the evidence sought to be discovered would be relevant under the facts and theories of a particular case, and cannot be obtained except through discovery." Accordingly, only "relevance" need be shown for discoverability; not that the "probative value substantially outweighs the danger of harm to any victim and of unfair prejudice to any party," as is required by Rule 412(b)(2) for admissibility.

A. The Discovery Sought Is Overwhelmingly Relevant to the Issues in This Litigation

Childhood sexual abuse, prior sexual trauma, and preexisting mental disorders on the part of a plaintiff are of extreme relevance in a sexual harassment lawsuit, for three reasons. First, they provide potent evidence to undercut Plaintiff's apparent claim that Defendants' actions were solely responsible for all of her present emotional troubles. Second, they can provide important clues to the genesis of the harassment dispute that may bear upon Defendants' liability, including whether the plaintiff is a "reasonable woman" (as opposed to a hypersensitive person), and whether she "welcomed" the conduct in question. Third, they are directly relevant to Plaintiff's credibility as a witness.

1. Prior Sexual Trauma and Other Preexisting Mental Disorders Are Highly Relevant to the Issue of Causation of Plaintiff's Alleged Damages

Plaintiff has accused Defendants of causing her to suffer severe and disabling psychological injuries. To put on a meaningful defense, Defendants must do more than merely say, "She's wrong." To the extent Plaintiff succeeds in convincing the jury that she has suffered physical and mental injuries, the jury will expect Defendants to offer alternative explanations for the source of Plaintiff's injuries. Defendants will have to provide expert testimony on this causation issue, and Defendants' expert will have to have access to Plaintiff's *entire* medical and psychiatric history to render an informed opinion. This is the only practical means available for challenging Plaintiff's theory of causation of this type of injury.

Courts have considered a plaintiff's history of childhood sexual abuse in determining the proper measure of damages in a sexual harassment case, for example. *See, e.g., McKinnon v. Kwong Wah Restaurant,* 83 F.3d 498, 70 FEP Cases 1037 (1st Cir. 1996) (affirming award of $2,500 in emotional distress damages to sexual harassment plaintiff, noting the relevance of plaintiff's having been sexually abused by her stepfather from age 5 to age 17); *Hurley v. Atlantic City Police Dep't,* 933 F. Supp. 396, 72 FEP Cases 1828 (D.N.J. 1996) (in reducing jury award of $575,000 for emotional distress to $175,000, noting plaintiff's history of childhood molestation and two abusive marriages).

If Defendants here are not permitted unrestricted access to information concerning potential alternative causes of Plaintiff's emotional distress, their one and only means of defense on the issue of causation of Plaintiff's alleged injuries will be eliminated, thus creating a ridiculously one-sided fight on the issue of damages. Defendants will be forced to sit mute in the courtroom, behind the screen of Plaintiff's "privacy" rights, while Plaintiff attributes her entire dysfunctional physical and mental condition to Defendants. Defendants will not be able to point, for example, to the overwhelming body of psychiatric research indicating that prior sexual trauma often causes chronic and severe psychological problems later in life.

For example, there is a well-documented connection between childhood sexual abuse and symptoms of depression and anxiety in adult life. *See, e.g.,* N. Zelikovsky & S. Lynn, *The Aftereffects and Assessment of Physical and Psychological Abuse, in* DISSOCIATION: CLINICAL AND THEORETICAL PERSPECTIVES 190, 202–03 (S. Lynn & J. Rhue eds., 1994) ("Adults who report a history of abuse are likely to report more depressive symptoms, anxiety, aggression and anger, and trouble with their interpersonal relationships than nonabused persons"); D. Sandberg et al., *Sexual Abuse and Revictimization, in* DISSOCIATION: CLINICAL AND THEORETICAL PERSPECTIVES 242, 259 (S. Lynn & J. Rhue eds., 1994) (describing a study showing that "child maltreatment was significantly related to depression, dissociation, and negative life outcomes");

C. Fine, *The Cognitive Sequelae of Incest, in* INCEST-RELATED SYNDROMES OF ADULT PSYCHOPATHOLOGY 161, 163 (R. Kluft ed., 1990) ("Feelings of depression and anxiety are by far the more common emotions described by these victims [of incest]"); D. Schetky, *A Review of the Literature on the Long-Term Effects of Childhood Sexual Abuse, in* INCEST-RELATED SYNDROMES OF ADULT PSYCHOPATHOLOGY 35, 41 (R. Kluft ed., 1990) ("Depression, low self-esteem, and feelings of being damaged are commonly reported among adults who experienced childhood sexual abuse").

Not only do victims of sexual trauma suffer a variety of psychopathology in later life, but they often incorrectly blame co-workers and other contemporaries for causing it. As one authority notes:

> The problems of incest victims . . . are often misattributed by the patient, and sometimes by the therapist, to ongoing daily problems in living . . . rather than being recognized as rooted in historical trauma and forced sexuality with a parent or someone in a quasi-parental or other familial role.

Fine, *supra,* at 162. As such, there is a substantial issue in this case of whether Plaintiff's current psychological condition is truly caused only by Defendants' actions, or whether instead prior traumas caused or contributed to it.[1] The assertions of Plaintiff and her psychiatrist are only the starting point; they are hardly the last word.

2. Prior Sexual Trauma Is Highly Relevant to the Issue of Whether Unlawful Sexual Harassment Even Occurred

In addition to causing obvious forms of psychopathology, prior sexual traumas can play a significant role in the development of personality, affecting the way in which a person perceives and reacts to co-workers and others. These include effects that are directly relevant to the legal issues presented in a sexual harassment case, such as causing the plaintiff to become hypersensitive to sexual cues, or causing her to "welcome" the sexual conduct or comments later characterized as harassment.

a. Hypersensitivity

A woman who is hypersensitive to sexual cues is anathema to the "reasonable woman," the standard by which workplace sexual conduct is determined to be sufficiently offensive to be unlawful.

---

[1]The same rationale would apply to prior mental disorders, as might be reflected in Dr. Freud's notes in terms of prior psychological treatment or counseling, prior psychiatric hospitalizations, prior suicide attempts or other self-destructive behavior, a history of eating disorders, prior substance abuse, and the like. The presence of any of these items would suggest that Plaintiff's present condition is, at least in part, attributable to a preexisting mental disorder.

In *Harris v. Forklift Systems Inc.,* 114 S. Ct. 367, 370 (1993), the Supreme Court decreed that to violate Title VII, harassing conduct must be "severe or pervasive enough to create an objectively hostile or abusive work environment." That the test is an *objective* one is highly significant; the mere fact that the plaintiff was subjectively offended—while a prerequisite—is not enough. The *Harris* Court stressed that the environment must be one that a reasonable person would find hostile or abusive.

The Ninth Circuit applied a similar standard in *Ellison v. Brady,* 924 F.2d 872 (1991), in which it stated:

> In order to shield employers from having to accommodate the idiosyncratic concerns of the rare hyper-sensitive employee, we hold that a female plaintiff states a prima facie case of hostile environment sexual harassment when she alleges conduct which a reasonable woman would consider sufficiently severe or pervasive to alter the conditions of employment and create an abusive working environment.

Id. at 879. Thus, if a sexual harassment plaintiff is a "hypersensitive" individual who, because of her psychological history or makeup, is offended by workplace conduct that a "reasonable" woman of normal sensitivity would not find offensive, such a plaintiff cannot prevail on a sexual harassment claim. *See also Zabkowicz v. West Bend Co.,* 589 F. Supp. 780, 784 (E.D. Wis. 1984) ("Title VII does not serve as a vehicle for vindicating the petty slights suffered by the hypersensitive"); *Hannah v. Philadelphia Coca-Cola Bottling Co.,* 1991 WL 34363, 56 FEP Cases 1325 (E.D. Pa. 1991) ("The employer has to be in a sense protected from the 'hypersensitive' employee").

Significantly, moreover, the "eggshell plaintiff" rule of common law tort jurisprudence, which holds that a tortfeasor takes his victim "as he finds her" and thus becomes liable for whatever harm he causes without regard to her hypersensitivity, does *not* apply to the issue of liability in a sexual harassment case. *Sudtelgte v. Reno,* 63 FEP Cases 1257, 1267 (W.D. Mo. 1994).

Considerable evidence has been developed in the field of psychiatry indicating that women with a history of childhood sexual abuse may display a hypersensitivity to sexual remarks in the workplace. For example, one woman, with no history of victimization, may not be troubled by a sexual proposition of a co-worker, and in fact may laugh it off or even find it flattering. Another woman, with a prior history of sexual abuse, would be more likely to react with anger or fear to the same proposition. This occurs because a woman with a history of childhood sexual abuse often develops a type of posttraumatic stress disorder as a result of that abuse that becomes chronic and integrated into her personality structure. Fear and hypervigilance resulting from the original trauma usually persist through the victim's subsequent life. *See* J. Herman et al., *Long-Term Effects of Incestuous Abuse in Childhood,* 143 AM. J. PSYCHIATRY 1293, 1293 (1986).

This fear and hypervigilance is as likely to be present in the workplace as in other contexts. As the author of one study of the characteristics of sexually abused women observes, "a woman who has been [victimized] is likely to have a heightened response to harassing remarks at work." She states: "What is trivial to one person may trigger PTSD [Post-Traumatic Stress Disorder] or a stress-response syndrome in another." J. Hamilton, *Emotional Consequences of Victimization and Discrimination in "Special Populations" of Women,* 12 PSYCHIATRIC CLINICS N. AM. 35, 42 (1989).

Thus, if Plaintiff was hypersensitive to sexual cues in the workplace, her instant claims of sexual harassment may fail. Defendants are at least entitled to explore this possibility at this early stage of discovery, and to put on expert psychiatric testimony on this issue if warranted. In *Lowe v. Philadelphia Newspapers Inc.,* 594 F. Supp. 123 (E.D. Pa. 1984), a racial harassment case, the court permitted testimony of defense psychiatrists—over the plaintiff's objection—on the issue of whether "the alleged harassment claimed by plaintiff is racial and is harassment at all." The defense psychiatrists testified that the plaintiff suffered from preexisting psychopathology that caused her to be "overly sensitive" and that she "may have overreacted to events on the job." The court maintained:

> Testimony concerning a . . . plaintiff's mental disorder which causes him or her to perceive criticism as harassment, and to perceive racial slurs where no racial motivation is present, is highly relevant to the question whether plaintiff's perception of racial harassment is correct.

Id. at 125–26. *See also Sudtelgte,* 63 FEP Cases 1257 (admitting psychiatric testimony to the effect that the plaintiff suffered from a paranoid personality disorder that adversely affected her ability to get along with co-workers and caused her to feel persistently "picked on").

b. "Welcomeness"

In *Meritor Savings Bank v. Vinson,* 477 U.S. 57, 68 (1986), the Supreme Court maintained that sexual conduct in the workplace must be "unwelcome" to be actionable. In *Henson v. City of Dundee,* 682 F.2d 897, 903 (11th Cir. 1982), the court defined "unwelcome" sexual conduct as that which is not "solicited or incited" by the plaintiff. Thus, even though a plaintiff may have regarded workplace conduct of a sexual nature as undesirable or offensive, if she consciously or even unconsciously incited the conduct, her harassment claim may not be viable.

A plaintiff's history of childhood sexual abuse is relevant to the issue of "welcomeness" because such abuse is known to cause the phenomenon of "repetition compulsion." This refers to the process by which a victim of childhood sexual abuse continues to recreate situations reminiscent of the original trauma. For example, a woman who has suffered from such abuse may interact in eroticized or seductive ways with the men she subsequently encounters. In the workplace, it is not uncommon for a woman with a history of childhood sexual abuse to behave in a sexually provocative manner with supervisors or co-workers. This is in part attributable to the fact that, because of her prior history of abuse, the woman may expect abuse, set herself up for it, and then find her worst fears confirmed.

This "repetition compulsion" is a common feature of the Borderline Personality Disorder, which is not only the most common personality disorder among sexual harassment plaintiffs, but it is also largely believed by the psychiatric community to be attributable in many cases to childhood sexual abuse. *See* J. Perry & J. Herman, *Trauma and Defense in the Etiology of Borderline Personality Disorder, in* BORDERLINE PERSONALITY DISORDER: ETIOLOGY AND TREATMENT 123 (J. Paris ed., 1993); J. Gunderson & D. Sabo, *The Phenomenological and Conceptual Interface Between Borderline Personality Disorder and PTSD,* 150 AM. J. PSYCHIATRY 19, 20 (1993); M. Stone, *Incest in the Borderline Patient, in* INCEST-RELATED SYNDROMES OF ADULT PSYCHOPATHOLOGY (R. Kluft ed., 1990); J. Herman et al., *Childhood Trauma in Borderline Personality Disorder,* 146 AM. J. PSYCHIATRY 490 (1989).

To illustrate how the phenomenon of "repetition compulsion" works, one authority explains:

> Many traumatized people expose themselves, seemingly compulsively, to situations reminiscent of the original trauma. These behavioral reenactments are rarely consciously understood to be related to earlier life experiences.

B. Van Der Kolk, *The Compulsion to Repeat the Trauma,* 12 PSYCHIATRIC CLINICS N. AM. 389, 389 (1989). As this authority continues:

> Some traumatized people remain preoccupied with the trauma at the expense of other life experiences and continue to *re-create* it in some form for themselves or for others. . . . Clinically, these people are observed to have a vague sense of apprehension, emptiness, boredom, and anxiety when not involved in activities reminiscent of the trauma.

Id. at 399 (original emphasis). *See also* S. Shapiro, *Trauma, Ego Defenses, and Behavioral Reenactment, in* SEXUAL TRAUMA AND PSYCHOPATHOLOGY 35, 39 (S. Shapiro & G. Dominiak eds., 1992) ("Many victimized adults appear to be addicted to a lifestyle of abuse").

As another leading expert has observed:

> It is the playing out of these themes of victimization that produces in large part the intense and unstable interpersonal relationships so characteristic of the borderline. *I would stress again that the victimization is seen mainly in the borderlines' ability to get others to do things to them, or upon them.* . . . Their abilities to get others to do things to them are often dramatic and obvious. . . .

J. KROLL, THE CHALLENGE OF THE BORDERLINE PATIENT 46 (1988) (emphasis added). This expert explains how a woman with a Borderline Personality Disorder might instigate sexual conduct in the workplace that might then become the basis of a sexual harassment complaint:

> The borderline performs an initial action to which others respond. The response may be predictable and within proportion to the seriousness of the initiating act, but often it is unpredictable and excessive, except in the sense that, predictably, others will take over and things may happen to the borderline to reinforce the victimization theme. In essence, the situation escalates rapidly. Often it is no longer the borderline who is out of control; it is the others. The borderline is then the indignant and hapless recipient of others' anger, irrationality, or inept attempts to help or rescue, or worse, the true victim of another's aggressiveness.

> Often the borderline need do no more than initiate a series of actions; sometimes, when the tempest begins to settle down, the borderline may provoke a little more, in order to heat the situation up again. . . .

Id. at 50–51. A sexual harassment plaintiff's history of childhood sexual abuse accordingly is of central relevance to the issue of whether she "welcomed" the sexual conduct of which she later complained.

3. Prior Sexual Trauma Is Highly Relevant to the Issue of Plaintiff's Credibility

Prior sexual trauma may impact Plaintiff's credibility in three respects. First, Plaintiff's allegations of harassment herein may be the product of misplaced rage against her earlier abuser. Second, Plaintiff's allegations may be wholly or partly a product of "pseudologia fantastica," or pathological lying. Third, Plaintiff's perception and cognition may be clouded by dissociation.

a. Borderline Rage

As noted earlier, it is commonly accepted within the psychiatric community today that childhood sexual abuse may cause a Borderline Personality Disorder to develop. One common feature of Borderline Personality Disorder is "borderline rage." Borderlines often exhibit rapid mood shifts, in which they suddenly vent intense anger against people around them, especially if they depend or previously depended on them. This anger is really a form of unresolved resentment that the borderline feels toward her father or other male figure who abused her as a child, but it is redirected at whomever in her present life might serve as a convenient target. Borderlines are especially sensitive to rejection; they react with rage against whomsoever they perceive as having somehow rejected them, and they often look for ways in which to obtain revenge. This helps to explain why a borderline, who previously acted friendly and flirtatious with supervisors and co-workers and who may have even initiated sexual-related conversations in the workplace, might suddenly change her mind and angrily accuse her colleagues of "harassing" her. As one authority has noted, this misplaced rage may actually cause a person to file a specious harassment suit. T. Gutheil, *Borderline Personality Disorder, Boundary Violations and Patient-Therapist Sex: Medicolegal Pitfalls,* 146 Am. J. Psychiatry 597, 598 (1989).

As Plaintiff apparently had a consensual sexual affair at one time with her alleged harasser in this case, Larry Low, it is extremely important that the potential that Plaintiff's allegations might be a product of borderline rage be investigated further. Defendants should be permitted to do so.

b. Pathological Lying

Another feature of Borderline Personality Disorder is "pseudologia fantastica," or pathological lying. Pseudologia fantastica is defined as "a syndrome characterized by a superstructure of some actualities erected on a foundation of fantasy." S. Snyder, *Pseudologia Fantastica in the Borderline Patient,* 143 Am. J. Psychiatry 1287 (1986). In other words, the essence of the accusation is a product of the patient's imagination, but some true details—such as when a meeting took place—are added to give a semblance of truth to the lie.

After describing a case that includes a false accusation of rape, the earlier-quoted authority discusses its relevance to litigation:

> The borderline patient may persuade legal authorities of his or her own innocence or of the authenticity of the allegations that he or she has made against others. *In the setting of the courtroom, the borderline patient may be quite convincing in his or her presentation of distortions or lies associated with pseudologia fantastica.*

Snyder, *supra,* at 1289 (emphasis added). With such an obvious and dire warning by one of the foremost experts in the area that the courtroom credibility of an individual with borderline personality may be suspect, all relevant aspects of a sexual harassment plaintiff's background—including her history of childhood sexual abuse—must be explored to determine whether she might have engaged in psuedologia fantastica in the course of reporting sexual harassment.

c. Dissociation

Even absent conscious lying, childhood sexual abuse still may impact a sexual harassment plaintiff's credibility in that many victims of such abuse suffer from a type of psychopathology known as dissociation. D. Sandberg et al., *supra,* at 257 ("dissociative pathology is associated with a variety of traumatic experiences, including severe childhood sexual and physical abuse"). Dissociation refers to a disruption in the usually integrated functions of consciousness, memory, identity, or perception of the environment. American Psychiatric Association, Diagnostic and Statistical Manual of Mental Disorders 477 (4th ed. 1994).

Incest victims may exhibit a variety of dissociative symptoms, which can "pervade every arena and influence every decision" in the incest victim's life. C. Fine, *supra,* at 171. These dissociative symptoms include cognitive distortions such as misassuming causality, distortions of self-perception, time distortion, and dichotomous thinking (in which a person or situation is viewed as "all good" or "all bad"). *Id.* at 166.

Again, with the obvious potential impact of dissociation upon a plaintiff's credibility at issue, Defendants should be permitted to inquire into this important area.

B. Even If Rule 412 Were to Be Applied Here, Evidence of Childhood Sexual Abuse Is Admissible, and Thus Discoverable, Under Rule 412

In *McCleland v. Montgomery Ward & Co.,* 1995 WL 571324 (N.D. Ill. 1995), the court admitted evidence of the plaintiffs' prior childhood and adolescent abuse, including sexual abuse, as evidence of a potential alternative cause for their emotional injuries. The court rejected the plaintiffs' motion in limine to exclude such evidence, in spite of the plaintiffs' argument that evidence of their prior childhood and adolescent sexual abuse was irrelevant and prejudicial. The *McCleland* court held that Rule 412 of the Federal Rules of Evidence does *not* apply to childhood sexual abuse where the defendant does not seek to introduce the prior abuse as evidence of the plaintiffs' sexual behavior or predisposition. Nonetheless, the *McCleland* court noted, even if Rule 412 were to be applicable, the probative value of the evidence substantially outweighed the danger of harm or undue prejudice. The court noted, among other things, that while the plaintiffs received extensive psychological treatment, their focus during that treatment was on their childhood abuse; neither mentioned to their therapists that they were being sexually harassed at work.

Similarly, in *Delaney v. City of Hampton*, 999 F. Supp. 794 (E.D. Va.), *aff'd*, 135 F.3d 769 (4th Cir. 1998) (table), the court granted the defendant's Rule 412 motion to admit evidence of the plaintiff's history of prior sexual abuse as a potential alternative cause of her emotional damages. The plaintiff alleged that as a result of sexual harassment she suffered Posttraumatic Stress Disorder requiring numerous hospitalizations and long-term psychiatric treatment. The court noted that the defendant's experts planned to testify that the plaintiff's prior sexual abuse contributed to the plaintiff's psychiatric problems. *See also Giron v. Correctional Corp. of Am.*, 981 F. Supp. 1406 (D.N.J. 1997) (permitting discovery of prior sexual abuse, noting possible relevance re causation of emotional damages).

CONCLUSION

If Plaintiff persists in her desire to lay out her entire dysfunctional physical and mental condition before the jury and attribute all of her problems solely to Defendants, due process requires that Defendants be able to meaningfully respond. Neither the psychotherapist–patient privilege nor FRE 412 stand as a bar to the production of Dr. Freud's records. Accordingly, Dr. Freud should be ordered to provide his records in their entirety without redaction.

Respectfully submitted,

FISHER & PHILLIPS LLP

BY: ____________________________

James J. McDonald, Jr.

Attorneys for Defendants
ABC Corporation
and John Doe

APPENDIX D

SAMPLE BRIEF IN SUPPORT OF MOTION TO COMPEL PLAINTIFF TO UNDERGO RULE 35 MENTAL EXAMINATION

James J. McDonald, Jr.
State Bar No. 150605
FISHER & PHILLIPS LLP
4675 MacArthur Court
Suite 550
Newport Beach, California 92660
(949) 851-2424

Attorneys for Defendants
ABC Corporation
and Richard Roe

UNITED STATES DISTRICT COURT
CENTRAL DISTRICT OF CALIFORNIA

JANE DOE,	) DOCKET NO. 999999
	)
Plaintiff,	) BRIEF IN SUPPORT OF DEFENDANTS'
	) MOTION TO COMPEL PLAINTIFF
	) TO UNDERGO RULE 35
	) MENTAL EXAMINATION
ABC CORPORATION,	)
et. al.	)
	)
Defendants.	)
______________________	)

INTRODUCTION

Plaintiff alleges in this lawsuit that she suffered severe emotional distress as a result of sexual harassment, and that as a result she had to seek psychiatric treatment. She also names her treating therapist as a potential witness in this case. Yet, she refuses to submit to a mental examination by an examiner retained by Defendants pursuant to Rule 35 of the Federal Rules of Civil Procedure absent several onerous and unworkable conditions, including that her attorney be allowed to attend the examination, that the examination be limited to 1-1/2 hours, and that if any psychological tests are to be administered that they be produced for her inspection prior to the examination. The Court should order Plaintiff to submit to the Rule 35 examination without conditions.

FACTUAL BACKGROUND

Plaintiff Jane Doe filed the instant lawsuit against her former employer, ABC Corporation, and several of its employees. While Plaintiff alleges 10 separate causes of action, including a claim for intentional infliction of emotional distress, all essentially involve her allegation that she was sexually harassed and wrongfully terminated from her employment.

Specifically, Plaintiff alleges in her Complaint that she was sexually harassed by a co-worker, Defendant Larry Low, with whom she admits she previously had a consensual romantic relationship. She alleges that as a result of such harassment, she "has suffered and continues to suffer physical injury, pain and suffering, humiliation, mental anguish and emotional distress. . . ." She further alleges that "as a proximate result of the conduct of the defendants," she began seeing Dr. Sigmund Freud, a psychiatrist.

Accordingly, counsel for Defendants by letter to Plaintiff's counsel requested that Plaintiff submit to a mental examination to be conducted by Milton Headshrinker, Ph.D., a licensed psychologist. Plaintiff's counsel declined to produce her client for such an examination, arguing that an examination is not warranted. Plaintiff's counsel later agreed to produce Plaintiff for such an examination, provided: (1) her attorney be allowed to attend the examination, (2) the examination be limited to 1-1/2 hours, and (3) if any psychological tests are to be administered, they be produced for her inspection prior to the examination.

As Dr. Headshrinker states in his declaration submitted herewith, the conditions which Plaintiff seeks to place upon her mental examination would greatly disrupt the clinical conditions necessary for a valid examination.

ARGUMENT

Plaintiff has squarely placed her emotional state in issue in this case. A Rule 35 mental examination is therefore appropriate, and the onerous restrictions that Plaintiff seeks to place upon her examination should be rejected.

I. PLAINTIFF HAS PLACED HER MENTAL CONDITION INTO ISSUE, WARRANTING A RULE 35 EXAMINATION

Rule 35 of the Federal Rules of Civil Procedure provides that when the mental condition of a party is "in controversy," the court may order the party to submit to a mental examination by a "suitably licensed or certified examiner." In

Schlagenhauf v. Holder, 379 U.S. 104 (1964), the Supreme Court established that a party may obtain a mental examination under Rule 35 upon a showing that the other party's mental condition is in controversy and that good cause exists for conducting such an examination. The *Schlagenhauf* Court went on to note, however, that a plaintiff who claims to have suffered a mental injury places her mental state in controversy and provides the defendant with good cause for an examination to determine the existence and extent of such asserted injury. *Id.* at 119.

Courts since *Schlagenhauf* have found a plaintiff's mental state to be "in controversy" where any one of the following factors are present: (1) a separate tort claim for intentional infliction of emotional distress, (2) the plaintiff's plan to offer the testimony of his or her own psychiatric or psychological expert at trial, (3) allegations of continuing mental or emotional injury, or (4) allegations of "severe" emotional injury. As *all* of these factors are present in this case, Plaintiff has plainly placed her mental condition into controversy and a mental examination is warranted.

A. Separate Claim for Intentional Infliction of Emotional Distress

A plaintiff's mental condition is unquestionably placed in controversy where a separate claim of intentional or negligent infliction of emotional distress is brought. *See, e.g., Sarko v. Penn-Del Directory Co.*, 170 F.R.D. 127, 131 (E.D. Pa. 1997); *Lahr v. Fulbright & Jaworski, L.L.P.*, 164 F.R.D. 204, 209 (N.D. Tex. 1996); *Ragge v. MCA/Universal Studios*, 165 F.R.D. 605, 608–09 (C.D. Cal. 1995); *Hirschheimer v. Associated Minerals & Minerals Corp.*, 1995 WL 736901, at *2 (S.D.N.Y. 1995); *Curtis v. Express Inc.*, 868 F. Supp. 467, 469, 66 FEP Cases 449, 450 (N.D.N.Y. 1994); *Bridges v. Eastman Kodak Co.*, 850 F. Supp. 216, 222, 64 FEP Cases 1100, 1104–05 (S.D.N.Y. 1994); *Everly v. United Parcel Serv. Inc.*, 1991 WL 18429, at *1 (N.D. Ill. 1991). The court in *Lahr* explained the rationale for this rule, which is that a claimant for intentional infliction of emotional distress "does not ask a jury to value the suffering that would ordinarily accompany a wrong. Instead, she raises mental anguish as the essence of the wrong, thereby making her mental condition an issue in the case." Accordingly, "[a] plaintiff who alleges an action for intentional infliction of emotional distress asserts a mental or emotional injury, and thereby places her mental condition in controversy on the basis of the pleadings alone."

B. Plaintiff's Use of a Mental Health Expert

A plaintiff also is held to put her mental condition in issue by indicating that she will call a mental health professional to testify at trial in her behalf. For example, in *Ziemann v. Burlington County Bridge Commission*, 155 F.R.D. 497 (D.N.J. 1994), a sexual harassment case, the court found that the plaintiff had placed her mental condition in controversy by retaining her own psychiatric expert, who was likely to testify on her behalf at trial. As the court noted, "[t]he decisions sanctioning evaluation by defense experts have generally entailed the plaintiff's introduction of psychiatric testimony at trial, which the defense is then permitted to rebut by testimony as to its own mental evaluation."

Similarly, in *Chaparro v. IBP Inc.*, 1994 WL 714369 (D. Kan. 1994), the plaintiff identified an expert witness who was expected to testify about the emotional impact of the allegedly discriminatory and retaliatory termination of her employment, as well as her treating physician, who was expected to testify about her treatment for depression. The court ordered a Rule 35 mental examination, finding that the plaintiff's intention to call an expert and her treating physician to testify on her behalf at trial indicated that she had affirmatively put her mental condition in controversy.

C. Allegation of Continuing Emotional Injury

Courts routinely have found a plaintiff's mental condition to be in controversy where there were allegations of ongoing mental or emotional distress. Several courts have adhered to the notion that there must be allegations of continuing mental or emotional distress or injury before a plaintiff's mental condition is considered to be in controversy. *See, e.g., Sarko v. Penn-Del Directory Co.*, 170 F.R.D. 127 (E.D. Pa. 1997); *Hirschheimer v. Associated Minerals & Minerals Corp.*, 1995 WL 736901 (S.D.N.Y. Dec. 12, 1995); *Ali v. Wang Labs*, 162 F.R.D. 165, 4 AD Cases 520 (M.D. Fla. 1995); *Ragge v. MCA/Universal Studios*, 165 F.R.D. 605 (C.D. Cal. 1995); *O'Quinn v. New York Univ. Med. Ctr.*, 163 F.R.D. 226, 228, 68 FEP Cases 1798, 1800 (S.D.N.Y. 1995); *Curtis v. Express Inc.*, 868 F. Supp. 467, 469, 66 FEP Cases 449, 450 (N.D.N.Y. 1994); *Bridges v. Eastman Kodak Co.*, 850 F. Supp. 216, 222, 64 FEP Cases 1100, 1104 (S.D.N.Y. 1994); *Jansen v. Packaging Corp. of Am.*, 158 F.R.D. 409, 66 FEP Cases 556 (N.D. Ill. 1994); *Ryzlak v. McNeil Pharm. Co.*, 38 Fed. R. Serv. 2d 443 (E.D. Pa. 1982).

D. Allegation of Severe Emotional Injury

Claims of severe emotional distress also are sufficient to place a plaintiff's mental condition "in controversy." For example, in *Chapparo v. IBP Inc.*, 1994 WL 714369 (D. Kan.1994), the plaintiff asserted claims of employment discrimination and retaliatory discharge, alleging "grievous emotional injury." The plaintiff also indicated that her treating physician as well as an expert would testify on her behalf at trial. The defendant then moved to compel a mental examination under Rule 35, arguing that the plaintiff's claim of severe emotional distress and the designation of the two expert witnesses placed her mental condition in controversy. The court granted the motion, noting that although the mere assertion of a claim for emotional distress does not by itself put the plaintiff's mental condition in controversy, here the plaintiff had identified two experts who would testify about her emotional condition and treatment, and more important, "[b]eyond a more conventional claim of emotional distress, she has alleged her distress to be 'severe and extreme.' "

II. THE EXAMINATION SHOULD PROCEED WITHOUT THE CONDITIONS PLAINTIFF SEEKS TO IMPOSE

Legal authority supporting the conditions Plaintiff seeks to impose on her mental examination are lacking. In fact, the weight of the authority rejects those conditions.

A. Presence of Counsel

The overwhelming weight of authority holds that a Rule 35 mental examination should be conducted outside the presence of counsel or other outsiders.

In an early case, the California Supreme Court echoed many of the same concerns. In *Edwards v. Superior Court,* 16 Cal. 3d 905, 130 Cal. Rptr. 14 (1976), the court refused to allow the plaintiff's attorney to attend the plaintiff's mental examination. The plaintiff had argued that her attorney's presence was necessary to protect her from improper questioning, to make the examination a more comfortable experience for her, and to ensure accurate reporting. The court rejected all three arguments. Concerning the plaintiff's claim that she needed counsel to protect her from improper questions, the court remarked:

> The analyst in a psychiatric examination seeks by careful direction of areas of inquiry to probe, possibly very deeply, into the psyche, measuring stress, seeking origins, tracing aberrations, and attempting to form a professional judgment or interpretation of the examinee's mental condition. Given such techniques and purposes we do not think that an attorney, no matter how well intentioned, can fairly and objectively monitor such an examination. Psychiatry is a discipline requiring highly specialized skills. Further, while properly objecting to a question on legal grounds, counsel does not necessarily possess the ability to define the psychiatric relevance of elicited answers. Many questions which would be legally objectionable, if posed in a courtroom, might be very relevant in the formulation of a sound psychiatric judgment.

Id. at 911, 130 Cal. Rptr. at 17. In answer to the plaintiff's argument that her counsel's presence was necessary for her comfort and emotional support, the *Edwards* court expressed its concern that the presence of others during the examination would be "distracting, if not disrupting," and noted that an examination must proceed free of such disruptions if it is to be valid. Finally, the *Edwards* court held that a verbatim account of all of the questions and answers at a mental examination is not necessarily desirable, as it might cause the examinee to react defensively and inhibit the "free, open and objective communication essential to an effective psychiatric examination."

In *Tirado v. Erosa,* 158 F.R.D. 294 (S.D.N.Y. 1994), the court similarly rejected the plaintiff's argument that the presence of her counsel and a stenographer was necessary due to the sensitive nature of the allegations in the case (unconsented sexual touching). It observed:

> Plaintiff also asserts that the subject matter is especially sensitive, but this consideration cuts both ways. On the one hand, plaintiff might not feel comfortable discussing intimate matters with defendants' psychiatric expert, but on the other it is not clear that having four people in the room rather than two will improve this situation. Plaintiff has made no showing that the presence of her male attorney and a complete stranger (male or female) taking down every word would make her any more comfortable.

Id. at 296.

A majority of courts in employment cases have disallowed the presence of plaintiff's counsel during the Rule 35 mental examination. *See, e.g., Breda v. Wolf Camera Inc.*, 78 FEP Cases 433, 435 (S.D. Ga. 1998); *Haensel v. Chrysler Corp.*, 1997 WL 537995 (E.D. La. 1997); *Farrell v. Shell Oil Co.*, 1995 WL 688795, at *2 (E.D. La. 1995); *Hirschheimer v. Associated Minerals & Minerals Corp.*, 1995 WL 736901, at *3 (S.D.N.Y. 1995); *Vinson v. Superior Court*, 43 Cal. 3d 833, 239 Cal. Rptr. 292, 44 FEP Cases 1174 (Cal. 1987); *Lowe v. Philadelphia Newspapers Inc.*, 101 F.R.D. 296, 299, 44 FEP Cases 1224, 1226 (E.D. Pa. 1983). *See also Wheat v. Biesecker*, 125 F.R.D. 479, 480 (N.D. Ind. 1989) (noting that majority rule is that plaintiff's attorney may not attend a Rule 35 examination). There is therefore no legal basis for Plaintiff's request to have her attorney present during the Rule 35 examination.

B. Limit on Duration of the Examination

Courts typically reject artificial limits on the duration of a Rule 35 examination. For example, in *Morton v. Haskell Co.,*5 AD Cases 272 (M.D. Fla. 1995), the court rejected the plaintiff's request to limit the mental examination to one hour, and in fact the court declined to impose any time restrictions for the examination. *See also Gavenda v. Orleans County*, 174 F.R.D. 272 (W.D.N.Y. 1996) (court refused to place time limit on examination).

As Dr. Headshrinker states in his declaration, an artificial limitation on the duration of Plaintiff's mental examination would greatly jeopardize his ability to conduct a clinically valid examination. As there is no legal justification for such a limitation, this proposed condition should be rejected.

C. Advance Disclosure of Tests

The difficulty with allowing Plaintiff to review the psychological test questions in advance of actually taking the test should be obvious. It is essential that Plaintiff take the psychological tests administered her by Dr. Headshrinker under scientific and clinically sound conditions. This precludes giving her an advance look at the tests. In *Ragge v. MCA/Universal Studios,*165 F.R.D. 605 (C.D. Cal. 1995), the court refused to order the defense examiner to disclose in advance the specific psychological tests to be administered. A similar result should apply here.

CONCLUSION

Plaintiff should be ordered to appear for a mental examination by Dr. Headshrinker without any of the conditions she seeks to impose.

Respectfully submitted,

FISHER & PHILLIPS LLP

BY: ______________________________
James J. McDonald, Jr.

Attorneys for Defendants
ABC Corporation
and John Doe

TABLE OF CASES

References are to footnote numbers in chapters (e.g., ***7:*** *39 refers to footnote 39 in chapter 7).* ***Pref*** *refers to the Preface.*

C

D

E

F

G

H

I

J

K

L

M

N

O

T

U

V

W

Z